ENCYCLOPEDIA OF
SUNKEN
TREASURE

John Wright

MICHAEL O'MARA BOOKS LIMITED

TO MY GODSON, DAVID BOLTON,
AND TO MARY JIGGINS AND CHRIS BLOM

First published in Great Britain in 1995 by
Michael O'Mara Books Limited
9 Lion Yard, Tremadoc Road
London SW4 7NQ

A CIP catalogue record for this book is available from the
British Library

ISBN 1-85479-908-8

Maps by Stephen Dew

Typeset by Florencetype Limited, Stoodleigh, Devon
Printed and bound by Clays Ltd, St Ives plc

CONTENTS

Australasia and the Far East

Europe

CONTENTS

Author's Acknowledgments

I wish to acknowledge the contributions of many libraries and museums, in particular: Mr. Goran Ekberg of the Sjöhistoriska Museet in Stockholm; Martine Bélanger and Diane Lemieux, Musée Maritime Bernier, Quebec; Helen Threlfall, Librarian, Maritime Record Centre of the Mersey Maritime Museum; Roland Brown, Research Assistant, University of Liverpool; Warren Delaney, Maritime Archaeology, Queensland Museum, Australia; Peter Harvey, Maritime Archaeological Unit, Victoria; Michael Green, Reference Archivist, Texas State Archives; Donald P. Zuris, Head Curator, Corpus Christi Museum of Science and History; Benjamin H. Trask, Librarian, Mariners Museum, Virginia; H.J.W. Stokes, Director, Australian Archives; Colin Bruce, Imperial War Museum; Robert Vickery, Bureau of Archaeological Research, Florida Department of State; Tommy Watts, Curator, Shetland Island Council; Brian Duncan Thynne, Hydrography Section, National Maritime Museum, London; Miss J. Olds, Librarian, Times-Media Ltd, Port Elizabeth, South Africa; Susan H. Karren, Assistant Director National Archives, Pacific Northwest Region, Seattle, Washington; Bob Power, Manager, Heritage Branch, New South Wales Government; Mike Nash, Maritime Archaeologist, Department of Parks, Wildlife & Heritage, Hobart, Tasmania; Dr Francine Wolterbeck, Christie's, Amsterdam; Royal Naval Museum, Portsmouth; Jeremy Green, Head, Department of Maritime Archaeology, Western Australian Museum; James Mallinson, Venture Capital Report Ltd; Kalmar Museum, Sweden; Guildhall Library, London; British Library, London.

I would also like to acknowledge my appreciation to the treasure divers who have written about their adventures, in particular Mel Fisher, Alex McKee, Robert Marx, Robert Stenuit, Kip Wagner and Peter Earle, to mention but a few; also, to the many marine archaeologists, without whose professional investigations and research much of our marine history would be lost.

I wish to make special thanks to William Braithwaite for giving me access to family files on the *Earl of Abergavenny*; Zoe Trumper of Performance Publications; Victor Vazquez for his research in New York; Rosemary Drysdale and Gus Spears of Easthampton, New York; the ladies at Billingshurst library; Tony Thompson and Jessica Thomas of Christie's; Ed Schneider of Christie's Images; Diana Lambley, Susan Pinder and Claudia Toledo.

I thank Cathy Randall of O'Mara Books for her patience and co-operation, my editor Rosemary Pettit and lastly Michael and Lesley O'Mara.

Picture Acknowledgments

The pictures in the plate section have been kindly supplied by Christie's Images, and show items that have been sold by various branches of Christie's, the fine art auctioneers, following their recovery from the sea.

The publishers are grateful to the following for permission to reproduce black and white pictures on the following pages: National Maritime Museum, pp. 17, 26, 29, 92, 101, 132, 148, 204;

Mary Evans Picture Library, pp. 41, 71, 139, 157, 168, 175, 195, 211, 219; e.t. archive, pp. 119, 135; P & O, p. 229.

AFRICA

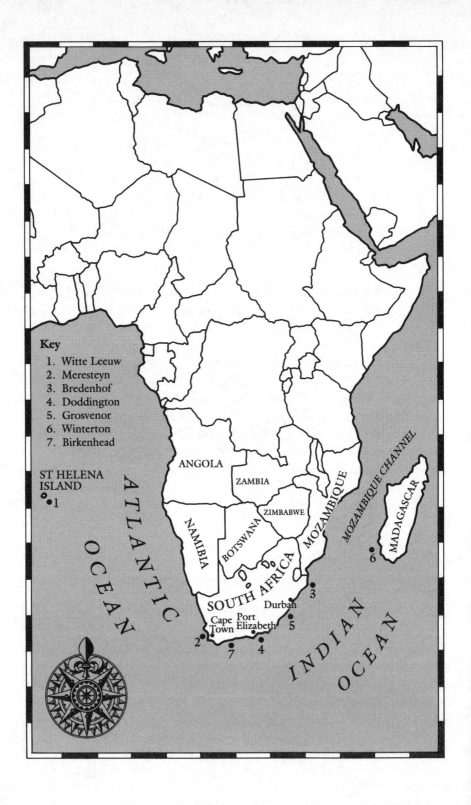

Key
1. Witte Leeuw
2. Meresteyn
3. Bredenhof
4. Doddington
5. Grosvenor
6. Winterton
7. Birkenhead

ST HELENA
ISLAND

ANGOLA

ZAMBIA

ZIMBABWE

NAMIBIA

BOTSWANA

SOUTH AFRICA

MOZAMBIQUE

MOZAMBIQUE CHANNEL

MADAGASCAR

ATLANTIC OCEAN

INDIAN OCEAN

Durban

Cape
Town

Port
Elizabeth

WITTE LEEUW

The Witte Leeuw, *meaning white lion, was a 750-ton galleon belonging to the Amsterdam Chamber of the Dutch East India Company. She was 150 feet long, with a 25-foot beam, and had a complement of 200 crew, soldiers and passengers commanded by Roelof Symoensen de Blom.*

AREA: *Sunk by the Portuguese in Kerk Baaij, now called St James Bay, St Helena Island, South Atlantic.*

The *Witte Leeuw* had spent two years trading in the Spice Islands before setting sail for Holland in 1613 in the company of three other Dutch ships. The *Witte Leeuw* carried a cargo of 15,171 bags of pepper, 1311 diamonds, other exotic goods and a large amount of Ming porcelain.

The four ships set sail across the Indian Ocean and round the Cape of Good Hope but, short of fresh water, they headed for the small volcanic island of St Helena. Holland and Portugal were at the time enemies, both countries being in dispute over rights to the Moluccas Spice Islands. The Dutch Governor General of the Dutch East Indies Jan Pieterszoon Coen, issued a directive: 'The commerce of the Moluccas, Amboina and the Bandas should belong to the company and no other nation in the world should be allowed to have the least part.'[1] Dutch and Portuguese ships frequently engaged each other in battle but, with the expansion of the Dutch East India Company and their increased number of ships, St Helena had become a dangerous port of call for the Portuguese.

Rounding the headland into St James Bay, the Dutch ships found two armed Portuguese merchantships: the *Casa Da Nossa Senhora Da Nazare*, commanded by Captain Jeronimo d'Almedio, and another galleon, the *Conceicao*. Taking advantage of surprise and their superior numbers the Dutch ships manoeuvred into position to attack the Portuguese.

Captain d'Almedio, judging wind and tide, warped the *Nazare* into a broadside position and readied his men. Sailing into the attack the Dutch ships met accurate cannonades from experienced gunners which devastated them. A Portuguese chronicler wrote later of the battle: 'Fought in such a way that one of the largest enemy ships was sent to the bottom, another was most marvellously battered and had to leave the fighting, her forecastle shattered, the other so ill treated that they had to flee leaving to our people a total victory.'[2]

The *Witte Leeuw*, badly damaged and holed many times on the waterline, sank at the entrance to the Bay. A Company letter to the Governor General of the Dutch East Indies in 1614 stated: 'The loss of the ship *Witte Leeuw*, near St Helena, when attacking two portuguese carracks which had there come to anchor . . . are mighty heavy blows for the company.'[3]

Robert Stenuit

Robert Stenuit had successfully salvaged Spanish and Dutch galleons and, in 1975, became interested in the wreck of the *Witte Leeuw*. Deciding to search for the wreck, with support from the National Geographic Society in Washington and the French underwater engineering company, COMEX, he formed a team of expert divers. In 1976 the expedition arrived at St Helena and began to search St James Bay. Within three days one of the divers located five encrusted cannons at a depth of 110 feet. Bringing the cannons to the surface and removing the encrustation they found the inscription: De Vereenichde Oost-Indig Comp (The United East India Company). Further diving revealed more cannons. Stenuit and his team surveyed and excavated the wreck site, recovering beautiful pieces of Ming porcelain of the Wai Li period, coins, silver artifacts, jewellery and gold ornaments.

Stenuit could find no timbers of the stern section of the wreck where most of the more valuable pieces of porcelain, jewellery and diamonds would be stored. During his search in St Helena he was sent a copy of an old document written by an English officer who witnessed the battle and described the last moments of the *Witte Leeuw*. This stated: 'His men still plying his ordnance . . . one of his pieces brake over his power roome, as some thought, and the shippe blew up all to pieces, the after part of her, and so sunke presently.'[4]

After seven months of diving, Stenuit and his divers found no diamonds. They believed them to be scattered somewhere on the seabed.

MERESTEYN

The Merestyen *was built in Amsterdam in 1693 for the Amsterdam Chamber of the Dutch East India Company. The* Meresteyn *carried 200 crew and soldiers commanded by Captain Jan Subbingh.*
    AREA: *Wrecked on the southwest side of Jutten Island at the mouth of Saldanha Bay, about 10 miles north of Cape Town, South Africa, Atlantic Ocean.*

The *Meresteyn* sailed out of Texel in Holland on 4 October 1701, bound for the East Indies with a large amount of gold and silver specie. Sailing on the northern route around the Shetland Islands into the Atlantic and south to Cape Town (a voyage which normally lasted 120 to 160 days), the *Meresteyn* encountered severe storms which drove her off course into the South Atlantic. Running short of food and water Captain Subbingh sailed eastwards to obtain a position from the African coast and to replenish supplies from the nearest available port. On 3 April 1702, with many of the crew dead and others suffering from scurvy, the lookouts sighted the African coast at Saldanha Bay, seventy miles north of Cape Town. The ship entered the bay in early evening and prepared to anchor between Jutten Island and Jut Point.

The captain, unaware of the currents and tides of the Bay, found his ship being swiftly driven towards the rocks on the west side of Jutten Island. Anchors were dropped to hold the ship but it was too late – the *Meresteyn* struck the rocks and sank in 14 fathoms of water. Ninety-nine survivors managed to reach the safety of the island where, the following day, they constructed a raft from the wreckage and landed on the mainland.

The Company had established a small station at Saldanha and the station keeper sent word to the Company Governor at the Cape, informing him of the sinking of the *Meresteyn* and the plight of the sick and injured survivors. A small ship, *Wezel*, under the command of Captain Volkert Shouten, was sent with supplies and instructions to salvage her valuable cargo.

On arrival at Saldanha Bay on 9 April, Captain Shouten offloaded the supplies and, with the *Meresteyn's* first mate as guide, began to search for the wreck. They took soundings 200 yards from the island but the *Wezel* was unable to approach any closer due to the rough sea and breaking surf on the rocks. Returning to the Cape Captain Shouten reported to the Governor that any attempts to salvage the treasure were useless, owing to the depth of the wreck and the violent surf.

In March 1971 a number of independent divers located the wreck. The brothers Reginald and William Dodds discovered a cannon and silver coins.

Bob Hayward, Barry Williams and Jock Dichmont also recovered small brass cannons, and a number of gold and silver coins.

These two groups worked on the wreck site over the years, recovering over 15,000 gold and silver coins. The *Meresteyn* was to be the most important coin wreck found on the coast of Africa.

BREDENHOF

The 800-ton Bredenhof *was built for the Middleburg Chamber of the Dutch East India Company in 1746; the ship was commanded by Captain Jan Nielsen with a crew of 260 men.*

AREA: *Wrecked on a reef 120 miles south of Mozambique and thirteen miles off the South African coast, Indian Ocean.*

1752 was a disastrous year for the Dutch East India Company; they had already lost two important merchantships, the *Geldermalsen* and the *Wapen Van Hoorn*. To make up for their losses, the Company sent three other ships, the *Kasteel Van Tilburg, Zuiderburg* and the *Bredenhof*, sailing to India at different times.

The *Bredenhof* was the last to sail from Holland, departing 31 December 1752, on her third voyage to Bengal via Cape Town and Ceylon. She carried a cargo listed as follows:

14 'Vaajes' [small casks] with copper 'Duiten' [farthing] and 30 chests with silver and gold. This was made up to 29 chests of bar silver, valued at 300,000 guilders and one chest with 5,000 gold Ducats valued at 25,000 guilders. The silver was set apart for Bengal to be minted into silver rupees. The alloy of silver bars was 11 pen, 20 gr and means 98.6% pure silver. One bar weighed 8 mark or 1.96 kilo. The value of one bar was about 208 guilders. Therefore the total value of the silver bar carried by the Bredenhof in 29 chests (50 per chest, making 1,450 bars), was approximately 301,600 guilders. The total weight of bar silver was approximately 2,840 kilos.[1]

On arriving at the Cape on 11 April 1753 nine of the crew disembarked due to sickness and 38 tons of wheat and wine were loaded for Ceylon. On 25 April the *Bredenhof* departed the Cape, sailing along the coast of East Africa where, in calm weather on the morning of 6 June, she drifted on to a reef.

Captain Jan Nielsen ordered the cannons, ballast and some cargo to be thrown overboard to lighten the ship.

The longboat and barge dropped anchors to winch the ship off the reef but, unable to clear the reef, Jan Nielsen then jettisoned the silver bars. The weather began to change and, by 10 June, a gale was blowing from the southeast. In desperation, everything heavy (including fourteen chests of silver) was thrown overboard. The following day the weather was no better, the wind had increased and the *Bredenhof*, still firmly wedged on the reef, began to break up. Rafts were constructed and the ship was abandoned; about 200 survivors landed on the coast. Captain Jan Nielsen saved five bags of gold. After two and a half months travelling along the desolate coastline, about 100 survivors arrived at a small Portuguese settlement. From the settlement a ship took them to Mozambique.

Pieter Bakker

One of the survivors, Pieter Bakker, who was first mate on the *Bredenhof*, hitched a lift in a Swedish ship from Mozambique to Surat in India. On reporting to the Company the directors gave Bakker a ship, the *Jonge Suzanna*, to pick up the survivors in Mozambique and to salvage any of the *Bredenhof*'s treasure. En route, Bakker met a Portuguese ship whose captain informed him that other Portuguese vessels had searched for the wreck and its treasure but nothing could be found. Bakker continued on his voyage and, on arriving at the wreck site, he saw anchors and cannons in shallow water but nothing of the chests of silver. Suspecting that the Portuguese had already recovered the silver he sailed on to Mozambique to pick up the remaining survivors.

Schuilenburg

Many of the survivors had reached Holland before the news of the unsuccessful salvage attempt by Bakker. It was decided by the Amsterdam directors of the Company to send the *Schuilenburg* with two survivors to assist in the location of the wreck. The captain of the *Schuilenburg* searched the reef with no success and returned to Holland in January 1756.

Marie José

In the 1980s a Caribbean company from the Cayman Islands made an extensive investigation of the history of the *Bredenhof*. In 1985 they contracted a

Captain Klaar of the *Marie José*, with a team of divers, to locate and salvage the treasure from the wreck.

After many weeks of searching and diving in the area where they believed the wreck to be, no sign of it was found. The divers were about to terminate the search when one of them found a small Dutch silver coin. On further dives they found a small anchor, a cannon and a major find of hundreds of silver ingots.

> We lay down a grid of bright yellow rope and started surveying and charting the area. We were plagued by dirty water and very strong currents. The tidal difference is 3 to 4 meters. We found another cannon and a large quantity of copper coins, 'duiten' all marked 1752 and from the Zeeland mint scattered all over the place. A few blocks of iron pig ballast were found, some lead sounding weights and a pewter plate lying next to one of the cannons.
>
> We were now worried about the lack of cannons in the area and, what about the anchors that had been thrown off to enable the survivors to winch the stricken vessel out of their perilous position? . . . We searched the area thoroughly and no more silver ingots were found. It made us wonder who it was that was able to salvage the chests soon after the wrecking. Was it the natives who were able to dive down and pick up the silver or was it the Portuguese Captains who plundered the wreck? One thing is for sure, part of the wreck drifted off and snagged 15 miles away and our modern day salvage team was able to pick up part of the silver cargo and copper coins.[2]

In December 1986, 542 silver bars were sold at auction by Christie's in Amsterdam for £138,000 ($203,000).

DODDINGTON

The Doddington *was chartered by the English East India Company in 1755, for service from England to the East Indies. Registered as 499 tons, her exact size is not known. She carried twenty-six guns and was captained by James Samson with a crew of seventy.*

AREA: *Wrecked on Bird Island, one of the small isles in the eastern part of Algoa Bay, near Port Elizabeth, Cape Province, South Africa, Indian Ocean.*

During the 1750s Britain and France were locked in hostilities that became known as the Seven Years' War. This war was fought in many regions, including India and the North American colonies.

In India, Robert Clive – in the service of the East India Company – became involved in the early campaigns against the French. The Royal Army of the East India Company was sanctioned by the British government and had established trading bases at Bombay, Calcutta and Madras. The French had settlements at Chandernagore, north of Calcutta; their headquarters were at Pondicherry, south of Madras.

The directors of the East India Company decided to authorize a military expedition in 1755, under the command of Clive, to be sent from England to Bombay; this was launched with the express idea of ending French influence in India.

Three of the Company's ships, *Edgecourt*, *Houghton*, and *Pelham* were assigned to transport the expedition. Two other ships were also chartered, the *Streatham* and the *Doddington*, in order to reinforce the small fleet.

The *Dodington* Carrys a large Quantity of Naval and Victualling Stores for the service of his Majesty's squadron as likewise cloathing and necessaries for his Majesty's Land Forces, all which you must take care are duly delivered to, and accounted for by the proper Officers, she also carrys about Two hundred Soldiers, part of whom consists of a Detachment from the Royal Regiment of Artillery, being One Company of about One hundred and seven Men Officers included, the remainder are Recruits for our Own Troop. Besides all which sundry Goods are laden on the Company's account for your Presidency, the particulars of which will appear by the accompanying Invoice and Bill of Loading; We have likewise sent on her sundry particulars for Bengal agreeable to an Invoice and Bill of Loading enclosed in the Packet directed to you, which, on her proceeding thither, must be carefully forwarded.[1]

The following gold and silver in her 'manifest of private gold and silver and wrought plate lycenced to be shipped on board the *Doddington* for St. George on account of the following vizt':

	OZr.DW.
For Robert Clive Esqr. Governor for Fort St.David	
One Chest of Gold, Marked R.C. No. I qt.	653 6 –
The Missionaries on the Coast in Silver	
One Chest D.M.Z. No.8	1,870 –

. . . Messrs. Walsh and Vansittart Do. G No.1   3,258 5 –
John Barrons Commissary & Paymaster to the Train of
Artillery
Do. J.B. No.1   3,663 –
Capt. Francis Ford to the Commanding Officer in being
of Colonel Adlercrons
Regiment Five Chests Marked J.A. No.1 at 5   18,591 –
Chas. Boddam Esqr. a Case of Wrought Plate   CB 444

Bullion Office, East India House
29th March 1755   Thos. Webb[2]

On your arrival at Fort St. George you are to deliver our President and
Council there all the Packets directed to them, with all the Bullion, Goods
and Merchandises on Board consigned thither, you are to land all
the Passengers and Soldiers, and in all things according to your Charter
Party.[3]

Robert Clive had established himself as a brilliant soldier. He was commissioned in March 1755 as a Lieutenant-Colonel of the Royal Army and
was then made Deputy Governor of Fort St David in Madras. He had been
ordered to lead the attack on the French at Pondicherry. In April 1755, Clive
was ready to sail to India and the ships assembled near Dover. Clive and his
wife boarded the *Streatham*. Their personal baggage, along with the gold and
silver, was stowed aboard the *Doddington*. The ship departed England on the
23 April with 200 soldiers and passengers.
    Captain Samson was given strict orders regarding the treatment of the
soldiers.

We have put on board the Gallons of Brandy for each soldier, which must
be duly distributed among them in proper quantities for their refreshment
and support.
    A detachment from His Majestys Royal regiment of Artillery being to
proceed to the East Indies in your ship you are hereby Ordered to afford
the Officers and Private Men all suitable Accomodations, and observe such
Conduct towards them, that there be no occasions given for discontent and
as we have given it in Charge to your Servants abroad to make particular
Enquiry into your behaviour of this Head, you may be assured We shall
highly resent any ill usage they may meet with on board your ship.[4]

The *Doddington*'s chief mate, Evan Jones, and the third mate, William Webb, both kept accounts of the voyage: Evan Jones describes the first part of the voyage.

April 23 sailed from the Downs, In company with the *Pelham, Houghton, Stretham*, and *Edgecote*, and in a week got clear of the Channel; in which time we found we had the advantage of the other ships in sailing; and this I believe made Captain Samson desirous of parting company. After leaving the Channel we lost sight of our consorts. . . . We met with nothing particular till May 14, when we made the island of Fortaventura, and the next day sailed between Teneriff and the Grand Canaria; on May 20, we discovered a sail, which proved to be the *Houghton*, and presently after made the island of Bonavista. The next day we got into Porto Prior Bay, where we found the *Pelham* and *Stretham*, who had arrived two hours before. Here we made with what dispatch we could in watering, and on the 26 May the *Edgecote* arrived. The next day we weighed and made-sail in company with *Pelham, Houghton*, and *Stretham*, leaving the *Edgecote* in the road; we kept company with the other ships a day, steering S by E2E which course the Captain thought too farr and by that means soon lost sight of them and saw them no more. . . . We had a Very pleasant Passage of 7 Weeks from St Jago To the Making of Cape Land, [and] On the 8th of July Took a Fresh Departure from Cape Lagullas, we Run to the E'ward in the Latitude of 35° 30' and 36° 0'0S. till I made [we had made by my Reckoning] 12° 45' E^t Difference of Longitude and by [the] Med^m of Six Other Journals 12° 50' Longitude and 35° 0'0 S Latitude. This day at Noon, the Captn Order'd the Course to be alter'd from E^t to ENE. Had Dirty Squally Weather with the Wind from SSW to SSE and a very Large Sea. We had at this Time two Reefs in the Fore Topsails and three in the Main, and all the Stay Sails Stow'd so that We Ran about 6 or 7 Knotts an Hour. At Midnight had About 70 Miles on The Board.[5]

The *Doddington* rounded the Cape of Good Hope on 8 July. She then made eastwards toward Cape Le Gullas. By 16 July the weather had become stormy; strong winds, rain and rough seas gave the *Doddington* a terrible journey. Captain Samson, erroneously thinking he was some 180 miles east of the coast and well into the Indian Ocean, changed course to east-northeast. His charts were incorrect and he was unwittingly making straight for aptly named Chaos Island. The chief mate Evan Jones's diary entry reads:

About a Quarter before One in the Morning, the Ship struck, and in less than 20 Minutes was entirely wreck'd. It was a dark and stormy Night, and the only Warning we had of our Danger was calling out, 'Breakers a-head and to Leeward.' The Helm was immediately put a-lee; but before she came quite Head to Wind, she struck lightly, and then stronger; at which Time the Sea broke directly into her forward, stove the Boats, and washed a good many People overboard. Altho' we used our best Endeavours to get her about, it was to no Purpose, the Sea breaking all over her, and she struck so hard, that the Mainmast went away by the board, and the Rest of the Mast soon followed. – We could see no Land.

The Ship continued lifting and striking with every Sea, till unfortunately she at last laid down on her Starboard Side, and soon parted; every Sea driving some Part of her away. As the Larboard Side and Quarter was now the only Place above Water, all those who could, got there; she still kept driving towards the Breakers, and the Sea was covered with her Wreck. As Captain Samson sat with me on the Quarter, he said he had prick'd off that Day at Noon, and judged himself 90 Leagues from the Land, and imagined this to be some unknown Rock, where possibly the *Dolphin* was lost. We expected every Minute to be washed off by the Sea, and Captain Samson bid us all Farewell, and hoped we should meet again in the next world.[6]

He continues:

Only 23 Being Saved out of 270 and Most of them Very Much Bruised, my Self Escaping with a Few Scratches. As Fast as we Mett Gott Close together as we Could to keep us warm, for it Was Bitter Cold, and Nothing on but a Wett Shirt. We had not Seated our Selves long on the Sharp Rocks, before we Was Vissitted by Some Seals, which Was Taken by the people who first Saw them, to be Wild Beasts. As they Came Nearer to us Some said they saw 4 leggs; and Took them to be Hoggs, by their Making a Noise much like a Hogg. It was all this Time so Dark that you Could Scarcely See the Rocks we Satt upon, and now it was that I first Thought of the Main [land], thinking it Impossible for Wild Beasts to be On a Rock in the Sea, how Soever was Obliged to be Content'd with thinking so Till day Light when we Found Ourselves upon a Small Island, tho it Scarce Deserves the Name, distant from the Main Land about 2 Leagues Surrounded by Severall Rocks, Some of them two Miles in the Offing on Which the Ship Struck.[7]

The twenty-three survivors remained on the island for seven months; they subsisted on a diet of fish, sea-birds' eggs and provisions that fortuitously washed ashore from the wreck. Evan Jones makes reference to the treasure: '. . . Unhappily there was a Chest of Treasure drove ashore from the Wreck, which the Officers wanted to preserve for the Proprietors, and the People wanted to divide, which occasioned great Disputes, and at last was divided in Spite of the Officers.'[8] This particular chest was probably that of Charles Boddam, listed in the manifest as containing 'Wrought Plate'. Another reference was made by Jones in his diary:

> Soon After this the Carpenter, and The Rest of the people was Informed by Bothwell, that the Treasure & Wrought Plate was Not to be Shared, Upon which Information Mr Collett & I was Call'd the greatest Rogues in the World, & Every One Swore it Should be Shared, and Everything Else that Came Ashore there belong[d] To Who it would. After Our days Work was Over and Every Body mett in the Tent to Supper. The Carpenter Asked me When the money and plate Was to be Shared which Surprised me greatly. Howsoever finding they Were Resolved to Share it, thought it Needless to deny my Intentions, Especially Since I found that Some I thought I could Trust, proved false.[9]

On Sunday, 29 September, after the Sunday service, the officers discovered that 'a Treasure Chest had been broke open, and two thirds of it taken out and concealed. Every body denied knowing anything of it.'[10]

The chief mate wrote:

> This may appear strange, that those whom danger had made religious should, at the same time, be guilty of theft, and that, too, in a situation in which the possession of gold could not contribute, in the slightest degree to their subsistence or their means of escape; but it should be remembered, that on a ship being lost, all the sailors lose their wages, and whatever is cast adrift is considered by the sailors as common property. The men, therefore, who ventured secretly to appropriate what they deemed their share of the treasure, were not conscious of acting dishonestly, but only designed to secure what they feared their officers would monopolise, and thus preventing disputes, which, in their circumstances, might terminate fatally.[11]

The *Doddington* was not the first ship to be wrecked on this particular island. In many eighteenth-century charts Chaos Island, now known as Bird Island, was incorrectly positioned. British naval charts, dated 1759, referred to the island as 'Confused Island'; its location was in the northwestern corner of Algoa Bay. As ships made landfall, especially at night or in bad weather, they were at risk of grounding themselves on the inhospitable shores of Chaos Island. As the *Doddington* survivors made their way around the island they discovered the remains of two wrecks: 'One seemed to be a Dutch ship, the other English; the latter least decayed, and by the iron-work seemed to have been much less than the *Doddington*. It plainly appears by Pieces of Glass, and other Things, that some unfortunate People had lived on that Place, and they could see the Remains of Habitation, by the Stones being regularly laid one on another.'[12]

It was decided to strip the wreck of her remaining timbers and search the island for usable wood and other pieces of wreckage that could be suitable in the construction of a boat. Amongst the survivors were Richard Topping, a ship's carpenter, and Henry Scantz, seaman, who had once been a blacksmith's assistant.

By February 1756, under the supervision of Topping and Scantz, they had succeeded in building a boat 30 feet by 12 feet. They named her *Happy Deliverance*. On Tuesday 17 February, Webb wrote in his journal: 'People employed all night in getting their things into the boat, and at high water hauled her out into the stream.'

On the 18th twenty-two persons boarded the *Happy Deliverance*: 'They all boarded her and left the barren roach, which we named Bird Island, having on board two butts and four hogshead of water, two live hogs, one firkin of butter, about four pound of biscuits a man, and ten days salt provisions at about two ounces a day per man, but quite rotten and decayed . . .'[13]

On 20 April 1756 they arrived at Delagoa River in Mozambique. Webb wrote: 'At four in the afternoon anchored in Delagoa river, in nine fathom, where we found the *Rose Galley* snow, Capt Chandler, trading for Beef and Teeth, of whom most of us begged a passage to Bombay.'[14]

John Lethbridge

John Lethbridge was the British pioneer of salvage diving. In the *Gentleman's Magazine* of September 1749 he wrote that he 'was prepossessed that it might be practicable to contrive a machine to recover wrecks lost in the sea'.[15]

He developed a primitive diving barrel in which the air supply could be replenished by means of a bellows. Lethbridge successfully salvaged twenty-seven chests of silver from the *Vansittart* using his 'diving engine'. In another letter dated 19 June 1757, he wrote to the East India Company proposing that he mount an operation to salvage the *Doddington*'s lost treasure:

> Sir, I have seen in the published papers that the *Dodington* Indiaman, was sometimes since wrecked on one island about 34 south and presuming she had a considerable quantity of treasure on board, I therefore take the liberty of troubling you with this, to request you to signify to the honourable East India Company that I am ready to serve them, in the recovery of the treasure lost, in case they are inclined to contract therefore, and if so, I should be glad to be informed what quantity of treasure was on board, and of what it consisted and what distance the ship was wrecked from the Cape of Good Hope, (where I have been on a diving expedition for the Dutch East India Company). I am the person that waited on you in March 1755, in order to contract for a diving expedition to the Isle of May, but was prevented by a contract subsisting with one Mr. Mill, which contract, I apprehend expires next spring, at which time, I should readily contract, for the recovery of the treasure, lost in the *Princess Louisa*; your answer hereto will vastly oblige.
>
> Your most humble servant, John Lethbridge.[16]

His request was refused and he died two years later at the age of eighty-three. An entry was made in the Wolborough Parish Register: 'Buried Mr. Lethbridge, inventor of a most famous diving engine, by which he recovered from the bottom of the sea, in different parts of the globe, almost £100,000 for the English and Dutch merchants which had been lost by shipwreck.'[17]

David and Gerry Allen

David and Gerry Allen were brothers from Port Elizabeth; both were experienced divers. In 1976 they found the wreck of the *Sacramento*, a Portuguese galleon which sank in 1647; they salvaged forty bronze cannons.

After their success they began to research the *Doddington*. The islands and reefs found in the eastern part of Algoa Bay are widely scattered over an area of nearly two square miles. The largest in the group is Bird Island, approximately 800 yards long and 600 yards in width with an elevation of about 35 feet. One and a half miles to the south lies Doddington Rock and East and West Rocks.

An entry in the *Indian Directory* of 1891 describes the rocks:

Between these rocks and islands the soundings are irregular, between 5 and 10 fathoms. During heavy weather, a tremendous sea rolls over the whole of this space, producing a surf truly terrific, the sea breaking in 8 and 10 fathoms water to seaward. It is necessary to give the Bird Island dangers a wide berth in passing, since it is difficult to distinguish between the sea that breaks into 10 fathoms, and that which rolls over the reefs. This is one of the most dangerous parts of the coast, especially to a stranger.[18]

The brothers chartered the *Etosha*, an 80-foot, 60-ton ex-fishing vessel; along with the Captain, George Braxton, and two other divers they sailed to Bird Island.

The weather was good and the sea calm. The group set up camp on Bird Island. Diving in a small area off Doddington Rock they found evidence of a wreck. David Allen describes the moment:

Below me, about twenty feet deep, lay a huge mound of what appeared to be about twenty tons of copper ingots. On top of that lay the ship's bow anchor, a huge fluked anchor perhaps twelve feet in length. Sticking out of that mountain of dull green copper were cannons . . . at a glance I could see all around bits and pieces of wreckage and cargo. On the upper side of the mount was a perfect bronze cannon six feet in length encrusted with white coral . . . lying on one side . . . lay a green patented brass carronade about three feet long. Later we were to find two more carronades . . . all around were large cannon balls, some a foot across.[19]

It was not until June 1977 that the divers managed to raise the first cannon. When they cleaned the coral from the barrel they found the crest of the Royal Crown and the initials of George II, king of England. Additional cannons brought to the surface confirmed that the wreck was that of the *Doddington*.

It seemed that the bow and stern had broken away from the midship section; the cargo then broke through the hold. The divers recovered 12 tons of copper, located twenty-six cannons and found large numbers of silver 'pieces-of-eight'. Although they found conglomerates of silver coins, they never located Clive's treasure chest of gold which would be worth today over £153,330 ($230,000).

The *Grosvenor* was dashed against a reef of rocks 400 yards off the east coast of South Africa during a violent storm on the night of 4 August 1782. 123 people survived the shipwreck but only nine lived through the terrible march along the inhospitable coast to the nearest settlement

GROSVENOR

The Grosvenor was built on the Thames by Wells of Deptford. She was launched in 1770 and chartered by the East India Company. She weighed 679 tons, her overall length was 120 feet and she was armed with twenty-six cannon. Her captain was John Coxon.

AREA: *Bay of Muscles, near the mouth of the Umzimvubo River, Pondoland, Cape Province, South Africa, Indian Ocean.*

The *Grosvenor* set sail from Portsmouth on 3 June 1780 bound for Madras, India. She arrived in Madras in January 1781; she then traded around various ports until 1782.

The *Grosvenor* departed India in March 1782, sailing for England via Trincomalee in Ceylon. According to her bill of lading she carried a general cargo of goods with an estimated value of £300,000. A letter sent to England from the company in Madras on 25 March states: 'The invoice by the Grosvenor amounts to S.P. (Star Pagodas) 162,378-22-69 (£64,951) and the register of diamonds to S.P. 243,44-31-69 (£9,737).'[2]

William Hosea, a wealthy official of the East India Company, was reported to have given the chief purser rough diamonds valued at 70,000 rupees, and £1700 in gold and silver coins for safe keeping.

According to company regulations Captain Coxon was allowed to carry 38 tons of his own 'privilege freight', the chief mate 8 tons, the second mate 6 tons and so on down to the ship's carpenter's allowance.[3]

Upon arrival in Trincomalee, the *Grosvenor* picked up extra cargo and passengers and continued on to England.

In Alexander Dalrymple's account to the East India Company Thomas Lewis, the foremast man, narrated that 'on 13 June the ship left Trincomalee. They saw no land after leaving Ceylon till the 4 August when the ship was lost.' At 8 pm on 4 August, by sea reckoning, when Thomas Lewis left the helm,

> the course was WNW with a fair wind; . . . in the middle watch the wind having come to the SW the 2nd mate had laid the ship on the starboard tack, but the captain came out and put the ship about again; he heard the captain say he was 300 miles from land by his account, which was the headmost; the wind having strengthened in the SW and blowing hard in squalls, . . . about half past 3 am he ws sent aloft to set down the foretopgallant yard, he thought he saw land and came down to tell, but he was sent up again, as they would not believe him; after the watch was relieved at 4 am . . . when he came from aloft about half past four, he saw the land plainly from the deck; but the 3rd mate . . . would not believe it, saying it was only the reflection of the sky and would not put the ship's head off to sea.[4]

A Mr Hubberly, the second mate's servant, was later to give the following account to the East India Company:

> In handing the topsails we saw two very large spreading lights, which Mr. Shaw, the second mate, who was the commanding officer of the watch, was made acquainted with, being so very strange. Various therefore

was the opinions of the persons on deck concerning them. At last we concluded they must be lights in the air, something similar to the Northern Lights. They soon after disappearing was taken no further notice of. We presently discovered it to be fires kindled by the natives some distance inland, for the purpose of burning the long grass, and cleansing the earth which was for several miles all on fire, and the cause of our losing sight of them were, we were approaching the land, thereby the hills on the coast obstructing our view. The gale still increasing with a high sea, Mr. Shaw deemed it most prudent to lay the ship's head to the eastward on the other tack, and consequently off the land, and for that purpose was veering the ship; but Captain Coxon, coming on deck at the instant, gave orders to let the ship remain with her head to the westward, which was towards the land. . . . At four a.m. the watch was relieved, Mr. Beale, the third mate relieving Mr. Shaw (Mr. Logie, the first mate being sick). Mr. Shaw informed Mr. Beale of the strange lights in the air, as he imagined he had seen, and cautioned him to keep a good look out. About half past four Thomas Lewis, seaman, since arrived in England, who had been detained at the foretop masthead, sending down the topgallant mast, came down on the forecastle and informed those who were stationed there that he thought he saw land under our lee bow. Every person directly looking out, some said they could observe land, others thinking it only a heavy squall, it appearing so high from the fogginess of the morning. We, however, as we approached it were soon satisfied. Mixon, a quartermaster ran aft and told Mr. Beale, commanding officer of the watch, that he could see land under our lee bow; but Mr. Beale said that he, Mixon, certainly was mistaken, and took no notice of it, not even so much as to give himself the trouble to go to the opposite side of the deck to examine it. Therefore Mixon after some hesitation went into the roundhouse, called Captain Coxon, and communicated the same, who instantly came on deck and gave orders to veer ship, and get her on the other tack with all possible dispatch. The boatswain had just time to pipe and call all hands, which, with the bustle on deck, soon brought them up. The helm was instantly put a-weather, the mizzen staysail hauled down, the fore-staysail hoisted, and every possible exertion used to get the ship on the other tack. Being on the larboard tack, we had wore round and brought the wind on the starboard quarter, and was in the act of hoisting the mizzen-staysail bring the ship to, when her larboard bow, dreadful to relate, struck against the rocks with such violence that we expected the masts to go over the side, which filled us all with the most terrible apprehensions, ... Our situation now was more dreadful, for excessive darkness being added to the violent squalls of wind and rain, accompanied with lightning, the surf breaking over the ship and rolling round us with a most terrible noise, the great surges dashing her against the rocks. ... There were at present about one hundred persons on and hanging about the quarter, the surf continually breaking over them, often washing some from their hold. We expected now the part of the wreck we remained on to go instantly to pieces, when we should all be entangled together amongst the fragments of the wreck, and those who could swim would stand no better chance than those who could not; ... Upon surveying our situation at daylight, we found the ship had first struck on the outermost part of a reef of rocks about two cables' length from the shore, which the sea broke over with a dreadful surf to the southward of us. The shore was bold, the cliffs steep, almost perpendicular. To the northward was a sandy pit ending in a low sandy point into which many things had drove. ... Betwixt three and four o'clock the stern of the ship went all to pieces, with nearly one hundred persons on it, a few coming on shore on different portions of the wreck, while the major portion of them when it separated, they remaining on the starboard quarter. It now drifted with them much nearer the shore, leaving the main body of the wreck breaking off the heavy sea.[5]

By five o'clock in the afternoon all survivors had reached the desolate and inhospitable shore of the Bay of Muscles.

Efforts were made to salvage the few provisions that were washed up along the shore. The captain explained to the castaways that a few days' rest could be allowed, but that they would then have to begin an estimated trek of seventeen days to the nearest settlement. Twelve weeks later, of the 123 who had managed to live through the shipwreck, only nine had survived the terrible march.

Sydney Turner

Sydney Turner owned two small vessels which traded out of Durban along the coast of Pondoland. On a trip to the area of the Ulambazo River he stopped to trade with local natives. An article later appeared in the *Natal Merchant Advertiser* on 24 February 1880. Entitled 'Relics from the Sea' it reported that: 'We were shown on Saturday some gold and silver coins which were picked up on the beach near the wreck of the *Grosvenor* by a gentleman (Mr. Turner) just returned from that very spot.'[6]

On 8 May the *Cape Argus* reported that a Mr S. Turner from Durban 'has now gone to the wreck with apparatus, dynamite, and men. Attempts are being made to secure the treasure known to be in the embedded hull of the *Grosvenor*.'[7]

Turner returned to Durban on 19 May. The following day the *Natal Mercury* published an article:

'By the S.S. *Adonis* which arrived yesterday, we are put in possession of some most interesting details in connection with the wreck of the ship *Grosvenor*, which took place ... about a hundred years ago. The report has long been abroad among the natives of the neighbourhood, that amongst the wreckage of the vessel could be found large quantities of gold coin and other valuable relics. Accordingly, Mr. Sydney Turner (of the firm Bennett & Turner) and Captain Beddoes of the Natal Pioneers, went to the spot about five weeks ago and have been engaged with a gang of kafirs in blasting with dynamite the rocks amongst which the wreckage lies. They have succeeded in finding, after some trouble, about fifty gold coins (supposed to be Spanish or Portuguese), about a hundred silver coins, said by Aboobaker Amod to have been coined 1200 years back, and a number of other trinkets and articles. We have not space today to follow further the details of Mr. Turner's researches, but promise our readers a fuller description of them tomorrow.'[8]

On 21 May 1880 the *Natal Mercury* carried a longer article, stating that the wreck of the *Grosvenor* occurred on a point of rocks about a mile north of the Itezani River, or about twenty-five miles on the Natal side of St John's River. The article continued:

Among the articles found was a large number of pistol and musket bullets, portions of crockery, brass ornamental work, glass stoppers, buttons, a gold clasp with the initials J.S.C., a copper plate, probably torn off a portmanteau, with the name of Buttall on it, a portion of gold ring, old battered specimens of silver and gold, and jewellery, and a button with the number 26 on it, supposed to be from a soldier's uniform, sleeve-links of Indian coins, and a lot of gold and silver coins. It is around these last-named that the chief interest at present centres. There are about fifty gold coins, about a hundred silver, and several copper ones. Many of the coins were found cemented into oxidized iron, the ship having been ballasted with pig-iron.

The gold pieces are about the size of a sovereign, but are much thinner; and although they have been so long exposed, several of them are in a wonderfully good state of preservation. . . . A number of little gold coins are quaint looking pieces, not unlike ordinary shirt studs [star pagodas]. . . .The silver coins are nearly all of one size – that of a shilling – and they appear to be of very ancient date. . . . Some Spanish coins appear to bear a date either about the year 1740 or 1770. . . .There is an idea in the minds of the local kafirs that a box of treasure is buried near the spot where the *Grosvenor* came ashore, but although a stone is said to have been marked to show where it is, there is as yet little clue to the whereabouts of the hidden prize. Nine of the cannon carried by the *Grosvenor* are lying among the rocks, as well as large quantities of iron ballast.[9]

A part of this article was reprinted in *The Times* of London on 29 June. Although Turner found a number of coins in poor condition, nothing of value was found that could offset his expenses; he discontinued his search.

Grosvenor Recovery Syndicate

Sixteen years later, in 1896, Alexander Lindsay, a Pondoland trader, was given several gold coins by local natives. On further enquiry he learnt that these coins had been found in the Bay of Muscles. Lindsay visited the bay and managed to recover 340 coins from the bottom of a rock pool. Nine years later, after the Boer War, Lindsay became a member of the Grosvenor Recovery Syndicate which was registered in Johannesburg. Its aim was to 'prospect, search for, win, get, quarry, reduce and prepare for market, all the treasure whether bullion, precious stones, bar gold or silver bars contained in the *Grosvenor* which was wrecked on the coast of East Africa, near St. John's river, in the year 1782'.[10]

A steam crane was purchased by the syndicate to remove the part of the reef where it was thought the *Grosvenor* lay; however, after the removal of 2000 tons of rock no trace of her was to be found.

Grosvenor Recovery Company

The objects of this company were to 'exploit and recover certain specie and treasure supposed to be contained in the hull of a certain ship being the wrecked East Indiaman formerly known as the *Grosvenor* now lying off the coast of Pondoland'.[11]

A dredger, the *Duiker*, was chartered by the company. She set sail for Pondoland; en route, in the Bay of Muscles, she struck a rock and had to return to Durban. The following month, with two divers on board, she returned to the site. The divers made a number of dives on the reef but, when a diver's airline was severed and he died, operations were terminated. The Grosvenor Recovery Company wound up its affairs and no further searches were made.

Grosvenor Bullion Syndicate

It was not until 1921 that the next attempt was made to recover the *Grosvenor* 'treasure'. Two Johannesburg businessmen, Martin and David Webster, formed the Grosvenor Bullion Syndicate Ltd. They issued a prospectus stating that 'information contained in documents will show the value of the treasure was £1,714,710 when it left Ceylon ... the *Grosvenor* lies within 100 feet of the nearest part of the shore, and is in only 18 feet of water, with from 6 to 10 feet of sand on top of her deck'.[12]

The prospectus also contained a 'list of treasures'. This stated 'the stones (precious stones, diamonds, rubies, sapphires, and emeralds) which are in 19 boxes were valued at £517,000. The gold bars number 720 and value £420,000. The silver bars number 1,450 (not valued) are stored amidships and specie (coins) to the value of £717,000 was stored in the lazarette as well as the savings of the passengers and crew.'[13]

£35,000 capital was raised by the sale of 700,000 shares at 1s each. The *Cape Times* of 10 September published an article entitled 'The Treasure Ship – Bold Bid for Prize of Two Million'.

In the first report of the directors on 28 December it stated that all pre-liminary work had been completed; diggers, machinery and equipment had all been purchased and put into use in order to salvage the 'treasure'. By the end of 1922 work was proceeding so slowly that the concerned shareholders had appointed a Cyril Campbell as their 'special commissioner' to investigate the company and all its operations. Campbell's report criticized the financial details of the company, including the paying of directors' fees and administrative expenses. One year later the Grosvenor Bullion Syndicate was no more.

Grosvenor Salvage Company

The Grosvenor Salvage Company Ltd was registered in Pretoria on 25 August 1938. An impressive prospectus was issued; the capital of the company was £75,000 divided into 5s shares. The objective was 'to take possession of articles recovered'. It was further stated that the value of the *Grosvenor's* cargo was now '£5,000,000'.

The company proposed building a breakwater 1300 feet around the reef where the wreck was supposed to lie. Upon completion, the sea water would then be pumped out and the wreck excavated. This construction would take six to seven months to finish. In December the site was surveyed and work began; by the following June 1000 feet had been dug out. In September 1939 war was declared in Europe, public interest in the *Grosvenor* waned and the operation ceased; today, nothing remains of the breakwater.

Grosvenor Salvage Company (Duckham)

This company was incorporated on 18 April 1946 and registered in Durban. The share capital was fixed at £50,000 and was divided into 120,000 ordinary shares of 10s each. The company's prospectus estimated the value of the *Grosvenor* 'treasure' at £5 million. F.W. Duckham, managing director, who was both a civil and a marine engineer, suggested that a special large Michigan crane should be brought over from the United States at a cost of £6000. The purchase, he proposed, would expedite the latest plan for finding the elusive wreck of the *Grosvenor*. Work was begun on improving the road out of the Bay of Muscles and, by May 1947, all was in place to begin the search in earnest. It then transpired that the company had not got the funds actually to purchase the Michigan crane. Various attempts were made to raise more finance. The following year the value of the 'treasure' was purported to be in the region of £7 million, but by 1949 all real funds were exhausted and salvage operations ceased.

On 30 May 1956 a small article appeared in the *Star* newspaper stating that five men had left Durban in yet another attempt to find clues to the location of the wreck of the *Grosvenor* and her elusive treasure. Nothing more was later reported.

WINTERTON

The Winterton *was an eighteenth-century British East India Company frigate. Her captain was George Dundas.*
   AREA: *Wrecked on a reef in the Mozambique Channel, six miles off the coast of Madagascar.*

The East Indian merchantship *Winterton*, commanded by Captain George Dundas, sailed from England on 2 May 1792 bound for Madras and Bengal. She had on board a quantity of gold specie to the value of £266,000[1], and carried a total of 280 persons, (crew and passengers), including ten women. *The Times* reported: 'The *Winterton* seems to have been marked for misfortune from the moment she was launched. On her first voyage, she sprung a leak, on her second, she was nearly lost within sight of port and on the voyage before last, the loss of 50 of her crew by sickness.'[2]

   The first part of the voyage to the Cape of Good Hope passed without incident. The *Winterton* arrived at False Bay on 18 July 1792 where passengers disembarked and rested as the ship took on fresh water and new provisions. On 10 August she left Cape Town sailing towards the Mozambique Channel. Captain Dundas intended to take the outer passage to India but, as the winds were invariable and contrary, he decided to make for the Bay of St Augustin and gave orders for the new course of east-northeast to be set, avoiding the dangerous Bassas De Indias Shoals. The Captain 'had two time pieces, one of which had served him in his former voyage, and by it he had constantly made the land with the greatest degree of exactness. From these and from several sets of lunar observations taken four days before – the whole of which coincided with the time-pieces – he concluded with confidence that at midnight they were eighty miles from the nearest part of the coast.'[3] The night of 20 August was clear, winds were moderate and the ship was making six knots; there was a new moon and a high tide, no sign of surf or breakers ahead.

   The first mate reported later: 'A little before three o'clock, he (the captain) pointed out to me the ship's place in a chart, which was then upwards of 60 miles (according to his idea) from land; and when he left the deck at three, directed me to steer N.E. .... if you see anything suspicious, act according,

At about 3 o'clock on the morning of 20 August 1792 the *Winterton* struck a hidden reef in the Mozambique channel. She was carrying a quantity of gold specie to the value of £266,000

without waiting to call me. Captain Dundas had not been off deck seven or eight minutes when the ship struck.'[4] She struck very hard and began to leak badly. Her bows quickly took on eight feet of water and the pumps could not keep pace with the encroaching seas.

Both the jolly boats and yawl were launched. A hundred yards astern they found five fathoms of water, the sails were thrown back in an attempt to get her off without success. The kedge anchor was carried to deeper water to try and heave her off the reef but again all efforts failed.

> Top-gallant yards and masts struck, the long-boat got out, the booms rafted alongside, and the deck entirely cleared. By the time these different operations were effected, day-light appeared, and discovered to us our situation, about six miles from land. . . . During the ebbing of the tide, the ship continued to beat with increasing violence, as the water diminished in depth: But about eight in the morning, she lay perfectly quiet. . . . So soon as we struck, the military recruits were ordered to the pumps. . . . But in the progress of the wreck, the bottom of the ship became so much shattered, that the pumps ceased to be of any avail.[5]

At 8 o'clock in the morning the rudder broke; it was then that Captain Dundas realized that the *Winterton* was truly lost.

As night fell the winds increased; the pounding surf smashed both the longboat and the jolly boat which had been moored astern. With these two boats lost it became impossible to attempt to salvage the treasure. As dawn came the *Winterton* began to break up and the remaining lower part of the ship was abandoned. 'Some of our soldiers and sailors had considerable sums of money. The amount of public treasure in the *Winterton* was near 400,000 dollars; and when the ship was entirely given up, any one who chose it might take as much as they could; but the weight made this hazardous.'[6]

Captain Dundas then ordered the crew to cut away the masts and spars to construct rafts. The beams of the poop were cut and the deck was shored up to form another raft, capable of holding sixty to eighty persons.

The Captain called the crew and passengers together and 'in a short speech made them acquainted with the situation where they were, as to latitude; the route they were to take after getting on shore . . . he insisted on the absolute necessity of paying strict attention to the commands of their officers'.[7]

As the wind increased the wreck was forced broadside on to the rocks, the port side was smashed in and the waves began to break over the stricken ship: 'The fatal moment now approached that was to separate many of us forever. The decks were falling in; large pieces of the wreck were dashed with such violence by the surf among us, as to endanger our lives; and, waiting for a favourable interval, we threw our raft overboard and jumped in.'[8]

Captain Dundas was washed through the quarter-galley and was never seen again. Fifty-three of the passengers and crew made it safely to the shore.

The *Winterton* treasure lies off Point St Felix 23° 30' South latitude. There have been neither official nor other reported attempts at salvage. But it is believed locally that fishermen have made dives in the area and have located some coins.

BIRKENHEAD

The Birkenhead *was built of iron and wood by the Laird Brothers of Birkenhead. She was launched in December 1845 and was 64 feet long with a displacement of 1918 tons. Typical of the period (in the transition from sail to steam) she was rigged as a three-masted brigantine and was also equipped with a funnel and two steam paddles. Although* Birkenhead *was originally built as a frigate and named* Vulcan *she was later converted to a troopship and renamed.*

AREA: *Sank off Danger Point about 50 miles southeast of Cape Town, South Africa, Atlantic Ocean.*

The Cape Frontier Wars, also called the Kaffir Wars, began in 1779 and continued intermittently for 100 years. These wars were fought between the European settlers in the Eastern Frontier Region of the Cape Colony and the native Xhosa peoples.

After the failure of several treaties, the eighth war broke out in 1846 and was to be the most costly in terms both of British casualties and money.

By the end of 1851 Sir Harry Smith, Governor and Commander-in-Chief of the Cape, requested reinforcements to bolster his depleted regiments. In response to Sir Harry's request, the *Birkenhead*, commanded by Robert Salmond, called in at several ports throughout the British Isles and recruited a selection of soldiers from ten different regiments. By 7 January 1852 the ship was on her way to South Africa; on board were twelve officers, three surgeons, and 479 non-commissioned officers and men. Twenty-five women, thirteen children and a crew of 130 made up the total numbers.

The *Birkenhead* also carried £240,000[1] in gold for the Army's payroll. The ship was overcrowded and living conditions were extremely unhygienic. Many persons became dreadfully ill and four women died.

On 23 February *Birkenhead* reached the Cape and anchored off Simonstown where the sick disembarked, and coal and fresh supplies were taken on board, along with thirty horses. Captain Salmond's orders were to take the troops up to Port Elizabeth at Algoa Bay and then to the Buffalo River some 500 miles further up the coast. On the evening of 25 February *Birkenhead* left for Port Elizabeth with 638 on board. The weather was fine with clear skies, a gentle breeze and calm seas. The ship cleared Cape Hangklip at 9.30pm and set a course south-southeast, making a speed of about eight knots. At mid-

The *Birkenhead* struck an uncharted rock off Danger Point in False Bay, about 50 miles from Cape Town in February 1852. Ten minutes after striking the ship broke in two. 445 of the 638 people on board were lost and a sum of £240,000 in gold went down with the ship

night the Second Master, Mr Davis, took over as Officer of the Watch. Able Seaman Thomas was at the helm, with two lookouts on the bow and leadsman Stone on the port-side paddle box sounding the depth at regular intervals as the ship was only four miles from the coast.

At 2am, as the *Birkenhead* approached Danger Point, the leadsman took a sounding and found bottom at 12 fathoms; moments later, the ship struck an uncharted rock. Stone was later to state '. . .that he was leadsman in the chain at one o'clock, but got no soundings. At about 20 minutes to two o'clock he got sounding in 12 fathoms, but before he got another cast, the ship struck, and he got seven fathoms alongside. Mr Davis was Officer of the Watch; the night was fine with smooth water. The land was seen on the port bow about four points.'[2]

As the ship struck the rock the iron plating was ripped open between the engine room and the forepeak. The lower troop deck was immediately flooded, drowning the trapped soldiers as they slept. Captain Salmond ordered the engines full astern in a desperate effort to free the *Birkenhead* from the rock, but, as she came off, she struck again and further tore the bottom and, in moments, the engine room flooded. Orders were given to throw the horses overboard and to lower the *Birkenhead*'s lifeboats. Although the ship was equipped with one large boat on either side of the paddle boxes, two eight-oared cutters on davits over the stern, two four-oared gigs on the forepart, and a 30-foot pinnacle midships, only the two cutters and one of the gigs were actually launched and cleared the ship. They held eighty persons.

Captain Wright of the 91st Regiment made this official military account during the subsequent enquiry:

Sir – It is with feelings of the deepest regret that I have to announce to you the loss of Her Majesty's steamer *Birkenhead*, which took place on a rock about two and a half or three miles off Danger Point, at 2 am. 20th February.

The sea was smooth at the time, and the vessel was steaming at the rate of eight knots and a half an hour. She struck the rock, and it penetrated through the bottom just aft of the foremast. The rush of water was so great that there is no doubt that most of the men in the lower troop-deck were drowned in their hammocks. The rest of the men and all the officers appeared on deck, when Major Seton called all the Officers about him and impressed on them the necessity of preserving order and silence among the men. He directed me to take and have executed whatever orders the Commander might give me. Sixty men were immediately put on to the chain-pumps on the lower after-deck, and told off in three reliefs; sixty men were put on to the tackles of the paddle-box boats, and the remainder of the men were brought on to the poop, so as to ease the fore part of the ship. She was at this time rolling heavily. The Commander ordered the horses to be pitched out of the port gangway, and the cutter to be got ready for the women and children, who had all been collected under the poop awning. As soon as the horses were got over the side, the women and children were passed into the cutter, and under charge of Mr. Richards, master's assistant, the boat then stood off about 150 yards. Just after they were out of the ship the entire bow broke off at the foremast, the bowsprit going up in the air towards the foretopmast, and the funnel went over the side, carrying away the starboard paddle box and boat. The port paddle box boat capsized when being lowered. The large boat in the centre of the ship could not be got at.

It was about twelve or fifteen minutes after she struck that the bow broke off. The men then all went up on the poop, and in about five minutes more the vessel broke in two, crosswise, just abaft the engine-room, and the stern part immediately filled and went down. A few men jumped off just before she did so, but the greater number remained to the last, and so did every officer belonging to the troops. All the men I put on the tackles, I fear, were crushed when the funnel fell; and the men and officers below at the pumps could not, I think, have reached the deck before the vessel broke up and went down. The survivors clung, some to the rigging of the mainmast, part of which was out of the water, and others got hold of floating pieces of wood. I think there must have been about 200 on the drift-wood. I was on a large piece along with five others, and we picked up nine or ten more. The swell carried the wood in the direction of Danger Point. As soon as it got to the weeds and breakers, finding that it would not support all that were on it, I jumped off and swam on shore.[3]

The fore part of the ship sank, leaving more than 350 men clinging to the slowly sinking poop deck. Benjamin Barber, assistant engineer, described the sinking:

About two a.m. on the morning of 26 February 1852 I was awoke by the ship striking, and ran into the engine-room, where I found Mr. Kitchingham, who was on watch, standing by the starting gear. He informed me he had just stopped the engines. We remained there until Mr. Whyham ordered the safety valves of the three boilers to be opened, which I did; shortly after, the order was given to turn astern, which was done; the fires were afterwards extinguished by the water rising rapidly in the engine-room. We then went on deck. Soon after, the ship parted; I went to the dinghy's fall, and lowered myself into the water, but the weight of the soldiers who clung on me forced me to let go, and take to some of the main rigging, where I remained until the ship went down, taking me with her. I came up again, and held onto some of the wreck, until picked up by Captain Wright and some more men on a part of the fore sponson, on which we succeeded in reaching the shore at about one p.m.[4]

It was only twenty minutes from the time the *Birkenhead* struck until she sank below the surface. As the poop-deck sank many men were clinging to the wreckage, only to be caught by sharks. 'Of those who swam, only a small percentage reached shore. Some died of exhaustion, others were entangled in the kelp or drowned, whilst many were gashed to pieces on the sharp rocks, that lined the coast.'[5]

The first news of the wreck of the *Birkenhead* reached Cape Town on the morning of 27 February. Two official documents were published:

To his Excellency Lieut-General Sir Harry G.W. Smith, Governor and Commander-in-Chief.

Sir, it is with much pain that I have to inform your Excellency of the total loss of Her Majesty's steamship *Birkenhead* at two o'clock in the morning of the 26th instant, near to Point Danger; and I regret to add that from the statement given by Dr. Culhane, assistant-surgeon of the ship, it would appear that only about 70 persons are saved out of 690 souls, nine of whom have landed, but the others are in two boats, and had proceeded seaward to be picked up by a sailing vessel. I have despatched the *Rhadamanthus* to the scene of this fearful disaster to afford all possible relief and to search for the missing boats. As it is possible they may be compelled to effect a landing, I would be glad if your Excellency gave instructions to the resident magistrates and field-cornets on the coast to keep a look-out for them, and render every possible assistance.

I beg to enclose Dr. Culhane's statement, and have the honour to be, your Excellency's most obedient servant. C. Wyvill, Commodore.

Since writing the above, the *Rhadamanthus* has towed in the Schooner *Lioness,* which vessel picked up the two boats mentioned. The sufferers, 116 in number, are at present on board the *Castor,* and the *Rhadamanthus* has again proceeded to the scene of the wreck. I annex a list of persons saved. Dr. Bowen, staff-surgeon, reports that several of the soldiers reached the land on rafts. C. Wyvill.

Statement of Dr. Culhane, of Her Majesty's Late Steamship *Birkenhead*'

That Her Majesty's steamship *Birkenhead* struck the rock at about 2 a.m. on the morning of the 26th of February somewhere near Point Danger, and in twenty minutes after filled and went down. The quarter boats were lowered, and about 65 persons got into them; the gig was also down. While getting the paddle box boats out the heave of the ship in sinking washed them away. Many were drowned before they could effect their escape to the upper deck. Dr. Culhane and eight men landed in the gig at Port D'Urban, where Mr. Phillipson has a store about thirty miles from the wreck. Nothing has been heard of the other two boats except that they pulled out to sea to get picked up by a sailing vessel.[6]

Of the 638 men, women and children on board 445 drowned. In documents relating to the court-martial Mr Richard Bevan Richards, the ship's master's assistant, stated the following relating to the *Birkenhead's* cargo:

Q. Do you know what the *Birkenhead* was carrying?

A. Yes. Troops, government stores and specie.

Q. Do you know how many troops?

A. Not exactly without looking at the records.

Q. Do you know what stores she had on board?

A. Yes, but not the quantity without the manifest.

Q. Do you know what specie she carried?

A. Yes, there were 120 boxes of specie but I cannot say except from the manifest what each or all the boxes contained.

Q. What did they contain?

A. Some 10,000, some 5,000 and some less in pounds, some gold and some silver.

Q. Did the boats stay by the wreck till daylight?

A. No, but nearly till dawn.

Q. Was any attempt made to save anything?

A. No, the vessel floundered too quickly.7

This statement confirmed that gold was certainly on the *Birkenhead*.

On 25 March 1852 an advertisement appeared in the *Government Gazette and Trade List Supplement*.

WRECK OF H.M. STEAMER *BIRKENHEAD*

Wrecked off Danger Point near the farm of Sir Robt. Stanford.

Also *Wearing Apparel*

On Monday morning next, the 29th instant, will be sold, by Public Auction, on the Beach of Danger Point the above Vessel, as she lies in the Sea, with rigging, spars, yards, &c, &c stores and provisions, and whatever may be on Board.

Consisting of Naval and Military Clothes, Shirts, Shoes, Stockings and whatever may have been washed on Shore from the above Wreck.

R.J. Jones, *Auctioneer*

On April 1852 the wreck was sold for £135 and the 'wearing apparel' for £100. In 1854 the wreck was again sold by public auction by agents of the

Admiralty to a Mr. H. Adams. Adams employed a number of divers in an attempt to salvage the gold with no success.

On 7 June 1862 the *Cape Argus* published the following article:

> The wrecked steamer *Birkenhead* – it is understood that a company in England has recently purchased this steamer, as she now lies submerged near Cape L'Agulhas, for 2,780 pounds: and that a number of artisans may shortly be expected to arrive for the purpose, if possible, of raising her. It will be in the recollection of many that at the time of the melancholy disaster – about ten years ago – she went down with a considerable amount of specie on board, and was then sold by public auction for 50 pounds to two gentlemen, who have since transferred their interest in her to the above company.[8]

Nothing further was reported.

Birkenhead Syndicate

The first syndicate was formed in 1893 by one of the survivors, G.A. Lucas, an ensign of the 73rd Regiment of Foot. He had settled in South Africa and become a prominent magistrate. The Birkenhead Syndicate offered shares at £10 each, but Lucas's attempts to salvage anything of value proved fruitless. In a letter dated 8 April 1902 Bernard Kilkeary, the paymaster sergeant of the same regiment, wrote to the Under-Secretary of War in London.

> Sir, Re: Wreck of the *Birkenhead*
>
> I beg respectfully to enclose for the perusal of the Rt. Honbll the Secretary of State for War a newspaper containing narrative supplied to me in connection with this wreck, from which I have purposely omitted any reference to the 'specie' on board which I understand was very considerable. The information which I possess upon this subject I shall place at the disposal of the proper government department upon request being made to me.
>
> I am sir your obedient servant. (SD) Bernard Kilkeary, Formerly Paymr-Sergt 73 Regt Late Mid-Ulster Artillery[9]

Mr Marzial of the War Office passed the letter to the Treasury department which replied to the Under-Secretary of State at the War Office:

> My Lord. I have laid before the Lords Commissioners of His Majesty's Treasury Mr. Marzial's letter of the 19th instant (114 MIS: 1336. FI)

forwarding a letter and enclosure (now returned herewith) from Mr. B. Kilkeary respecting specie alleged to have been on board the troop-ship *Birkenhead* at the time when that vessel was wrecked in February 1852. I am directed to refer to the correspondence I noted in the margin, and to acquaint you for the information to the Secretary of State for War that, as a result of enquiries I made in 1893, it was impossible to say what amount of public treasure, if any, was on board the *Birkenhead* at the time of the wreck.[10]

In 1935 the Sorima Company of Genoa explored the site; their salvage attempts were abandoned due to bad weather conditions.

Second Birkenhead Syndicate

In 1936 the salvage rights were acquired by a Mr Tromp van Diggelen who was granted a permit to 'search for and operate abandoned vessels along the coast of the Union and to take possession of all articles or things of value which he may find'.[11]

He formed the Second Birkenhead Syndicate and published this prospectus:

> Despite unfavourable weather, enough material has already been salvaged from the wreck of the 'Birkenhead' to prove that the Syndicate's method of free-diving is the only correct one for the type of work that is here demanded. With the coming of better weather conditions during the Summer, and owing to exact plans of the sunken vessel having been supplied by the Maritime Museum in London, work can be continued with great confidence and plans are being made for extensive recoveries. Enough copper has already been found to bring in a considerable amount when it is brought up to the surface; anchors, and other valuable relics, have been 'buoyed' to be salvaged later.
>
> The vessel contained much military equipment as well as a great variety of articles of value. The most efficient methods will be employed to 'comb' every part of the wreck and much gold coinage should be recovered 'loose' as many men had their pay, in gold sovereigns, on their persons when they were suddenly drowned below decks. Hundreds of sea-chests will also be explored for valuables and golden coins. Every corpse that floated ashore carried sovereigns in a belt or in pockets of clothing; over 600 soldiers and sailors had received pay on the day before the catastrophe.[12]

It was not until the summer of 1957 that the salvage vessel *Penta* anchored off 'Birkenhead Rock' and Nicholas Dekker, the chief diver, made his first investigation of the wreck.

Dekker found and recovered the bow anchor and located the paddle wheels, stanchions and ventilators, but was unable to find the stern half where the gold was supposed to be stored. Despite an extensive search of the wreck site, the stern section was never found and the Birkenhead Syndicate gave up further operations.

Depth Recovery Unit and Aqua Exploration

The Depth Recovery Unit, headed by Dr Allan Kayle, successfully applied to the South African National Monuments Council in 1983 for salvage rights.

Dr Kayle signed a contract with Aqua Exploration in a joint venture, establishing a strong team of divers and equipment; salvage operations were to be supervised by the National Maritime Museum. In 1984 the group set up a base camp near Danger Point. Working from ski-boats the divers began their preliminary exploration of the wreck site. In the first three months the divers found a number of cannons, the remains of the paddle wheels and the broken section of the stern partly buried under sand and coral.

It was not until 1986 that the main salvage operations began when the tug *Causeway Adventurer*, fully equipped with diving apparatus and diving bell, secured herself with three seven-ton anchors above the wreck. Diving to a depth of 100 feet the divers sifted tons of sand and silt, finding ship's artifacts, bottles, porcelain and the first gold coins. Twenty-seven gold sovereigns, minted between 1821 and 1837, included George IV with laureated head (1821), Victoria with unicorn (1850), William IV (1837), George III with St George & the Dragon on reverse (1820).[13]

Over 111 gold sovereigns were found but the bulk of the treasure was never located. The Ministry of Defence in Britain said officially 'that it could not confirm or deny the rumour of gold aboard'.[14]

THE AMERICAS

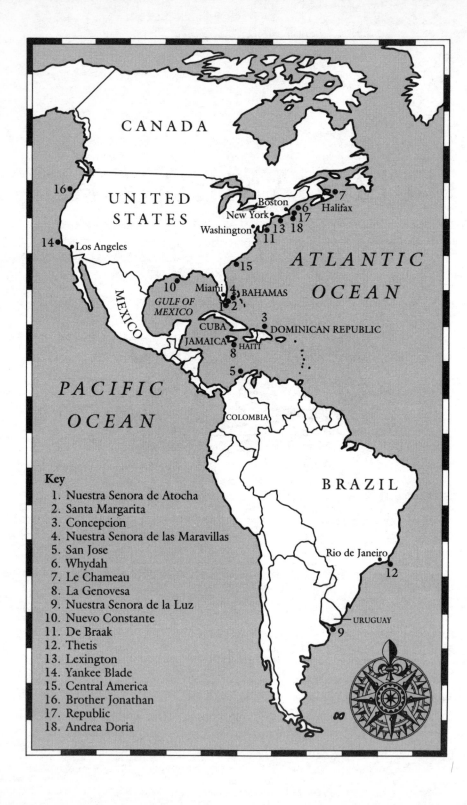

CANADA

UNITED STATES

16•

14• Los Angeles

Boston
New York•
Washington•

7•
6•
17
18
13
11

Halifax

ATLANTIC OCEAN

15•

10
Miami 4
2

BAHAMAS

MEXICO

GULF OF MEXICO

3

CUBA

DOMINICAN REPUBLIC

JAMAICA
8

HAITI

5•

PACIFIC OCEAN

COLOMBIA

BRAZIL

Rio de Janeiro
12•

URUGUAY

9•

Key
1. Nuestra Senora de Atocha
2. Santa Margarita
3. Concepcion
4. Nuestra Senora de las Maravillas
5. San Jose
6. Whydah
7. Le Chameau
8. La Genovesa
9. Nuestra Senora de la Luz
10. Nuevo Constante
11. De Braak
12. Thetis
13. Lexington
14. Yankee Blade
15. Central America
16. Brother Jonathan
17. Republic
18. Andrea Doria

NUESTRA SENORA DE ATOCHA

The Nuestra Senora de Atocha *was built in Havana in 1620 by the master shipwright Alonso Ferreria. She was a typical galleon of the period with a raised forecastle, towering sterncastle and square sails. She weighed 550 tons and was armed with twenty bronze cannons. The* Atocha *was commanded by Captain Bartolomé De Nodal and carried a crew of 155, eighteen trained gunners, eighty-two soldiers and forty-eight passengers; Vice-Admiral Pedro de Espanza was Senior Officer.*

AREA: *Wrecked on the reefs at the Marquesas Keys, twenty miles west of Key West in the Straits of Florida, USA.*

The *Nuestra Senora de Atocha* sailed from Cadiz on 23 March 1622. The *Atocha* was part of the outward-bound fleet sailing to Havana and Portobelo in Panama, carrying wine, cloth, iron, general merchandise and over half a million pounds of mercury. The fleet arrived at the Isthmus of Panama on 24 May where the ships unloaded their cargo.

In June the *Atocha* was joined by seven other galleons, eight galleons alto-gether escorting seventeen ships, merchantships and three pataches (armed guard vessels) that made up the Tierra Firma treasure fleet. This fleet was commanded by the Marquis de Cadereita in the flagship *Nuestra Senora de Candelaria*, and set sail for Cartagena to pick up additional gold and silver before continuing to Spain via Havana. At Portobelo and Cartagena, silver-master Jacove de Vreder supervised the loading of the *Atocha*. The total cargo consisted of 161 ingots of gold, each weighing anywhere from 6 to 77 troy oz, and 901 ingots of pure silver: 'approximately 250,000 silver coins of various denominations were aboard the *Atocha*; output of the royal mints at Potosi, Lima, Mexico city, Santa fe de Bogota, and Santiago de Chile. Historians estimate that the value of these coins . . . could total between 46 and 115 million dollars.'[1]

Also in her cargo were a large number of uncut emeralds from Colombia. During the Spanish conquest of South America large quantities of emeralds were taken from the Incas of Peru but their mines were never located by the Spanish Conquistadores. The only other source of South American emeralds was the famous Muzo mines near Bogota, Colombia.

Many of the passengers aboard the *Atocha* were wealthy Spanish officials, merchants and religious dignitaries carrying religious objects made in gold and silver studded with precious stones.

The three main galleons carrying the bulk of the treasure were the *Atocha*, her sister ship, *Santa Margarita*, and the flagship, *Nuestra Senora de Candelaria*. Each ship carried an immense amount of treasure; the total value at today's prices has been estimated to be in the region of £250 million ($400 million). The Spanish Crown owned many of the most productive gold and silver mines that were to be found in the New World. Legally, each gold and silver bar had to have an assayer's stamp and a circular mark of the Royal Seal, indicating the quinto or royal fifth. This tax or 'registered treasure' for the Spanish Crown was recorded in each ship's manifest. Many corrupt officials took advantage of the seemingly endless stream of treasure that made its way to Spain; they under-valued treasure and carried quantities of 'unregistered treasure' to avoid the King's 20 per cent tax. The penalty, if one were caught, was severe: 200 lashes and ten years in the galleys as an oarsman. Both the *Atocha* and the *Santa Margarita* carried a large amount of unregistered treasure. On 3 August 1622 the fleet departed Cartagena and made for Cuba. When the ships arrived in Havana on 22 August they made ready to be supplied with fresh water and provisioned for the homeward voyage to Spain. The hurricane season was well underway. An old Caribbean adage serves to outline the threat of hurricanes:

> June, too soon
> July, stand by
> August, come they must
> September, remember
> October, all over.

But the fleet was six weeks behind schedule and departed Havana on 4 September. The ships sailed northeast then tacked north into the Florida Straits in order to pick up the Gulf Stream current. About seven on the morning of 5 September gale-force winds rose out of the northeast and quickly increased to hurricane force (gale force 10). The fleet was scattered but, by midnight, when the wind clocked around to the south, the ships were blown towards the Bajos de los Martyrs (Bank of the Martyrs, now the Florida Keys). Many of the galleons lost their sails and had to cut their masts away. The merchantship, *Nuestra Senora de la Consolacion*, capsized and sank; the *Nuestra del Rosario*, along with one of the pataches, were wrecked on Loggerhead Key in the Dry Tortugas. The *Santa Margarita* lost her foresail, and broke her main-mast and tiller; she was swept across the reefs at the Cayos del Marquez (Marquesas Keys).

A contemporary account describes the situation: 'But as waves roule after

Philip IV who ascended the Spanish throne in 1621. He inherited a vast empire
with possessions on four continents, together with a huge national debt. The
treasure fleets bringing vast quantities of gold and silver to Spain from the New
World were a financial lifeline, helping to fund wars against the Dutch and
the French

waves, one mischiefe followes another: for presently the wind turned to the
south ... then they feared another misfortune, to be thrust or hurried into
some creeke or bay of the coast of Florida ... and then there was no hope
but either splitting on the sand, or perishing on the shore.'[2]

Three miles to the east of the *Santa Margarita*, the *Atocha* was driven on to
the same reefs; badly holed by the coralheads she sank in 55 feet of water.
Of the 265 souls aboard the *Atocha*, 260 (including the Admiral and the senior
pilot) drowned. Two slaves, two ship's boys and a seaman were rescued the
following morning by the longboat from the *Santa Cruz*. A Captain Bernardino
de Lugo, commander of the infantry force on the *Margarita*, and one of the
few wreck survivors, was later to report: 'At seven in the morning he saw one
league to the east of his galleon the one named *Nuestra Senora de Atocha* ...
dismasted except for the mizzen mast. While he watched, she went down and
... nothing could be seen of the ship.'[3]

The battered remnants of the fleet limped back to Havana to repair rigging, sails and hulls. In total, seven ships were lost, including three treasure galleons. The loss of so much treasure was of great concern to the Spanish Crown as the economy had become based on the gold and silver mined from New Spain and New Granada. While the *Candelaria* was in Havana being overhauled, the Marquis de Cadereita held a meeting with officials to plan salvage from the *Atocha*, *Santa Margarita* and *Rosario*.

Early Spanish Salvage Attempts

A translated excerpt from a letter written by the Marquis de Cadereita to King Philip IV outlines the first salvage attempt made in 1622:

> On the 15th of the same month the Governor, ministers and pilots of the army and fleet met to reach an agreement to prepare the ships in order to search. . . . It was decided the Captain Gaspar de Vargas would go to make the recovery from the two lost galleons, and to search for the lost one around the Tortuga Keys, which he went out to do on the 16th September with three 'pataches' and two 'chalupas' (smaller ships). Having reached the right place, he discovered the small mast of the 'Almiranta' [Atocha]. . . . The galleon was in a depth of 10 'brazas' of water. The divers went down to enter the silver compartment, which could not be accomplished because the portholes and hatches were locked and the decks were in one piece. . . . He then left to search for the Santa Margarita. The buoy was not found, neither was the ship. A storm kept them from working further. He headed for the Tortuga Keys in search for the Nuestra Senora del Rosario which he found stranded in one of the keys, on the 24th of September, and found on the land its people and on a nearby key a 'patache' of the fleet. . . . They took out all the silver and twenty pieces of artillery.[4]

Following Captain Vargas's 1622 attempts at salvage, Francisco Nunez Melian was contracted to salvage in 1624 by King Philip. The King was anxious that both the *Atocha* and the *Santa Margarita* should be located and their respective treasures be repossessed by the Spanish Crown as soon as possible. Melian wrote of his progress to King Philip:

> Your Royal Highness: Without any delay I am advising you of the diligence in the search of the galleons 'almiranta' and Santa Margarita. I left this harbour May 26 very well supplied with three armoured frigates, two

boats and one patache, accompanied by more than 100 men-of-war and all the necessary equipment for the search of the 'almiranta', for which I had already carefully looked with dredging instruments and diving bells following the information given me by the pilot major Captain Antonio de Gobea, who embarked with me because he is the best pilot in the whole Indies.

The knowledge and diligence of the pilot major has been valuable and he has helped me greatly in the search of the 'almiranta'. He has, however, fallen again in sickness and being near death I was compelled to bring him back to this city, although not wishing to stop the search for the 'almiranta' and the Santa Margarita.[5]

In 1626 Melian finally found the *Santa Margarita*, but the location of the *Atocha* eluded him. A few further unsuccessful searches were made but in 1688 the Casa de la Contratacion (Board of Trade) listed the *Atocha* as still missing. In time the ship was forgotten.

Mel Fisher: Treasure Salvors

Although Mel Fisher was born in Indiana, California was to provide him with his introduction to diving and salvage investigation. By the mid 1950s he had taken part in several Caribbean expeditions. In 1963 Fisher sold his engineering business and moved himself and his family to Florida; he eventually met Kip Wagner and the two men formed Treasure Salvors, Inc. In 1964 they found two important wrecks from the 1715 Spanish treasure fleet and from these two ships 2500 gold doubloons were recovered. Kip Wagner left Treasure Salvors Inc. and started his own salvage company.

In 1966 Fisher became interested in, and began to research, the fate of the 1622 Tierra Firma treasure fleet – he was particularly interested in the *Atocha*. Information that he found in early Spanish documents referred to Cabeza de los Martires in the Cayos del Matecumbe as the wreck site of the *Atocha*. In modern-day terms this indicated to Fisher that Matecumbe Key, lying near Middle Key between Key West and Key Largo, could well be the *Atocha*'s resting place. Accordingly, Fisher set up an intensive search operation using Middle Key as his centre point. Treasure Salvor's search boat, *Holly's Folly*, scanned and plotted the eighty-five-mile stretch of reef from Matecumbe Key up to Key Largo. In spite of this thorough search no evidence was found to suggest that *Atocha* was lying beneath the sea's surface.

Mel Fisher was by nature an optimist and an opportunist. He sold all that he owned and gambled his capital on finding the galleon. When his money had all been spent he managed to fire others with his dream and put more funds together to finance salvage vessels and divers. There were times when crew and divers received no pay; these times lasted up to three months.

Fisher contacted the historian, Dr Eugene Lyon, a specialist in Spanish Florida, and hired him as a consultant. Fisher told Lyon, 'Put me within a quarter of a mile of the *Atocha* and I'll pay you $10,000.'[6]

Lyon went to Seville to research Spanish documents of the period in the Archivo General de Indias. He discovered that the actual reference to the *Atocha*'s wreck site was given as the Cayos del Marquez. However, the cross-reference, that of Cayos del Matecumbe, was a very general seventeenth-century navigational point and actually referred to all the islands found along the southern tip of Florida. To compound further the question of location it could be shown that, by the eighteenth century, charts had started to show that the Cayos del Marquez seemed to be more consistently located some seventy miles west of Key West. Lyon then located Melian's account of his 1624 search and salvage attempts.

In September 1970, armed with Dr Lyon's information, Treasure Salvors moved operations down to Key West. Fisher made for the Marquesas Keys and plotted out the new search area; a fifty-mile stretch of water reaching from Moon Shoal to Sandy Key. Months of fruitless searching began. In a review of all the documents it appeared that they had been exploring on the wrong side of the Keys. The search was quickly moved to the west side of the Marquesas Keys. After a year of searching *Holly's Folly*'s magnetometer detected a large metal object in an area known as Quicksands, near the outer reef. A 12-foot Spanish sheet anchor was discovered and raised to the surface. When the divers went back down they found a silver coin and three lengths of gold chain. A few days later, the support ship, *Virgilona*, using more sophisticated equipment, uncovered two unnumbered gold ingots; these could have been 'unregistered cargo' contraband. There was still nothing to show whether or not this was indeed the elusive *Atocha*.

Over the next eighteen months gold ingots, silver and gold coins, swords, daggers and numerous miscellaneous artifacts were recovered. On 14 July 1974 the conclusive find was brought to the surface: three silver ingots numbered, respectively, 569, 794 and 4584. When these were checked against the Cartagena manifest the number 4584 was found to correspond to that seventeenth-century packing list; the *Atocha* was at last a confirmed find.

As the salvors moved towards Hawk Channel, southeast of Quicksands, nine bronze cannons each marked with the Spanish royal crest and the symbols '31 Q 10 L' ('31 quintals and 10 pounds'), dated 1607, were discovered in the deeper water. These cannons were also identical to those on the *Atocha*'s gun-list.[7]

But at dawn on 20 July 1974 disaster struck: a leaking bulkhead and a faulty valve combined to capsize the salvage boat *Northwind*. Of the eleven crew eight survived, but Fisher's son, daughter-in-law and another diver all drowned.

This tragedy did not deter Fisher from his single-minded search for more of the *Atocha*'s riches. Over the following decade Treasure Salvors concentrated efforts in the area where the main bulk of the treasure was purported to lie. In early 1985 the lower hull was located in 62 feet of water. This showed that she had drifted over seven miles from where she originally sank. There, amongst the smashed keel and hull timbers, lay ballast stones mixed with an abundance of treasure.

Duncan Mathewson, Treasure Salvors archeologist, said: 'We recently found a sea chest that belonged to the pilot of the *Atocha*, Martin Jiminez, and it contained another astrolabe, gold dust, gold nuggets, silver coins and a 41 foot gold chain he was smuggling back to Spain.'[8]

Fisher was jubilant; the total find for 1985 was as follows: '130,000 silver coins, 956 silver bars with an average weight of 1,000 ounces or more, 315 emeralds, 115 small gold bars ranging in size from six to 77 troy ounces, 15 gold chains, 67 gold coins and 22 other items of gold and jewels. . . . The following year the divers recovered another 2,500 emeralds, 35 gold bars, 85 silver bars and an assortment of other artefacts.'[9]

Mel Fisher told the *New York Times*: 'I would say that the optimum value we hope we can sell it for sometime in the distant future is $183 million.'[10]

On 14 June 1988, at Christie's in New York, a few treasure items were put up for auction: 'A silver gilt two-handled cup was sold for $165,000, a gold two-handled cup for $275,000 and a five-foot long chain weighing 2 pounds (1kg) made $319,000; the total amount auctioned raised $2.58 million.'[11]

There are still many items that remain to be valued and sold. The state of Florida has laid claim to the treasure. The sheer value of the treasure, as well as the length of time involved, have both served to create a complicated scenario that is still unfolding.

Fisher was not the only person searching in the twentieth century for the seventeenth-century wreck. A number of salvage companies and treasure

hunters who knew of the wreck and her estimated value were all methodi-
cally searching in and around the Florida Keys. Burt Webber, Art McKee and
Kip Wagner were just three of the determined professionals who were dogging
Fisher's footsteps.

Fisher also found the *Santa Margarita* but his finds were not free of frustration, litigation and violence. The Federal Government contested his claim
and argued that the *Atocha* was public property. It was only in 1978 that the
US Court of Appeal upheld a lower court ruling in favour of Treasure Salvors.
Fisher made many enemies, four people died, including 'one diver [who] was
murdered when he tried to barter his share of the *Atocha* treasure for cocaine'.[12]
Another diver tried to hijack 50 lbs of gold.

The lure of treasure is strong and brings with it diversity and complications.
After sixteen years, and an investment of $10 million (£6.7 million), Mel
Fisher had realized his dream – the finding of treasure valued at many millions
of dollars from the richest seventeenth-century ship ever to be salvaged.

SANTA MARGARITA

The Santa Margarita, *built in* Vizcaya *for the Indies trade, was the sister ship of the* Nuestra
Senora de Atocha *and was part of the 1622 Tierra Firma treasure fleet. She was a galleon of
630 tons, armed with twenty-five cannons. She carried a crew of ninety-one plus sixteen officers and
152 soldiers, commanded by Captain Bernadino De Lugo.*

AREA: *Wrecked on the Marquesas Keys, four miles west of the wreck of the* Atocha *in Hawk
Channel, twenty miles west of Key West, Florida, USA.*

In late May 1622 the *Santa Margarita*, along with the *Atocha* and twenty-six
ships, assembled at Portobelo in Panama. They were part of the Tierra Firma
treasure fleet bound for Spain. Gutierra De Espinosa, the silvermaster, directed
the loading of the *Margarita's* treasure, 'accounting for 419 silver ingots,
118,000 silver coins, 34 ingots of gold weighing 1,488 ounces'.[1]

As with the *Atocha* there was a large amount of unregistered treasure, carried
unofficially so as to avoid the King of Spain's 20 per cent duty. Wealthy
Spanish dignitaries were also taken on as passengers and each brought with
him his own private treasure. Two Jesuit priests and a wealthy merchant, Gaspar

De Rojas, who was transporting eighty-four silver ingots (part of his personal fortune), and Don Francisco De La Hoz Berrio, governor of Spanish Venezuela, made up the complement of private passengers.

The fleet set sail and arrived in Havana, via Cartagena, on 22 August 1622. Once there the ships were reprovisioned and the Marquis de Cadereita made immediate plans for swift departure as the fleet, weeks behind schedule, was sailing at the peak of the hurricane season. By 4 September the chief pilot, Lorenzo Vernal, predicted excellent weather and the Marquis decided that the fleet could depart the following day. The twenty-eight ships left Havana and sailed northeast, then tacked against rising headwinds. By 5 September the winds had increased to hurricane force; each ship was forced to make her own way in the terrible weather. The whole fleet was blown by the gales to the treacherous coral-based Florida Keys. Both the *Atocha* and the *Margarita* were within sight of each other as the surges and tides drove them towards the Marquesas Keys. The *Margarita* reduced sail. As she struck the reef her mast broke and the whole ship was thrown across the reef and into shallow water where she broke up and sank. Of her crew, passengers and soldiers only sixty-seven survived by clinging to the scattered wreckage.

Early Spanish Salvage Attempts

Shortly after the *Atocha* and the *Santa Margarita* were wrecked, Captain Gaspar De Vargas was commissioned by agents of the Spanish Crown to locate and salvage the great store of wealth that had sunk with the two ships. His divers were able to locate the *Atocha*, but were unable to gain access to her treasures. The *Margarita*'s location was to elude Vargas and he had to abandon his search. In 1624 Francisco Melian was instructed by King Philip IV to seek out the two ships. Melian was never able to relocate the *Atocha*, but did find the *Margarita*. Captain de Gobea led his divers in several efforts to gain entry to the wreck and to salvage at least some of the treasure. The diving conditions were far from ideal and, as the weather worsened, Melian wrote to his king: 'Because of the severity of the winter and the outline of the galleon being concealed below a sandbank, since the currents had shifted, it had made fruitless the labours of Captain de Gobea.'[2]

In 1627 diving attempts were resumed with the following result:

The opinion of this pilot major and of the diver Antonio de Sosa is that the galleon *Santa Margarita* broke in half with the chambers where the silver was stored falling off to the right and that the missing silver was in the quartel. All excess ballast of the ship was removed leaving hardly anything inside helping us to further confirm that the majority of the silver was contained in the missing quartel and when we finally discovered its location, it was so very buried in the sand and so difficult to reach that if God does not help us it will not be possible to retrieve anything. However, a little to the west and near the spot of ballast, the divers discovered 37 ingots of silver, 3,172 pieces-of-eight reales, 67 marks of worked silver, and 34 copper plates.[3]

Over the following three months Melian and his crew worked at salvaging the Santa Margarita. In his 'Report of treasure recovered from the galleon Margarita in the Cayos de Matacumbe between May 8 1626 and August 31 1627' he lists: '350 large and small ingots of silver; 64,750 pieces-of-eight reales; 10 pieces of worked silver, including a plate and a small vase, four silver lamps, 3 silver vases, 1 silver cup, 1 silver salt cellar. . . .'[4]

In return for his loyal service King Philip granted Melian the governorship of Caracas, Venezuela.

Mel Fisher: Treasure Salvors

In 1970 Treasure Salvors began its search for the Atocha in the area around Quicksands on the Outer Reef of the Marquesas Keys. Fisher used data that was based on evidence from Captain De Lugo who had reported to the Royal Commission in Havana in 1622, just days after the storm that had devastated the fleet. De Lugo stated that, as he made his escape from the stricken Margarita, he saw the Atocha sinking 'one league east'. The Spanish divided a degree of latitude into seventeen and a half leagues of four miles each, the English divided it into sixty nautical miles or twenty leagues. The Spanish league is slightly longer than the English league and the mile a little shorter. Using the location of the Atocha as a pivot, Fisher systematically combed the area 'three mile east' of the Atocha. He used two of his dive-support vessels, the Swordfish and the Virgilona. It was not until 1980, when a diver spotted a large mass of ballast stones, and a silver ingot marked RX 4718, belonging to Gaspar De Rojas, that the Santa Margarita became a confirmed find.

As the divers removed the stones they discovered ship's timbers and copper nails buried in the sand. A twenty-three-foot section of a Spanish galleon was excavated. An airlift was brought in. Along the ribs and deck timbers were hidden six silver ingots each weighing 60 lbs. There was a solid mass of silver coins fused together by the seawater oxidizing the silver; this lump weighed 105 lbs. Numerous silver and gold coins lay scattered over the seabed and in between the broken ribs and hull timbers. The markings and the tally numbers were authenticated by matching them with the silvermaster's list. As the divers dug around the smashed hull more and more treasure was uncovered. Forty-three gold chains totalling 180 feet, one 12-foot long with a weight of 6.5 lbs, were found. The treasures were dispersed along a 3000-yard trail marked by gold and silver coins. The recovered treasure from the *Margarita* represents about one third of her original cargo and is valued at $20–30 million (£13–20 million). Mel Fisher has stated that 'much of the treasure may still be lying on the bottom of the sea'.

NUESTRA SENORA DE LA PURA Y LIMPIA CONCEPCION

Nuestra Senora de la Pura y Limpia Concepcion, *better known as the* Concepcion, *was a nao or merchantman of 600 tons. Built in Havana in 1620 she was fitted out as a galleon in 1639. She was 140 feet long, armed with forty cannons and carried 532 passengers and crew. Seventeenth-century Spanish galleons were slow and difficult to manoeuvre. The* Concepcion *was no exception.*

AREA: *North Riff of the Ambrosian Bank (Silver Bank), west of the Silver Bank Passage and north of the Dominican Republic, Caribbean.*

On I June 1639 a contract was signed between the Spanish Casa de la Contratacion (Board of Trade) and the owner of the *Concepcion*, Don Tomas Manito. He agreed to charter the vessel to the Spanish Crown (King Philip IV) for the voyage from Cadiz, Spain to Veracruz, New Spain (Mexico) to escort the returning silver fleet. Two silver fleets were dispatched each year: one sailed in the spring for Veracruz, and the other sailed in August for Cartagena on the mainland of South America. After wintering in the colonies, the two fleets would rendezvous in Havana for the trans-Atlantic voyage. The Spanish silver fleets were a natural target for Spain's enemies, particularly the English and the Dutch, and much of Spain's maritime resources lay in the protection of her fleets. The Spanish economy relied heavily on the safe arrival of the gold and silver bullion.

When the *Concepcion* had completed her structural modifications, enabling her to carry more cannons, she was examined by the Board of Trade officials and given clearance to sail in the position of *capitana*, the ship of the Captain-General of the Fleet. The *Concepcion* sailed down the Guadalquivir River to the Bay of Cadiz; there the Captain-General, Roque Centeno y Ordonez, welcomed on board his most distinguished passenger, the Duke of Escalona, the recently appointed Viceroy of New Spain. On 21 April 1640 the fleet of twenty ships assembled in the Bay of Cadiz and set sail for New Spain.

No major incidents were recorded during the outward voyage and the fleet arrived safely at Veracruz on 24 June 1640. In keeping with the overriding policy of protecting the treasure fleets, the new Viceroy commissioned eight new galleons to be constructed; these would be known as the Armada de Barlovento and would serve as escort ships for the returning treasure fleet.

A year passed and the new ships were not ready. The existing fleet languished in the harbour, rotting and ill maintained. Their sails and cordage were perishing and their hulls were increasingly infested with shipworm.

Even though there was delay at Veracruz, gold and silver continued to arrive at the royal warehouses from the Indian mines and temples. The Captain-General died and Juan de Campos was promoted in his place with Don Juan de Villavicencio as Vice-Admiral. Villavicencio had been senior captain of the Mexican fleet and was a man of experience. Campos was an insolent and intolerant man, more concerned with the transactions of gold and commerce than with his duties as a senior naval commander. Villavicencio and Campos disliked each other.

The Armada de Barlovento had its own commander, Fernando de Josa Suarez, in the lead ship *Rosario*.

In early July 1641 Campos received urgent instructions from the Viceroy who was most anxious that the fleet should return to Spain within the year, leaving before the hurricane season in mid August. Campos gave orders for the ships to be overhauled. The *Concepcion* was badly in need of repair; she was careened and rotten timbers hastily replaced and new rigging installed; she was brought to harbour to be loaded with her cargo.

There are wide discrepancies as to the amount of gold and silver that the *Concepcion* actually carried. Pedro de Medina, the silvermaster of the ship, reported that she carried 550,000 pesos of the King's silver and 500,000 of unregistered cargo[1] – so-called private trade goods. The first mate, Francisco

Granillo, who was in charge of stowage, claimed that the amount of unregistered silver totalled more than that of the King. He also reckoned that the total quantity of registered silver was 4 million pesos, a weight of 140 tons. The estimated worth of this was then £1 million.[2] Additionally, there was a small amount of gold and jewellery.

Captain-General de Campos made the *San Pedro y San Pablo* his flagship and Villavicencio, who had been senior captain of the 1635 treasure fleet, was appointed to the *Concepcion*. As he took command of the ship, he expressed his overriding concern as to the seaworthiness of the vessel; repairs had been made, but she was twenty years old and in an overall state of deterioration. A meeting was held with the ship's officers and a decision was made to sail to Havana. Once there it was agreed that a complete refit would be carried out. By 23 July the cargoes had been loaded, and the treasure ships and their escort set sail, bound for Havana.

After a stormy passage they arrived in Havana on 27 August at the beginning of the hurricane season.

While in Havana, Villavicencio gave Campos his assessment of *Concepcion*. He asked Campos for more time to repair her leaking hull, suggesting that the fleet set sail for Spain after the hurricane season. Campos dismissed this request and ordered the fleet to sail to Spain; he was also aggravated by the latest order from the Viceroy to wait in Havana for the Tierra Firma treasure fleet that was on its way from Cartagena. The two fleets were to rendezvous and make for Spain together. The Tierra Firma fleet was commanded by Francisco Diaz Pimiento who had invaded the English colony at Old Providence Island in the early summer of 1641. He had sailed with twelve ships and 2000 men and had captured 700 Englishmen, together with forty cannons and half a million pesos in plunder.[3] Pimiento was returning to Spain a hero and Campos had no wish to be obscured by such a man. The fleet sailed on 13 September. Before the day's end Villavicencio had to signal to the Captain-General that the *Concepcion* was taking on water so rapidly that her pumps could not keep ahead of the increasing flow; the sternpost had broken and planks had given way. Campos ordered the fleet back to Havana where more repairs were carried out. Villavicencio then proposed to Campos that the treasure should be transferred to another ship; Campos refused and the fleet, once again, set sail; by now it was 20 September.

The route from Havana to Spain was due north into the Florida Straits, along the eastern seaboard towards the Carolinas. A course would then be set eastwards to the Azores and then on to Cadiz. The numerous reefs and shoals between Florida and the Bahamas were poorly charted and strong currents set vessels perilously close to the jagged Florida Keys.

On the morning of the 28th the wind changed from northeast to south, bringing rain and rough seas. By nightfall the storm had intensified to hurricane force, huge waves slammed into the *Concepcion* and opened her seams, destroying the repairs to her sternpost and planking.

Three merchantmen had sunk during the night and many of the escort galleons were dismasted and damaged. The *Concepcion* was still afloat, but the pumps could now no longer hold back the water which flooded her lower hold. The mainmast was cut away and cannons were thrown overboard to lighten the stricken ship. On the first day of October the storm had passed, the day was clear and calm but no other ship was in sight. Villavicencio gave orders to repair the damage. Holes were patched, seams recaulked, timbers replaced. The pumps were double-manned and the water level was reduced to a few feet. Villavicencio knew that the ship could not possibly make the trans-Atlantic voyage, so he decided to sail for the Spanish port of Puerto Rico near Anegada Island. The senior pilot estimated that the position of the *Concepcion* was due north of Puerto Rico. Villavicencio argued that it was not possible to have sailed that far east and that the ship's position was far more likely to be to the north of Hispaniola. The pilot protested that his degree of error could not possibly be so large. Spanish maritime regulations stated that the captain had to accept the pilot's judgment as supreme in matters of navigation. Dramatically, Villavicencio called for a silver bowl of water; in front of the crew he washed his hands of the responsibility and then gave the order to turn south.

Villavicencio stated: 'I, along with the other practical persons, felt that it was not possible to have gone such a long way or to be as far to windward as the pilots made out and affirmed.'[4]

In early Spanish charts the Abrojos (the English called them Abroyes) were a series of reefs and shoals extending over a wide area from Turks Island to Puerto Rico. In later charts they were located in a square or diamond pattern twenty miles south-east of Turks Island and sixty miles north of Puerto Plata in Hispaniola. Due to their shape, the reefs later became known as Handkerchief or Mouchoir Bank. The reefs further eastwards were named Ambroshia or Ambrosian Banks by William Phips and later called Silver Banks.

On the evening of 30 October the night was clear with a moderate wind when, suddenly, the *Concepcion* struck the Abrojos Reefs. Desperate efforts were made to kedge her off the reef, but she remained hard and fast. On the second day the wind came up and pushed her further upon the reefs; her stern wedged between outbreaks of rock and she began to break up.

Only one longboat had survived the hurricane. Realizing their situation was perilous, seven small rafts and one large raft were hastily constructed from deck planking and other ship's timbers. The pilots were confident of sailing the thirty miles to Anegada Island, the nearest land; in fact, Anegada Island was over 400 miles to the east.

On the third day the weather grew steadily worse with heavy rain and huge waves breaking over the wreck. The quarter-deck collapsed, leaving only the poop-deck above water. At four in the morning the wreck slid to one side and Villavicencio gave orders to abandon ship and make for the rafts. Thirty-three survivors, along with Villavicencio, took to the longboat which drifted away from the wreck. Seventy persons made it to the large raft; those clinging to the wreck or unable to reach the rafts perished.

Three of the smaller rafts never reached land and the largest, with seventy survivors, was never seen again. After twenty-two days at sea, the longboat landed on the coast of Hispaniola. Of the 532 on board the *Concepcion* 117 survived.

The other galleons of the Armada de Barlovento were all badly damaged before reaching the safety of various ports in Cuba, Hispaniola, Puerto Rico and Florida. Of the merchantships four sank, five were wrecked on the coast of Florida and only one ship arrived safely in Spain.

The Stanley Brothers

By 1657, at the age of seventeen, Sir John Narborough had spent four years in the navy serving in the West Indies and it was in Jamaica that he first heard stories about the loss of the *Concepcion*. In the summer of 1682 two men, Sir Richard White and Captain Isaac Harmon approached Narborough, who was then one of the Commissioners of the navy. White and Harmon presented a proposal based on documents known as 'The Spanish Directions' written by the pilot of the *Concepcion*. Narborough introduced the two men to King Charles II; the result of the meeting was a royal commitment to wreck-hunting. By law, the King had a right to a royalty of 'things taken up from the bottom of the English Seas'. The King's Admiralty instructed the Navy Board in October 1682 to find a suitable ship. It was reported back to the Admiralty:

Wee thinke it fitting also to acquaint you that His Majesty's sloop the Bonetta now at Deptford (which is about the burthen of this vessel) may with a small charge and in a little time be fitted for the sea. Her dimensions are as followeth vizt. length by the keel 61 feet, breadth 18 feet, depth in hold five feet, draught of water 4 feet 6 inches, burthen 57 tons. And in case she shall be judged a proper vessell for this designed voyage to the West·Indies it will save His Majesty the charge of buying another for that use.[5]

Captain Edward Stanley was put in command of the Bonetta with his brother Peter as sailing master and pilot. The Bonetta was to be accompanied by the frigate H.M.S. Falcon, commanded by Captain George Churchill, brother of the later Duke of Marlborough. The two ships set sail from England on 30 April 1683 bound for the West Indies with sealed instructions 'to take note that ye orders which I had received . . . to search for the "rack" in the "abroxes".'[6]

Arriving off the north coast at Puerto Plata in Hispaniola on 3 July 1683, the ships then sailed sixty miles north to the reef. The 'Spanish Directions' stated 'the wreck lay about a cable's length from ye edge of the banke.'[7]

The first days were spent investigating the edge of the bank running southeast about half a mile from the breakers, but nothing was found. The weather began to deteriorate with heavy squalls and the two ships sailed to Port Royal in Jamaica on 17 August. Two further expeditions were made that year. The following year in April 1684 the Bonetta returned to the Abrojos accompanied by the sloop William and Mary but found no evidence of the Concepcion.

Stanley became obsessed with finding the wreck, returning with Harmon five times to the reef between April and June. On 18 June Stanley wrote in his journal 'I have noe hopes of finding ye wrack.'[8]

Stanley returned to Jamaica where he met Tom Smith who had been a sailor on a ship sailing from Barbados bound for New England. Smith told Stanley that when his ship struck a reef he saw bars of gold and silver lying on a ledge below the surface of the water. Stanley was so impressed with the details of Smith's story that he took him to Colonel Molesworth, Governor of Jamaica. Smith was cross-examined by Molesworth who became convinced of the validity of his account. Smith was prepared to sign into Articles 'to be hanged if he did not show them the wreck'. On 2 April 1685 Smith signed a deposition stating

that he this deponant in April last being in a small bark named ye James and Elizabeth with four men more of which James Ulin was master and being bound from Barbados to New England passed between the island Mona and Hispaniola and within three days after they passed from Cape Caberoon being the northernmost part of ye easternmost end of Hispaniola . . . they fell in accidentally (on ye 15th or 18th of said month of April) with a reefe of rocks, one of which was about fifty foot high, the rest being low, and most even with the water, upon one of which being flat, they saw several sowes and piggs of silver heaped up upon one another, and allsoe one barre of gold, and within forty foot from that rock whereon the silver lay upright wedged in between two rockes, upon which there was a dispute between the master and company whither they should send their boats on shore for ye silver, in which time a gale sprung up and blew very fresh . . .[9]

The Governor wrote to London informing the Lords of Trade and Plantations of his decision to send the *Bonetta* to the wreck site. Molesworth did not accept Smith's Articles to be hanged if he did not locate the silver and gold but if he failed he was 'to serve ye King seven years in his ships of warr without pay, and to submit his body to such corporal punishment as I shall think fit, which I have threatened him to be very terrible and severe'.[10]

Captain Stanley was given his sailing instructions: 'Make ye best of your way towards ye ledge of rock to ye eastward of Handkerchief Reefe, and there use your best endeavour for ye finding of a Spanish wrack, and ye several bars of silver and gold sayd to be landed out of said wrack upon a flat rock neer unto it.'[11]

The *Bonetta* departed Jamaica at the end of January 1685, sailing along the south coast of Hispaniola through Mona Passage northwest towards the Navidad Reefs. Stanley sailed around the reefs for several days before bad weather forced his ship back to Puerto Plata. On 1 May, reprovisioned, he sailed to the eastern side of the Ambrosian Bank searching for the fifty-foot-high rock.

Once again, adverse winds and heavy seas forced Stanley to head back to Jamaica. Undaunted, he set off again, determined not to give up the search, and made numerous trips to the reefs. But on 23 November 1685 Stanley gave up the search. Molesworth wrote: 'He hath been several times in a great deal of danger beating upon the rocks without meeting with the markt rock which they lookt for, and with such hazard of their lives as wholly discourages him from prosecuting it further.'[12]

Stanley returned to England on 19 July 1686. Thomas Smith vanished from the records and it seems he was never punished.

William Phips

One of the most spectacular successes in treasure salvage of the period was that of William Phips. He was born in Montsweag, Maine, in 1651, the son of James Phips, a poor immigrant armourer from Bristol, England. William Phips left home at eighteen and made for Boston where he became apprenticed to a ship's carpenter. According to his biographer, Cotton Mater, even by the age of twenty-two he could still not read or write. When Phips completed his apprenticeship he found employment with a shipbuilder. He was a hard worker and managed to marry a well-to-do society widow. At twenty-four he had his own ship and was involved in trade between Boston and the West Indies. As he reached his thirtieth year he obtained qualifications both as a naval engineer and as a navigator.

On his voyages to and from the West Indies William Phips first heard of the wreck of the *Nuestra Senora de la Pura y Limpia Concepcion*. Fired by reports of vast amounts of treasure, he decided that he would attempt to locate the wreck. Unable to find finance in Boston Phips left for England and made representations to the English government; he was then introduced to the Duke of Albermarle and Sir John Narborough. Both men were wealthy and well connected. Having obtained their financial backing, as well as their personal support, it was then possible to find 'gentlemen adventurers' who would invest further funds in the project. Albermarle secured four major investors and a warrant from James II; dated 18 July 1686, this validated a search for three years in return for which the Crown received one tenth of the treasure.

> We were gratiously pleased to grant to our right trusty and right entirely beloved cousin and councillor Christopher Duke of Albermarle, all wrecks, jetson and flotsam and lagan and goods derelict riches, bullion, plate gold, silver, coyne, barrs, piggs of silver, ingotts of gould merchandises and other goods and chattles . . . wrecked or lost by shipwreck or otherwise in or upon any of the rocks, shelves, shoals seas or banks to the windward or ye north-side of Hispaniola or about the islands or Gulf of Florida in America.[13]

Two ships, the *James and Mary* of 200 tons, commanded by Phips, and the small frigate, *Henry of London*, weighing 50 tons and captained by Francis Rodgers, left England on 26 September 1686.

By 10 November 1686 the ships had anchored in Carlisle Bay, Barbados, then sailed south to Porto Plata, Hispaniola. In order that a safe, yet thorough, search be made of the treacherous shallows, a ten-oared dugout was built. On 13 January Phips began to navigate the North Riff which forms the northern edge of the Ambrosian Bank (Silver Bank). A John Taylor who had been ship-wrecked on the North Riff in 1644 had made some descriptive remarks about the nature of the water: 'This is a bank of flat rocks, some on level with water, and called boylers whereon the water seems to boil, between the rocks is 9 and 10 fathom of water.'[14]

Captain Rodgers approached the eastern end of the reef: 'Then began to meet with ye boilers very thicke, being 10, 8, 6 and some not 4 foot under water, soe that wee were forct to keep a man att topmast heade to conn her through.'[15]

He managed to anchor in 10 fathoms of water. He had searched six miles from east to west and he found no evidence of the wreck:

This day towards 4 a clock Mr. Rogers came in who gave us to under-stand that they had been on the bank and had two or three days fair weather they searched the bank and told us they had don as much as any man could do and also that at 10 a clock in the morning standing from the bank to the southward they were at evening imbayed amongst a parcel of boylers they knew not off where they were forced to Anchor all night and by Gods blessing it being a very small breeze of winds all night in the morning they got cleare of them.[16]

The following day, on 20 January, Captain Rodgers weighed anchor and searched the southern edge of the reef using the dugout and the longboat. A few hours later the boats returned,

bringing us happy and joyfull of ye cannew's findeing ye wrecke, their being in her Mr. Coule [Covill], Francis and Jonas, ye 2 dieverrs. For which blessing wee returne infinite praise and thankes to Almighty God. Our boate carryed [away] with her chaine and grapnell, a new buoy rope, a new buoy, with severall wooden buoyes, and 2 longe oares, to fix uppon ye wrecke that wee might the better finde her when wee came on ye banke next. . . . Most part of her timber is consum'd away, and soe over growne with curlle [coral] that had itt not been for her guns shee would scarce ever been founde, itt being at least 45 years since shee was lost and ye richest ship that ever went out of ye West Indies.[17]

The journal of the *James and Mary* recorded on 8 February: 'This morning our Captain sent our long boat on board Mr. Rogers which in a shoart time returned with what made our hearts very glad to see which was 4 sows, I bar, 1 champene, 2 dowboyes, 2000 and odd dollars by which wee understood that they had found the wreck.'[18]

By early April Phips and his divers had salvaged over 25 tons of silver. By 19 April the weather was beginning to deteriorate. Provisions were getting low and the divers were exhausted. Phips gave orders for the ships to sail to Turks Island. On 2 May, with provisions stowed, they sailed to England. On 9 June they anchored at Gravesend on the Thames. A naval guard was placed on board and the *James and Mary* was escorted to Deptford. The officers of the Royal Mint weighed the silver and gold and took the King's tenth. The total weight of the silver recovered was 68,511 lbs and 7 oz. There were 25 lbs of gold and a few pieces of jewellery. The total value was then listed as £205,536; at present day prices Phip's treasure would be worth over £2 million ($3 million). The Royal tenth was £20,553; the Duke of Albermarle received £43,534; Sir John Narborough, along with four others, each received £21,766 and William Phips got £11,013. The remaining sum was divided amongst the crew.[19]

Phips became a hero and was invited to Windsor by James II. He was knighted and in 1691 appointed the first Royal Governor of Massachusetts. On 18 February 1695 he died, aged forty-four, and was buried in London in the church of St Mary Woolnoth. His tombstone was inscribed:

Near this place is interred the body of Sir William Phips, knight, who in the year 1687, by his great industry, discovered among the rocks near the Banks of Bahama on the north side of Hispaniola a Spanish plate-ship which had been under water 44 years, out of which he took in gold and silver to the value of £300,000 sterling: and with a fidelity equal to his conduct, brought it all to London, where it was divided between himself and the rest of the adventurers. For which great service he was knighted by his then Majesty, King James the 2nd, and at the request of the principal inhabitants of New England, he accepted of the Government of the Massachusetts, in which he continued up to the time of his death; and discharged his trust with that zeal for the interests of the country, and with so little regard to his own private advantage, that he justly gained the good esteem and affection of the greatest and best part of the inhabitants of that Colony.

Seaquest International

Burt Webber came from the small farming town of Annville, Pennsylvania. He learnt to scuba-dive in his early teens and enrolled at the Diving Training Academy in Miami. In 1961 he began working with the diver, Art McKee, at his Museum of Sunken Treasure on Plantation Key in Florida. After several years of diving for wrecks in Florida and Caribbean waters Webber met Jim Haskins, coin dealer and expert in Spanish colonial and maritime history. Haskins was very keen to begin a search for the *Concepcion*. He had found documents that suggested 'that Phips could not get into the stern section of the wreck which is grown over with coral'.[20]

Short of funds for a salvage operation, Webber was introduced to Warren Stearns, chairman of a firm of investment bankers based in Chicago. Stearns became interested in the proposed project and raised the finance for an expedition to search for the *Concepcion*. In 1977 Seaquest International was formed. 'Seaquest started with an initial outlay of $450,000, about 30 investors putting an average of $15,000'.[21] Webber obtained a salvage licence from the Dominican Republic and converted the *Samala*, a British ex-minesweeper, into a salvage vessel. Accompanied by a crew of divers, he set sail for the North Riff of the Ambrosian Bank. Frustration and disappointment were to lie ahead; after eighty-two days, using the most sophisticated equipment, six wrecks were located, none of them the *Concepcion*.

Jim Haskins had heard of Peter Earle, a teacher at the London School of Economics who was writing a book on the *Concepcion*. He flew to London to discuss the salvage project; Earle was to provide Haskins with vital information – a copy of the log of the *Henry*: 'A journal of our voyage intended by divine assistance in the ship Henery, Francis Rogers Cmdr., bound for ye Ambroshia Banks on ye north side of Hispaniola, in company with ye James and Mary, Capt. Wm. Phips Cmdr. both in pursuit of a Spanish wreck, in which search God bee our Guide.'

The log of the *Henry* gave Webber and Haskins a smaller search area, concentrated on Half Moon Reef. With extra money raised by Stearns, plus an extension on the salvage lease, the *Samala* returned to the Ambrosian Bank and renewed the search. After they had anchored 150 yards from the position noted in the *Henry*'s log Webber made his first dive. 'I swam around one of these coralheads and into the next grid survey we had buoyed out and there it was, the magnometer started to produce magnetic anomalies as I swam in and out of the canyons.'[22]

On excavating the site Webber and his divers found silver and gold coins, Ming Dynasty Chinese porcelain cups and gold chains. Using an airlift the divers located a chest 8 feet below the sand. On bringing it to the surface Webber discovered a false bottom filled with gold coins.

More than 60,000 gold and silver coins have been located, along with jewellery, gold chains and other valuable objects.

Warren Stearns, when asked about the cumulative value of the find, 'declined to put a value on the tons of gold and silver coins and bullion, artifacts and porcelain salvaged from the *Concepcion*, only conceding: "It's many millions of dollars."'[23]

It is now estimated that the value of the treasure will exceed £27 million ($40 million) in total.

NUESTRA SENORA DE LAS MARAVILLAS

The Nuestra Senora de las Maravillas *was a Spanish galleon of 800 tons. She was Don Matias de Orellana's Admiral's ship, belonging to the 1656 Tierra Firma treasure fleet under the command of the Marquis de Montealegre in his flagship, the* Jesus Maria.

AREA: *Struck the western edge of the Little Bahama Bank, twenty-five miles from Memory Rock and forty-five miles north of West End on the Grand Bahama, Caribbean.*

The *Nuestra Senora de las Maravillas* departed Mexico in late 1655 with 700 passengers and crew; she was one of the largest galleons of a fleet of nine treasure ships sailing to Spain. On the homeward voyage the fleet stopped at Portobelo and Cartagena where the *Maravillas* picked up an immense amount of treasure before sailing on to Havana. Most of the treasure was stored in the stern of the ship (gold and jewels were generally placed in the Admiral's cabin) and large amounts of coin and bullion were in the lower aft hold. The fleet left Cartagena, arriving in Havana twenty-six days later where the *Maravillas* underwent repairs before sailing to Spain.

On 1 January 1656, the fleet departed Havana Harbour and sailed towards the Florida Keys where the ships would pick up the Gulf Stream flowing northwards, then turn west to the Azores and Spain.

On the night of 4 January, sailing up the Straits of Florida just off the Bahamas, the *Maravillas* found herself in shallow water. A cannon shot was fired to warn the following ships of the danger. The *Jesus Maria*, the nearest ship, turned as the *Maravillas* tried to manoeuvre to deeper water; in the confusion and darkness the *Jesus Maria* smashed into the *Maravillas*. Don Diego Portichuelo de Ribadenevra, a Spanish priest on the *Maravillas*, recorded later:

> I found some alarmed, others confused and everyone giving opinions about what should be done. On account of new sails, the *Maravillas* had made good speed, and was close to the *Capitana* [i.e. the flagship, the *Jesus Maria*] when that vessel fired a cannon shot to warn the accompanying flotilla to change course. She then turned away from the danger, but in so doing rammed the *Maravillas* as she attempted a slow and cumbersome manoeuvre. The impact ... broke through our planks from the top of the waterline to the holds, making splinters out of all of them.[1]
>
> The confusion of the people was so great that they did not realise the importance of the sails to get them out of danger, and instead occupied themselves in trying to stem the water pouring into the ship ... with the sails idle, the currents rapidly drove the ship towards the banks. She bumped against the rocks so forcefully that her seams began to crack. Though the people were bailing with four pumps and pails, the water rose as high as the second deck. Up to that time I heard confessions from many people, among them Admiral Don Matias de Orellana, who told me that we would surely die and that I should grant absolution to everyone ...[2]

Admiral de Orellana, understanding his ship was severely damaged, headed for shallower water in the hope of beaching her, but the galleon struck a reef and broke in two. The bow half sank on the reef and the main stern section drifted away. Next morning, fifty-six survivors were rescued out of the 700 persons on board.

The *Jesus Maria*, her bow badly damaged, attempted to continue her voyage to Spain but a storm off the Florida Keys forced her to change course and return to Cartagena. On arrival, the Marquis de Montealegre reported the loss of the *Maravillas* to the Governor of Cartagena, Don Pedro Zapata. Realizing the importance of the loss of treasure, the Governor sent a squadron of six ships, under Captain Juan de Somovilla Texada, with the assistant pilot of the *Maravillas* and pearl divers from the Isle of Margarita, to recover the treasure. Arriving at the wreck site on 1 June, Texada found the scattered remains of the galleon but the shifting sands had covered most of the wreck and treasure; nevertheless, the pearl divers did find a number of silver and gold bars and coins.

Robert Marx and Seafinders

In the early 1960s Robert Marx, a marine archaeologist and treasure hunter, began to research the 1655 Tierra Firma treasure fleet. In the General Archives of the Indies in Seville, Marx located many documents concerning the loss of the galleon *Maravillas* but, in particular, he found a book published in Madrid in 1657 written by one of the survivors, Don Diego Portichuelo de Ribadenevra, keeper of the Holy Metropolitan church in Lima. De Ribadenevra wrote a detailed account of his journey from Lima to Mexico and the sinking of the *Maravillas*.

It was not until 1972 that Marx formed Seafinders Inc., financed by eleven businessmen with a lease from the government of the Bahamas that they would receive 25 per cent of any treasure recovered. For four months the salvage vessel *Grifon* searched the area of the Bahama Bank with a magnetometer; many wrecks were located but nothing to indicate a Spanish galleon.

As chance would have it, when pulling up the *Grifon's* anchor one day, two Spanish-type ballast stones were wedged on the anchor. On investigation the divers found, at a depth of only 30 feet, other ballast stones and a gold coin dated 1655. The following day, four large anchors and two bronze cannons were located bearing the coat of arms of Philip IV. Marx had found the bow section of the *Maravillas*. Using a prop wash, the divers cleared a hole to a depth of 30 feet, finding over 600 silver coins, three large silver bars and silverware. On the fifth day, Marx and his divers brought to the surface an immense amount of treasure: 'Five tons of silver bars, around fifty thousand silver coins, twelve gold discs weighing eleven pounds each, more than a hundred gold coins, many exquisite pieces of jewellery, hundreds of uncut emeralds, a large ivory tusk and about half a ton of other artefacts.'[3]

For the next six weeks, gold and silver treasure continued to be brought to the surface. As the *Grifon* was packed with treasure but short of food and water, Marx and his team were forced to head for their home port at Fort Pierce.

On the last few days before returning to Fort Pierce, Marx began to search for the main stern section where the major part of the treasure would be stored. At a position some distance away from the bow section Marx found evidence of the stern; keeping the location secret, the *Grifon* returned to port.

Marx later stated: 'She is a very unusual wreck ... probably the richest galleon that ever went down in shallow waters ... from the documents we found that she had 20 chests of pearls on board. We found a lot of emeralds, but we haven't found any pearls yet . . .' Marx and his team recovered 'about $2 million worth of treasure and artefacts, and that's an estimate. We have mostly silver coins and bars - but we also have gold, jewellery, emeralds and many, many invaluable historical items such as navigation equipment, ships fittings and military gear.'[4]

On reaching Port Pierce, Marx was notified that the Bahamian Government had discontinued Seafinders' salvage permit. Marx stated: 'We thought she was in international waters, but just to be safe we got a lease from the Bahamian Government and worked through them on the find . . .'[5]

The Bahamian Government had kept the discovery of the *Maravillas* a secret but word leaked out and questions were raised in Parliament. A statement from the Government said: 'The Bahamian Government is taking every step to ensure that the treasure and artefacts that have been transported to the US, are returned to the Bahamas.'[6]

Marx duly returned the treasure but stated on 2 December: 'The Ministry of Transport asked us to return the treasure we had in Florida to the Bahamas until this thing was settled. We did, like dummies, and took it over in two plane loads this week . . . now we find they've seized all the artefacts and treasure, suspended our lease and have a gunboat sitting over the wreck-site to keep us off it.'[7]

After over four years of legal battle, the Bahamian Government reluctantly parted with Seafinders' share. Ironically, the US Government informed Marx that the wreck site was in international waters and that there had been no need to apply to the Bahamas officials for a salvage permit.

Herbert Humphreys and Marine Archaeological Research

During the following years a number of salvage companies began to search for the stern section of the *Maravillas* without much success.

Marine Archaeological Research (Marex), formed by Herbert Humphreys in 1984, was one such company.

In 1988 Marex and RV *Beacon*, a high-tech salvage vessel with a team of technicians and divers, rediscovered *Maravillas*'s bow section and recovered 5000 silver coins, 13 feet of gold chain, jewellery and gold ingots, as well as evidence indicating that the stern section drifted north leaving a trail of scattered treasure.

Humphreys continued excavating the wreck site, bringing up gold, silver and emeralds, the largest emerald weighing 100.85 carats.

The *Maravillas* is estimated to carry on board £700 million ($1,050 million) worth of treasure. In 1992 Humphreys sent a consignment of treasure to auction at Christie's in London; this sale raised £453,871 ($681,000). The centrepiece of the auction was a gold cross studded with sixty-six perfect square-cut Colombian emeralds which sold for £231,000 ($346,500).

So far, Herbert Humphreys and his divers have recovered over £3 million ($4.5 million) in treasure.

Still to be found, if the *Maravillas's* records are accurate, is a 1800 lb solid gold statue of the Madonna and child, a 400 lb gold table encrusted with precious gems and twenty chests of pearls plus gold and silver ingots.

Humphreys says: 'I have seen the stuff that dreams are made of.'[8]

SAN JOSE

The San Jose *was the flagship of the Tierra Firma treasure fleet in the year 1708. There were seventeen ships in this particular fleet which sailed out of Cartagena. She was armed with sixty-nine cannons and carried a crew of 600.*

AREA: *Southeast of the Isla de Baru, off the Bancos del Tesoro (Treasure Banks) near Cartagena, Colombia, Caribbean.*

In the early part of the 1700s Captain Charles Wagner had distinguished himself engaging Spanish ships between the Azores and Cadiz. In January 1706 Wagner was sent from England to take up his new appointment as Commander-in-Chief of the West Indian Fleet. He was based in Kingston, Jamaica, with orders to seize or destroy any Spanish ships trading in that area of the Caribbean. Over the following two years Wagner had several small successes. In April 1708 he set out aboard HMS *Expedition*, a seventy-gun warship. *Expedition* was accompanied by HMS *Kingston* (sixty guns), captained by Timothy Bridge, HMS *Portland* (fifty guns), with Captain Edward Windsor, and a small fireship, *Vulture*. His mission was to patrol the Colombian and Venezuelan coasts seeking out Spanish treasure ships that were sailing out of Cartagena.

After weeks of roaming the southern Caribbean, Wagner's ships spotted sixteen vessels, three of them heavily armed warships of the Spanish treasure fleet: the *San Jose*, a sixty-gun flagship, commanded by the Captain-General of the fleet, Don Jose Fernandez De Santillan; the *San Joaquin*, captained by

Antonio Ordaz y Perez, carrying sixty-four guns, and the *Santa Cruz* of fifty guns. They were sailing along with six merchantships, two French merchant-ships and three smaller vessels.

At the beginning of the 1700s, the yearly shipments of gold and silver to Spain had been interrupted by hostilities in Europe; as a result, the royal ware-houses at Portobelo in Panama had accumulated a large amount of treasure. In 1706 two of the largest and most heavily armed galleons of the Spanish fleet arrived in New Granada, along with a number of merchantmen, to collect the backlog of gold, silver and other merchandise.

The Spanish fleet was loaded at Portobelo and sailed on to Cartagena. The *San Jose* and the *San Joaquin* were estimated to be carrying '12 to 14 million'[1] pieces-of-eight in gold and silver divided evenly between them.

Late in the afternoon of 8 June 1708, the two fleets engaged in battle near the Isla de Baru off the coast of Colombia. An English report describes the action.

> ... finding they could not weather the Baru, a small island, so as to stand in for Carthagena, they stretched to the Northward with an easy Sail, and drew into an irregular Line of Battel, the Admiral who wore a white Pendant at the Maintop mast Head, in the Centre, the Vice Admiral, with the same Pendant at the Fore-top-mast Head, in the Rear, and the Rear-Admiral, who bore the Pendant at the Mizen-top-mast Head, in the Van, about half a mile from each other, there being other Ships between them. Of the seventeen, two were sloops, and one a Brigantine, which stood in for the Land; two others of them were French Ships, which running away, had no Share in the Action.[2]

At five in the evening, with a northeast breeze, Wagner positioned his ships and tacked to seaward of the three warships. The *Expedition* first attacked the slow-moving *San Jose* with a close-range broadside. The *Kingston* manoeuvred into position and fired a volley at the *San Joaquin*. Captain Bridge of the *Kingston* later stated: 'When we got abreast of the Vice-Admiral, the Commodore called us to engage him so we bore down within about half-gun shot and gave him a broadside in which his main topsail yard came down and afterwards fired shot at him but he fell astern.'[3]

The *Expedition* continued to attack the *San Jose*; casualties and damages were heavy on both sides. For two hours the battle raged with the two ships exchang-ing close-range cannon fire; then there was a sudden blast of flame – shot from the *Expedition* had struck *San Jose*'s powder magazine. A massive explosion occurred, showering the *Expedition* with burning rigging and spars. The *San Jose* sank almost immediately; of 600 crew only eleven survived.

Captain Bridge recalled: 'At 7 I saw a ship blow up, where upon my great surprise all I thought it my duty to make saile to use the utmost of my endeavour in saving him self and which others possible I could in making saile as the smoke blew away I discovered the Commedore to my great satisfaction and finding the *Expedition* foretack I stood after them supposing they might receive some damage from some part of the wrack that blew up, they being so very near.'[4] Although *Expedition*'s sails and rigging were badly damaged, Wagner tacked to give chase to the *Santa Cruz*.

Wagner caught up with the slower Spanish galleon. After four hours of tacking and cannon fire the *Santa Cruz* finally surrendered. Wagner gave orders to the *Portland* and the *Kingston* to pursue the *San Joaquin* which was making for Cartagena and had managed to sail well out of cannon range. According to evidence given later by Thomas Thompson, boatswain of the *Portland*,

> a gale sprang up about noon and we gained in the chase of the Spaniard. ... when we got within a mile of him, the *Kingston* took in her small sails hauled up and furled the mainsail, upon which we shortened sail also. We chased the enemy an hour afterwards and when we were near enough the *Kingston* fired a broadside. We tacked in return and gave the Spanish Vice-Admiral our broadside, then following the *Kingston* who made what sail he could to sea and the enemy stood in for Cartagena.[5]

Due to the *Kingston* and *Portland* being near to the coast and sailing in uncertain waters, first the former and then the latter gave up the chase. The *San Joaquin* slipped safely into Cartagena Harbour. This was reported to Wagner who passed the information to the subsequent court-martial: ' "Between two and three in the afternoon we were very near the west end of a shoal called the Salmedinas which lay about three leagues off the castle at the entrance to Cartagena Harbour, and so near the enemy at the same time so that we might engage him ... but the captain refused to go after him within the shoal." Captain Bridge of the *Kingston*, referring to Captain Windsor of the *Portland*.'[6]

The English ships returned to Jamaica with the Spanish treasure that they had managed to capture from the *Santa Cruz*: 'Thirteen chest of pieces of eight, and fourteen piggs, or sows of silver, was all that could be found.'[7]

When, in July, the English fleet arrived back in Port Royal, Jamaica, Wagner immediately signed court-martial papers with regard to the conduct of Captains Windsor and Bridge. It was alleged that these two men were both guilty of poor judgment, misconduct, and failure properly to engage the Spanish fleet (a possible breaching of the Articles of War). Privateers of the time, although 'licensed to plunder', were also held accountable under these Articles and could be prosecuted for failure to comply.

> Captain Edward Windsor commander of Her Majesty's ship *Portland* being tried for not doing his duty in the late action with the Spanish Galleons on the coast of Cartagena in New Spain on 28:30 of May last. It did appear that the said Captain Windsor was slack in his duty by not bearing so near the enemy as to keep sight of some of them when they were engaged on the 28 at night. That upon chasing the enemy the next day by signal from the Commadore he left off chase and bore down to the *Kingston* in the evening when he ought not to have done so, and that on the 30 when the *Kingston* and *Portland* chased the Vice-Admiral of the galleons near Saladena he shortened sail before he came up with the said and did not pursue the chase of the said ship so far as he might have done, but it appeared that he was lead into these mistakes through want of judgement and having too great regard to Captain Bridge of the *Kingston* as a senior officer. This court having duly considered the whole matter do find him guilty of the breach of some part of these Articles of War and of the said offence do dismiss him the said Captain Edward Windsor from being captain of Her Majesty's ship the *Portland* signed Charles Wagner.[8]

In addition to Captain Windsor being found guilty, Captain Bridge of the *Kingston* was also tried:

> And it did appear by evidence upon oath that the said Captain Tim Bridge did not use his utmost endeavour to engage and take the enemy the night of 28th of May, and that he did too negligently pursue the chase of the Spanish vice admiral the 29th and 30th, and that he left the chase when within shot of the said Spanish ship doubting the pilot's knowledge and being near the shoals called the Salmedinas, though the pilot offered to carry the ship within said shoal after the said vice admiral. But no want of personal courage being alleged against him, this court does only find him guilty of breach of part of Section 12 and 14 of the Articles of War. And for the said offence do dismiss said Captain Tim Bridge from being captain of Her Majesty's ship the *Kingston*.'[9]

Thomas Handasyd, the then Governor of Jamaica, sent an account of the skirmish to the Council of Trade and Plantations:

I herewith send your [Lordships] a list of the galleons, and the other vessels that were with them, when they were attack'd by Mr. Wager. I understand Mr. Wager intends to bring the two Captains that were then with him to a triall, as soon as the ships expected from Great Britain arrive, that they may be able to make up a Court Martiall: By the account that I have had from my own Officers that were on board those ships, and the Lieutenants of them, Mr. Wager has had very foul play, but that will be best known when the Court Martiall meets. The traders that are lately come from Porto Bell, say, that the Spaniards laugh at them and tell them that two of our men of war, one of 60, the other of 50 guns, dare not attack their Vice Admiral of 64 guns (the *San Joaquin*), that they only ffired now and then their chase gunns at him, and then sailed ahead of him and gave him their stern guns, at so far distance as not to do him any damage, and never came up to give him a broadside. This talk is enough to concern any true Englishman.[10]

According to the Royal Council of Cartagena the captured *Santa Cruz* carried 3 to 4 million pesos. The *San Jose* sank with an estimated '5 to 7 million gold and silver pieces of eight'[11], some nine miles southeast of the Bancos de Tesoro (Treasure Banks). Antonio Ordaz y Perez, Captain of *San Joaquin*, later reported to the Council of Cartagena: 'They were relatively close to the great shallow and a map illustrating this position mentions the spot where the Great Galleon was lost with approximately 3 million pesos in gold.'[12]

Sea Search Armada

In 1981 the Sea Search Armada, a Chicago-based group of investors headed by Warren Stearns, made a proposal to the Colombian Government: the group stated its interest in commencing salvage operations on the *San Jose* and offered an equal split of any treasure found. According to Sea Search's archivist, Dr Eugene Lyon, 'The bronze cannons, some weighing two tons, give the ship an unusual magnetic signature, which Stearns said he is certain that Sea Search's deep-diving submarine, *Auguste Piccard*, detected during several passes over the site ... calculated that the ship had come to rest under 800 feet of water.'[13]

Up to the present time no treasure has been recovered. Sea Search estimates the gold and silver coins, ingots, plate, jewellery and religious articles to be valued at at least £650,000 ($1 million).[14]

WHYDAH

The Whydah was named after the old African slave port at Ouidah in present-day Benin. She was a British-built slaving galley of 300 tons, armed with twenty-eight guns and launched by the Royal African Company. The Whydah was captured by Samuel Bellamy in February 1717 and used as a pirate ship.

AREA: *Grounded and sank on a sandbar 500 feet offshore at Marconi Beach, near Wellfleet, Cape Cod, Massachusetts, USA, Atlantic.*

Samuel Bellamy was probably born in Dorset in England, but very few facts can be found relating to his background. Bellamy arrived in Eastham, Cape Cod around 1715; possibly he had relatives or connections in the area. He met up with Paul Williams from Newport, an educated man whose father had been the Attorney General of Rhode Island.

Bellamy and Williams sailed to Jamaica and joined Governor Heywood's expedition in 1716 to salvage the treasure from the *Grifon*. This was a French ship, sailing with the Spanish treasure fleet, which sank in a hurricane near Fort Piece off the coast of Florida in 1715, carrying an estimated 9 million pesos in gold and silver.

The expedition having failed, Bellamy and Williams joined two pirates, Captain Benjamin Hornigold of the sloop *Mary Anne* and the Frenchman Captain Louis Lebous[1] in the *Postillion*. Near Havana they captured two Spanish brigantines carrying cargo of little value.

Hornigold had a disagreement with Lebous regarding tactics, and refused to plunder English ships. With their differences unresolved, Hornigold and twenty-six of his men separated from Lebous in one of the captured ships. He later 'came in' under the King's proclamation of 5 September 1717 which offered pardon to those pirates who surrendered within a given time.

Bellamy and Lebous became partners, sailing to the Virgin Islands where they captured two ships, the *Sultana*, commanded by Captain Richards, and a sloop, commanded by Captain Tosor. Bellamy took command of the *Sultana* and appointed Williams Captain of the sloop.

In documents in the Suffolk County files in Massachusetts, dated 6 May 1717, John Brown, a 'forced seaman' on board Lebous's sloop, describes the pirates' exploits:

Off Cape Corante they took two Spanish Briganteens without any resistance, laden with cocoa from Ma[l]aca. The Spaniards, not coming up to the pirats demand about the ransom, were put ashoar and their Briganteens burn'd. They sailled next to the Isle of Pines, where meeting with three or four English Sloops empty, they made use of them in cleaning their own, and gave them back. From thence they sailled in the latter end of May to Hispaniola, where they tarried about 3 months. The Examinate then left Leboose and went on board the Sloop commanded formerly by Hornygold, but at that time by one Bellamy, who upon a difference arising amongst the English Pirats because Hornygold refused to take and plunder English Vessels, was chosen by a great majority their Captain, and Hornygold departed with 26 hands in a Prize Sloop, Bellamy having then on board about 90 men, most of them English. Bellamy and Leboose sailled to the Virgin Islands and took several small fishing boats, and off St. Croix a French Ship laden with flower and fish from Canada, and having taken out some of the flower gave back the Ship. Plying to the Windward the morning they made Saba they spy'd two Ships, which they chased and came up with, the one was commanded by Captain Richards, the other by Capt. Tosor, both bound to the bay. Having plunder'd the Ships and taken out some young men, they dismist the rest and Tosors Ship and made a man of War of Richards's, which they put under the command of Bellamy, and appointed Paull Williams Captain of the Sloop. Next day they took a Bristol Ship commanded by James Williams from Ireland laden with provisions, and having taken out what provisions they wanted and two or three of the Crew let her goe. Then they parted with their French consort at the Island of Blanco.[2]

At the end of February Bellamy and his crew sailed in the Windward Passage, between Cuba and Hispaniola and seized the English ship, the *Whydah*, carrying £20,000 in gold and silver.[3]

Captain Lawrence Prince in a ship of 300 Ton called the Whido, with 18 guns mounted, and fifty men, bound from Jamaica to London, laden with Sugar, Indico, Jesuits bark[4] and some silver and gold, and having given chase thre daies took him without any other resistance than his firing two chase guns at the Sloop, and came to an anchor at Long Island.[5] Bellamy's crew and Williams's consisted then of 120 men. They gave the Ship taken from Captain Richards to Captain Prince, and loaded her with as much of the best and finest goods as she could carry, and gave Captain Prince

A slave ship taking a new consignment aboard. The *Whydah* was originally built to
carry slaves from Africa to the Americas and took its name from Quidah in Benin, a
port on the west coast of Africa. The ship was captured by the pirate Samuel
Bellamy on her maiden voyage

about twenty pounds in Silver and gold to bear his charges. They took 8
or 10 men belonging to Captain Prince; the Boatswain an two more were
forced, the rest being volunteers.[6]

Bellamy took over the *Whydah*, transferring ten cannons from the *Sultana*.
With Williams commanding the small sloop they headed for the Virginian
coast; en route they seized a small ship off Haiti.

They took an English Ship hired by the French, laden with Sugar, Indico,
and having taken out what they had occasion for, and some of the men,
dismist her. Then they stood away for the Capes of Virginia, being 130
men in company, and having lost sight of the Sloop the day before they
made the land, they cruised ten daies, according to agreement between
Bellamy and Williams, in which time they seized three ships and one Snow[7],

Two of them from Scotland, one from Bristol, and the fourth a Scotch
Ship, last from Barbadoes, with a little Rum and Sugar on board, so leaky
that the men refused to proceed further. The Pirats sunk her. Having lost
the Sloop they kept the Snow, which was taken from one Montgomery,
being about 100 Ton, and manned her with 18 hands, which with her own
Crew made up to number of 28 men; the other two Ships were discharged
being first plundered.[8]

By 26 April sailing between Nantucket Shoals and St George's Bank, Bellamy
seized the *Mary Anne* from Dublin, commanded by Andrew Crumpstey, sailing
to Massachusetts from Madeira with a cargo of wine. Bellamy ordered
Crumpstey and five of his men to board the *Whydah* and sent over seven armed
pirates to commandeer the *Mary Anne*. About four o'clock that afternoon a
thick fog came up and the ships hove-to; by 10 o'clock that evening the winds
increased to gale force from the east with heavy rain. The ships separated. In
a deposition by Thomas Fitzgerald and Alexander Mackonochie of the *Mary
Anne* it was stated:

They discovered a large Ship, and her Prize, which was a Snow, astern, an
the large Ship came up with the said Pink[9] Mary Ann, between nine and
ten, and ordered us to strike our Colours, which accordingly we did, and
then they shot ahead of us, and braced too, and hoisted out her boat and
sent seven Men on board, Armed with their Musquet, pistols and Cutlashes
(with Men are now in Boston Gaol) and they commanded the said Capt.
Crumsty to take his papers and go aboard the said Ship . . . presently after
the pyrates had hoisted their boat on board the great Ship, they gave Orders
to the Pyrates on board the pink to steer North Northwest after them,
which Course they followed till about four a Clock in the afternoon, and
then the large Ship whereof Capt. Samuel Bellame was Commander, and
the snow and pink lay too, it being very thick foggy weather, And about
half an hour after four a Clock a sloop came up with Capt. Bellames Ship
and he hoisted out his boat and sent several men on board the Sloop and
soon afterwards, Vist. about five a Clock, the Commander of the snow
bore away, and came under the stern of Capt. Bellames Ship and told him
that they saw the Land; And thereupon Capt. Bellame Ordered the Pyrates
on board the Pink to steer away North, which they did, and soon as it
began to be dark the sd Capt. Bellames Ship put out a light astern and
also the snow and the sloop and the pink had their lights out; and about
ten a Clock the weather grew thick and it lightened and rained hard and

was so dark, that the pinks Comp. Could not see the shore till they were among the Breakers, when the Depon't Fitz Gerald was at helm, and he lost sight of the Great Ship, Snow and Sloop.[10]

The *Mary Anne* grounded and sank near Orleans, Massachusetts. The *Whydah*, making her way up the coast and unable to seek refuge of a port, cast out the bower anchors to try and ride out the gale. Dragging the anchors with the sea swamping the ship, Bellamy decided to cut the ship loose and run her ashore. Unknown to Bellamy a sandbank lay between the ship and the shore. The *Whydah* struck the sandbank with the waves battering her broadside; she keeled over to her legside and capsized.

In the Boston *Newsletter* dated 6 May 1717 the Governor of Massachusetts issued a proclamation:

Where a Ship of The Burthen of about three hundred Tons, Mounted with Twenty eight Guns, Manned with One hundred & thirty Mew, Commanded by Samuel Bellame, said to be an English man, a Reputed Pyrate, has lately Infested and Annoyed the Coast. And on Friday the 26th of April last past in the Night time the said Ship was cast on Shore in a Storm on the back side of Cape Codd, against the middle of the Table Land, and broken to pieces, the most of her Men drown'd: on Board of which Ship there was Money, Bullion, Goods and Merchandize of considerable value, much of which has been taken up before Information thereof was given to any in Authority; And it is very probable that much more may be recovered.

I do therefore with the Advice of His Majesty's Council strictly charge, command and require all Justices of the Peace, Sheriffs, Constables, and other His Majesty's Officers and subjects; within this Province, to use their utmost Endeavors and Diligence to Seize and apprehend, or cause to be seized and apprehended, any Person or Persons belonging to the said Pirate Ship, their Accomplices and Confederates, with the Money, Bullion, Treasure, Goods and Merchandizes taken out of the said Ship, or any of her Apparel, that shall be found with them, or any of them, or in the possession of any others; and to carry such Person or Persons before One or more of the Members of the Council or other of His Majesty's Justices of the Peace to be imprisoned and Proceeded against as the Law directs. And all persons whomsoever are hereby strictly forbidden to Countenance, Harbour, Entertain, Comfort, Conceal or Convey away any of the said Ships Company, or any of their Money Treasure, Goods or Merchandize, as they will answer the same at their utmost Peril.[11]

Only two of the *Whydah* crew survived; the remaining 144 perished. The two who survived were John Davis, aged twenty-two, a Welsh shipwright and John Julian, an Indian born on Cape Cod and acting as pilot. They were taken to Boston and put in irons in Stone Jail. The seven pirate survivors from the *Mary Ann* were as follows: 'Simon Van Vorst aged twenty four, born in New York, John Brown twenty five, from Jamaica, Thomas Baker twenty nine, born Flushing, Holland, Hendrich Quainton twenty five, from Amsterdam, Peter Cornelius Hoof thirty four, from Sweden, John Sheenan twenty four, born Nantes, Thomas South thirty, born Boston, England.[12] All were tried with piracy. Thomas South was acquitted, the others found guilty and sentenced to be hanged. They were executed on 15 November at Charleston Ferry within the flux and reflux of the sea.'[13]

Barry Clifford

Barry Clifford was a former high school history teacher turned professional treasure hunter. He formed Maritime Explorations with a group of investors who put in $6 million to locate and salvage the *Whydah*. After two years' search along the coast near Wellfleet, Clifford was granted permission in 1984 to excavate two miles of sea floor. He relied in part on information by Cyprian Southack, a colonial sea captain, pilot and notable map maker of the time, who wrote to Governor Shute of Massachusetts in May 1717:

> May 2 at 2 Afternoon I sent Mr. Little and Mr. Cuttler to the Rack. they Got their that Night and Capt. watch till I came the Next morning. at my Coming there I found the Rack all to Pices, North and South, Distance from one a Nother 4 Miles. Sir, whear shee Strock first I se one Anchor at Low water, sea being so Great Ever sence I have ben here, Can not Come to se what maye be their for Riches, nor aney of her Guns. she is a ship a bout Three hundred tuns. she was very fine ship. all that I Can find saved Out of her, is her Cables and som of her sailes, Cut all to Pices by the Inhabitances here. their has ben at this Rack Two hundred men at Least Plundering of her. sum saye they Gott Riches Out of the sand but I Can not find them as yett. Sir, what I shall Gett to Gather will be to the Value of Two hundred Pounds. If your Excellency Pleass to send the sloop to Billingsgatt for itt, is Carted Over Land to that Place. Sir, here has been 54 wit men and 4 Negros Come a shore Ded from the Rack. If their be aney News by the Pirritts at boston whear the money is, I humbley

Desier Your Excellency menets of what Place in the ship itt was in, for I am in Great hops. whare the Anchors are the money is I fancy, and weather Per mett I have Got a whale boat to fish for itt and Things for that service.[14]

Clifford and his divers discovered the *Whydah* 30 feet below the surface and 500 feet off Marconi Point, exactly where Southack reported the wreck. Working from the 70-foot diving vessel, *Vast Explorer*, and the larger ship, *Maritime Explorer*, the divers located cannons, gold and silver coins scattered over a 200–300-foot area. No firm evidence from the finds indicated that the wreck was that of the *Whydah* until, in 1985, divers found a bronze bell inscribed 'The *Whydah* Gally 1716' with the symbol of a Maltese cross between each word. Also located were '4,500 to 6,000 coins most of them in silver ... 180 50 pound bags of silver and gold dust'.[15]

Barry Clifford estimated 'that the finds might be worth $5 to $10 million [£2.8 to £5.6 million]'.[16]

LE CHAMEAU

Le Chameau *was an eighteenth-century three-masted, 600 ton, forty-eight gun French transport sailing ship, 133 feet long, carrying 233 passengers and a crew of 100. She was commanded by Jean Charles Percheron.*

AREA: *Sank during a gale when she struck a rocky reef now known as Chameau Rock, off the coast of Cape Breton Island, Nova Scotia, Canada, Atlantic.*

The French transport ship, *Le Chameau*, departed the French port of Rochefort in July 1725, bound for the colonial fortress at Louisbourg in Nova Scotia. She carried gunpowder, weapons and military supplies, plus 300,000 livres in coin as pay for the troops of New France.

As the *Chameau* approached the eastern end of Cape Breton Island she ran into a gale; at 4am on 26 August she struck a submerged rock and was dashed to pieces, drowning all her crew and passengers.

The Commandant of the fortress at Louisbourg sent out a search party under a French privateer, Pierre Morpain, finding only bodies on the beaches at Kelpy Cove and scattered wreckage along the coast. It was not until the following year that Morpain began to attempt to search for the treasure of

Le Chameau. Dragging a primitive grapnel, he recovered a cannon and two anchors, but no treasure.

In 1914 the SS *Ragna*, a 1000-ton steamship, sank after striking Chameau Rock. The insurance company sent a diver down to survey the *Ragna*; in his investigations he claimed to have seen a number of gold and silver coins in rock crevices. On finishing his survey, he planned to recover the coins but drowned a few days later.

Two other salvage attempts were made years later; however, no treasure was found.

A. Storm, D. Maceachern and H. Macleod

Alex Storm emigrated to Canada from Holland and settled in Cape Breton, working as a diver salvaging copper, brass and other non-ferrous metal from wrecks off the coast. While working on a wreck near Chameau Rock, Storm spotted several cannons and eroded cannon balls. Cleaning the surface of one of the cannons he made out the bust of Louis XV and the date, 1724. On his next dive he found a silver fork and a silver four-livre coin. Storm had retrieved the first evidence of the wreck of *Le Chameau*.

In March 1965 Storm applied to the province of Nova Scotia, for a period of three years 'to search for treasure trove over a certain area of land underwater off the island of Cape Breton and to recover and to retain any treasure trove found therein by him upon payment to the provincial Secretary of a royalty at a rate of ten percent of the value thereof'.[1]

From the Federal department of transport he also obtained a letter giving permission to keep anything of value without handing it over to the Receiver of the Wrecks.

Storm approached two friends, Dave Maceachern, a surveyor, and Harvey Macleod, a railway engineer, to join his project. Each investing $600, they bought diving equipment and an old 35-foot fishing vessel, the *Marilyn B II*. Working from the small fishing village of Little Lorraine, four and a half miles from Chameau Rock, the three men began their search for the wreck.

From their research and surveys it appeared that the *Chameau*'s superstructure and upper deck had broken away from the hull and lower deck. At Chameau Rock they first located twenty-eight cannons. Storm wrote: 'It seems certain sure now that the twenty eight cannon by the rock slipped out of the ship on its first impact. The rest must have stayed with the hull, and so the hull must be somewhere else and not by the rock.'[2]

Having discovered nothing more around the original search area by Chameau Rock the divers began to search for the remains of wreckage which would indicate the direction of the hull and upper deck. Working in a west-northwest direction from the rock, Storm recorded: 'On this course it did not take long before I found plenty of cannon balls, cannon and lead partridge shot. I sighted our last underwater marker and then I proceeded (out of the marked grid area) and I came to a high ridge on the base of which was a lot of iron work and lead shot. . . . I am sure we are getting hot.'[3]

By the end of August a 2000-foot-long trail from the *Chameau* had been found; this suddenly terminated with no other signs or wreckage: 'Again nothing was seen. Disheartened, we proceeded back to the place where, as near as we could guess, we found our last traces of wreckage. On the way down I spotted a dark shape on the bottom. I investigated.'[4]

The dark shape, made up of ballast stones, was over 200 feet long by 8 feet high and 15 feet wide. Standing out from the stones were the rotted timbers of the *Chameau's* hull. More cannons were discovered and, searching in the surrounding rock crevices, Storm found clusters of gold and silver coins. In the weeks that followed, 11,000 silver coins, 2000 gold Louis d'or, silverware, ceramics and pewterware were discovered.

On 11 December 1971, the first of the treasure was sold in New York for $200,000 (£84,000); the total amount of treasure recovered is estimated to be in the region of between $700,000 to $1 million (£467,000 to £667,000).

The bulk of the treasure is still to be found near Chameau Rock.

LA GENOVESA

La Genovesa, also known as the Nuestra Senora del Carman, *was a Spanish galleon, built in Genoa. She carried fifty-four cannons and 400 passengers, soldiers and crew commanded by Captain Francisco Guiral.*

AREA: *Wrecked northeast of Banner Reef in the San Pedro Banks, also known as Las Viboras, ninety miles southwest of Jamaica. Banner Reef takes its name from the English barque* Banner *which sank on the reef in 1880.*

La Genovesa sailed from Boca Grande Harbour of Cartagena on 18 August 1730, bound for Havana on her way to Spain. She carried a large amount of treasure which consisted of '367,247 pesos in silver, 134,444 pesos in gold, 11 gold bars, 177 marks, 7 ounces of silver ware, 54⅙ ounces of gold ware, 12 marks, 2 ounces glossed silver'.[1]

Sailing out of Cartagena *La Genovesa* set course northwest to Havana. The first landmark would be the small Cays of the Pedro Banks – the Pedro Banks were known to the Spanish as Las Viboras (the Vipers) – a hazardous coral reef about 45 miles long. At the eastern end of the reef lie four Cays: Northwest Cay, Middle Cay, Southwest Cay and South Cay, known locally as Rocky Cay which represent la Cabeza de la Viboras (the head of the Viper).

The *Genovesa* headed north to Havana, picking up a southeasterly wind. On the seventh day the wind had increased to gale force and at 5pm the lookout sighted Las Viaboras nine miles ahead. Driven east by the gale the galleon entered the shallow water of the Banner Reef, her rudder struck the reef and was torn away, and the wind swung the ship around smashing her lower stern. The galleon sank between two reefs in 14 feet of water. Battered by the surf the ship began to break up. With darkness approaching Captain Guiral ordered rafts to be constructed while he and his second-in-command, Don Francisco Lagett, sailed with seventeen crew to the nearest small cay (Sandy island) where they spent the night. Returning to the reef in the morning, and finding no trace of the ship or any of the survivors, they set sail for Port Royal in Jamaica, a distance of roughly seventy-five miles.

Oliver Cromwell captured Jamaica from the Spanish in 1656 and within a few years its capital, Port Royal, had become a centre for piracy until the earthquake of 1692 which destroyed two thirds of the town. Port Royal was rebuilt and maintained its importance as a base for English ships.

After the war of the Spanish succession (1701–14) Spain and England were at peace and Spanish ships en route to Spain passed unmolested by British shipping.

In reaching Port Royal Captain Guiral reported the loss of his ship to Admiral Charles Stuart of the Royal Navy. After resting for a week Guiral was given a small sailing ship and provisions to return to the reef to salvage any treasure and search for survivors.

Arriving at the wreck site Guiral found the remains of tangled rigging and broken spars washed up on the reef; in searching the area at low tide he could see the outline of the bow section lying on its side with the broken stern half facing the heavy surf. By concentrating diving efforts on the stern section, where the bulk of the treasure was stored, the divers recovered a number of treasure chests.

Admiral Stuart dispatched the Royal Navy frigate, HMS *Experiment*, under Captain Henry Reddish, to assist in the salvage. The *Experiment* anchored in calm water close to the reef; Captain Guiral transferred a large amount of recovered treasure to her. HMS *Experiment* was joined by another Royal Navy ship, HMS *Tryal*, and diving continued intermittently for several months. Sixteen of the fifty-four cannons were recovered, as well as five anchors and more gold and silver coins. The ships returned to Port Royal on 7 February.

HMS *Adventure*, commanded by Lord Muskerry, sailed to Cadiz where he handed over to Spanish officials a total of '34,069 pesos in gold escudos and silver 4 reales, 4,000 pesos in gold 2 escudos (1,000) 119,856 pesos in 101 silver bars equal to 14,935 marks, 4 oz. 25,296 pesos in 11 small bars of gold, 1 complete bar, 2 half bars and 1 gold piece. 64570 pesos in gold 2 escudos (16,142) 9000 pesos in silver coin, 256 pesos total'.[2]

Art McKee

Art McKee was a professional treasure diver who had been successful in salvaging a number of Spanish galleons in the area around the Bahama Banks. McKee became interested in the *Genovesa* in the mid 1950s when he first visited Banner Reef; he made a number of dives but found no evidence of the galleon. In 1979 Jack Haskins, another treasure diver, showed McKee copies of documents from the London Public Records Office; one of these was the log of HMS *Tryal*, which stated: 'Anchored within two leagues of sloop working wreck, and 4 leagues from Savannah Key bearing East by South, I sent the Lieutenant over in the pinace to inform himself of where the wreck lay. 20th September – at noon the wreck bore south east by south, and the Savannah key east north east four leagues, anchored by ye wreck, it bore south east by east and Savannah Key east north east.'[3]

In later English navigational charts many former names had been changed, Savannah Cay became Southwest Cay and Button Cay, a small 10-foot-high white mound of coral, was renamed South Cay.

Jack Haskins joined McKee's expedition sailing in the 54-foot converted fishing boat, *Polaris*, captained by Deryck Mills. The *Polaris* anchored 200 yards to the northwest of Banner Reef and two rubber inflatables searched the area indicated in the *Tryal*'s log. The diver found a large pile of ballast stones and sixteen cannons in 14 feet of water – but no evidence that they belonged to the *Genovesa*.

Jack Haskins began a sweep of the area with a metal detector and picked up small silver bars weighing between 2–3 lbs; moving near to the edge of the ballast stones he located more silver bars. In the first day's diving Haskins recovered twenty-one small silver bars, one 80-lb silver bar and three silver coins.

The next day the weather changed, forcing the *Polaris* to return to port. Art McKee never returned to Pedro Banks; he died nine months later of a heart attack. It is difficult to estimate the total amount of treasure recovered from the *Genovesa*.

NUESTRA SENORA DE LA LUZ

Very little is known regarding the origins of the Nuestra Senora de la Luz, *although it is understood that she was a Portuguese galleon of over 200 tons sailing under licence to the Spanish Crown.*

Her wreck was originally known as El Preciado, *a legendary galleon, carrying a vast treasure, reputedly sunk by an English pirate ship in 1793. Local legend has it that an Irish gunner by the nickname of 'Little Red' accidentally fired a cannon and hit the* Preciado's *powder magazine; the ship blew up and immediately sank. Although there is confusion about the wreck's identity, experts now believe from ship's fragments that the treasure belongs to the* Nuestra Senora de la Luz.

AREA: *Sank near Montevideo off La Playa de la Mulata, Uruguay, Atlantic.*

The *Nuestra Senora de la Luz*, under licence to the Spanish Crown, set sail in 1752 from Buenos Aires to Cadiz via Montevideo. Her registered cargo consisted of gold and silver coins to the value of 1,071,000 pesos; in addition it was reported that she was carrying unregistered specie worth 200,000 pesos hidden in her powder magazine.[1]

On 2 July 1752, the *Luz* anchored off Montevideo in the Rio de la Plata, five miles from the harbour. Loaded with her valuable cargo and ready to sail, she was struck by a violent storm which swept her away from her anchorage and wrecked her on the northern coast with no survivors.

Rubén Collado

Rubén Collado operated a salvage company under licence from the government of the Republic of Uruguay and found his first gold coin in April 1992.

Since then 1650 gold coins, 320 silver coins and forty gold ingots have been recovered[2] with an estimated value of between £2.5 and £3 million ($3.75 and $4.5 million).[3] Much still has to be salvaged.

NUEVO CONSTANTE

The Nuevo Constante, *a Spanish galleon of 470 tons originally belonged to the English company of Bervickes-Timmerman; at that time the ship was known as the* Duke of York. *In 1764 she was purchased by the widow and daughter of Francisco San Gines, a prominent Spanish merchant from Cadiz. The ship was renamed* Jesus Nazareno, *but was better known as* El Nuevo Constante. *The bill of sale states she measured 102 feet on the keel with a 30-foot beam, a standard three-masted rig with mains and topsails on the fore and mainmast. The* Constante *carried twelve cannons with a crew of eighty-eight under the command of Captain Julian Antonio de Urcullu.*

AREA: *Ran aground during a hurricane off the coast of Louisiana near Cameron Parish and Constante Bayou, USA, Gulf of Mexico.*

On 7 December 1765 the *Nuevo Constante* was loaded at Cadiz with a general cargo bound for Veracruz in Mexico. The cargo consisted of wine vinegar, iron plough shares and nails; the main cargo included 1334 sheepskin bags filled with mercury, placed in wooden boxes each weighing 150 lbs.[1]

Mercury was also known as quicksilver and was an important product in the Spanish colonies; it was widely used in the amalgamation process for the extraction of gold and silver, and was vital to the Spanish economy.

The *Nuevo Constante* set sail, with one other galleon, and arrived in Veracruz on 27 February 1766.

By early May the galleon was prepared for her return voyage to Spain and was loaded with 2,058 'pigs' or ingots of copper weighing 112,655, 30,680 pesos in silver coins, 5,000 pesos in gold coin and over 160 pounds in silver bars.[2] These are valued at over £700,000 ($1 million) at today's prices.

The *Nuevo Constante* was to join the homeward fleet of ships under the command of Augustin de Idiaquez; this included his flagship *Santiago la Espana el Jason*, two other merchantships, *La Perla* and *El Triumfante*, and the royal warship, *El Dragon*, carrying the Marquis de Croix, the Viceroy-designate for New Spain. After many months of delay the fleet finally departed Veracruz on 21 August when they were joined by another ship, the *Corazon de Jesus*.

Ten days later, on the evening of 1 September, east of Cape Negrillko, Mexico, the fleet ran into a violent storm. On the fourth day the fleet had lost contact with each other and the *Corazon de Jesus* lost her mast and rigging, and was wrecked on the Louisiana coast. The *Nuevo Constante* was leaking badly, the sea water rising to the level of the pumps. Captain De Urcullu realizing it was only a matter of time before his ship sank, headed for the nearest land. The galleon ran aground 180 miles east of the Spanish port of Balize in Louisiana, stranding herself in 10 feet of soft mud 500 yards from the marshy shoreline.

The Captain sent several of the crew in the longboat to reconnoitre the shore to find high ground. Locating a suitable camp site about a mile from the wreck the crew salvaged as much of the supplies and cargo as possible. Once the camp had been established the captain ordered the longboat to sail to Balize and notify the Spanish authorities to rescue the castaways.

On hearing the news the Governor of Louisiana, Antonio De Ulloa, sent several ships to the rescue of the castaways and the survivors of the *Corazon de Jesus* which was wrecked some fifty miles to the west of the *Constante*.

Two ships, the schooner, *El Diquiblot*, commanded by William Moore, and another vessel, reached the survivors in October.

In 1785, during the mapping of the Louisiana coastline by Jose De Evia, a reference was made to the wreck: 'I followed the coast from here 27 miles toward the west, to the Bayu Del Constante. It was so called because of a vessel of this name having been lost opposite it in the month of September of the year 1766, in a southeast hurricane. It sailed from Veracruz.'[3]

Free Enterprise Salvage Company

Curtis Blume, a fisherman, shrimped in Louisiana waters in his boat, the *Lady Barbara*. In an area now called the Constante Bayou, in the winter of 1979, Blume caught three copper ingots in his shrimp net.

Blume mentioned the copper ingots to a friend and fellow shrimper, Steve Smith. Returning to the site and using a dredge at 18 feet, they brought to the surface more copper ingots, ballast stones and a number of gold and silver ingots. Blume and Smith, recognizing the importance of their finds, notified the state authorities.

Blume formed the Free Enterprise Salvage Company with four other men; the agreement with Louisiana state established that the state would pay for the archaeological work and receive twenty-five per cent of the artifacts, with the company paying salvage costs and receiving seventy-five per cent. Salvaging the wreck began in 1980; sidescan sonar produced a clear outline of the remains of the wreck. On excavating the wreck the divers found the intact lower section of the hull and deck timbers. A total of twenty-seven moulded silver discs, weighing 80 lbs, were recovered, along with 50 lbs of gold bullion with an estimated value of $500,000 (£246,000).[4]

DE BRAAK

HMS De Braak *was a British privateering vessel of 255 tons. Built in England in 1781 as a single-masted vessel but later converted to a two-masted brig, she had been constructed for the French Navy. When war was declared against France she was sold to the Dutch. Holland was then occupied by the French and so the* De Braak *was incorporated into the British Navy. She was commanded by Captain James Drew and had a crew of eighty-three.*

AREA: *Foundered off the Delmarva Peninsula, a mile off Cape Henlopen in the Delaware Bay, USA, Atlantic Ocean.*

In March 1798 HMS *De Braak* was consigned to join a convoy of British ships sailing to North America; on her voyage out, two strange ships were sighted and the *De Braak* was ordered to pursue and investigate their colours. Finding that one was a British Navy ship sailing along with a captured French vessel, the *De Braak* altered course in order to rejoin the convoy. Unable to re-establish contact she made her own way to Delaware, capturing the *Don Francisco Xavier*, a Spanish merchantman en route.

The *De Braak* sailed into Delaware Bay where she was caught by a sudden squall and capsized on 25 May 1798. *The Times* described the loss:

> Philadelphia, May 28. By Mr. Vincent Low, who arrived from Cape Henlopen yesterday afternoon, we have received the melancholy news of the loss of his Britannic Majesty's sloop of war *De Braak*, Capt. Drew, which overset in Old Kiln Roads about four o'clock last Friday afternoon. She was at the time, under the mainsail and reef top-sails, just about to cast anchor, a mile from the light-house, her boat alongside waiting for the Captain who intended to go on shore at Lewes Town; a sudden blow of wind laid her down on her beam-ends; she immediately filled and went down, with Capt. Drew, his Lieutenant, and 38 officers, sea-men and

marines. The rest of the ship's company, about 25, including the boatswain, escaped in the boats, and several were taken up by a pilot boat.

. . . The crew of the *De Braak* consisted of 83 persons in all, about half of whom were saved, including those who were in a prize she had taken. The Officers left alive are the Prizemaster, a Midshipman, and the Boatswain. The accident altogether is a most melancholy one, but it is greatly heightened by the circumstance of the Captain's Lady being so near as New York, where she was every hour in anxious expectation of the happiness of meeting him. The prize lies at the Fort.[1]

J. Potter in his *Treasure Diver's Guide* quotes from a Halifax newspaper: 'HMS *De Braak* we are informed, was capsized off the Cape of Delaware, returning from a successful cruise on the Spanish Main: She had on board . . . an immense amount of treasure consisting of gold and silver bars and precious stones, and also eighty thousand pounds in English gold taken on board at Jamaica for transportation to England.'[2]

In H.T. Wilkins's *Treasure Hunting*, published in 1932, the value of the treasure is estimated to be between £1,500,000 and £3,000,000.[3] The admiralty dispatched HMS *Assistance* under Captain Oakes Hardy to assess the possibility of raising the *De Braak*. Captain Hardy wrote on 22 July 1798:

I have the honour to enclose a dispatch from Vice Admiral Vanderput partly relative to the raising his Majesty's sloop Braak. I am sorry to learn that she is driven into 13 fathoms water and must from being so violently shook, be full of sand and mud, so as to render any exertions to sweep under her bottom very uncertain in their effect, and also very equivocal whither the expense would not be very great of the undertaking, so much as to outweigh the returns to government. The only mode I can think of is to offer a certain handsome salvage to any who may undertake the business . . . signed Oakes Hardy[4]

In a document found in the Public Records Office in London, Hardy also writes:

. . . having duly considered the propensity of weighing [raising] the Braak, am of the opinion that no time should be lost in expediting vessels of the following description with the necessary apparatus hither . . . the Braak lays in 13 fathoms of water on hard ground . . . the necessary tackle for raising her would be two cables of 13 inch – four hausers of 7 inch – four setts of heavy down blocks that will receive the said hausers – four vessels not less than 80 tons each – which must be well found with ground tackle – half a dozen of stout loof tackle will be necessary – the falls to be 3½ or 4 inch falls. N.B. As many good pumps as can be got well fitted will be wanted – and by no means omitted. Oakes Hardy[5]

After two months all attempts to raise and salvage the *De Braak* proved unsuccessful and further operations were discontinued.

In Gary Gentle's book, *Shipwrecks of Delaware*, fourteen attempts to salvage the *De Braak* are listed:[6]

1880–1882.	International Submarine Company.
188?.	Ocean Wrecking Company.
1887.	Pancoast Expedition.
1888.	Captain Jeff Townsend.
192?.	Captain Charles Adams, U.S.N.
1932.	Ralph Chapman of Merritt, Chapman & Scott.
1935–1936.	Charles N. Colstad Expedition.
1952.	Charles Johnston, Rodney King, and George Shockley.
1962–1963.	William Strube.
1965–1968.	D & D Salvage Company.
1970.	Tracy Bowen Associates.
1973.	HMS De Braak Salvage Company.
1979.	Edward Westlake.
1981.	Sting Ray Inc.

Sub-Sal Inc.

Mr Harvey Harrington, a commercial diver, formed a syndicate with a number of investors from Nevada to locate and salvage the *De Braak*.

After three years of research and exploration the divers discovered the first evidence of a wreck: copper sheathing, rudder hinges, bilge pumps. The wreck was confirmed when they found a gold ring belonging to Captain James Drew, with the inscription, 'In memory of my brother, Capt. John Drew, drowned 11 January 1798, age 47'.[7] The Captain's twin brother, John, had died four months before his own death on 25 May.

The 84-foot-long ship lay at an angle of 20 degrees with its three decks collapsed one on top of the other.

The *Los Angeles Times* reported: 'Since July, seven divers working around the clock in 80 feet of water have brought up tons of artefacts, including more than 100 18th century escudo pieces, doubloons and pieces of eight, each coin is worth $1,000 to $5,000 and Harrington hopes to find enough to make a profit on the $500,000 that the Nevada firm has already poured into the search.'[8]

Harrington was accused of not complying with Sub-Sal's contract with the Division of Historical and Cultural Affairs. Sub-Sal was alleged to have removed gold coins and then to have recorded lesser items as substitutes. The US District Court ordered an investigation and Harrington was censured for removing property owned by Sub-Sal and the state. He was subsequently disallowed from selling any of *De Braak*'s treasure. By the end of 1984 Sub-Sal was insolvent.

Drew Associates

John Davidson, a New Hampshire real-estate developer, bought out two of Sub-Sal's original investors. He paid off debts of over $100,000 and became principal stock holder, forming Drew Associates.

A 90-foot fishing trawler was purchased and equipped with a 6-inch vacuum hose. After months of work they had recovered over 3500 artifacts but little treasure. It was then decided to raise the hull, using a lifting cradle, and to dredge the area below. After a complicated and expensive salvage operation the hull was raised and dredging was carried out to a depth of 14 feet. A few more coins were located along with artifacts that were of historical interest. At the end of 1986 expenditure had reached $3,000,000 (£2 million); the total number of coins recovered was less than 600, each with an estimated value of $1000 (£680). Davidson halted the salvage operation.[9]

Davidson maintains that there is still treasure scattered around the wreck site. 'I predict that the legend of the *De Braak* will live on, and that whether I continue to chase the rainbow or not someone will come along with new equipment one of these days and start looking for the treasure all over again.'[10]

THETIS

HMS Thetis *was a forty-six-gun frigate built in Pembroke, Wales in 1817. It had a complement of 300 officers and men, commanded by Captain Samuel Burgess.*

AREA: Sank after hitting the rock cliffs at Cape Frio, approximately 100 miles north of Rio de Janeiro, Brazil, Atlantic Ocean.

In the early 1800s, many merchants from South American countries began to send to England considerable quantities of bullion and coin in exchange for British goods. British commercial interests were based at the British Station in Rio de Janeiro.

The first of these shipments occurred in 1820 when the frigate *Hyperion* carried $1,000,000 from Callao in Peru, via Cape Horn and Rio to Spithead in England.[1] The conveyance of bullion and specie in British warships from South American ports continued for over fifty-five years.

HMS *Thetis* sailed out of Rio de Janeiro on the evening of 4 December 1830, bound for England, 'having on board gold and silver bars, and other treasures of various descriptions, amounting in value to about 810,000 dollars, the greater part of which she had brought round from the Pacific to Rio, where she received a small additional quantity, the whole being shipped on account of merchants and others in England.'[2] Departing Rio, the weather was overcast with heavy rain and thick patches of fog, the wind to starboard.

The following morning the weather worsened. Captain Burgess recorded in his narrative: 'At one o'clock am, it then bearing north west by west about three or four leagues – during the day after the fog cleared up, it rained considerably and was very dark all round particularly in the north west. . . . At half past one, the wind being scant, I ordered her to be kept east by north from the cross sea appearing to impede her progress and at 2 east north east was the course given, she having then run about 19 miles – then under the idea that she was nearly abreast of Cape Frio and twenty miles off. . . .'[3]

At seven in the evening, the fog returned with heavy rain. By eight, the fog had thickened to the extent that it was impossible to see the length of the ship. Captain Burgess ordered extra lookouts posted and sails trimmed; he then retired to his cabin.

At 8.15 the lookout from the cathead called out 'breakers ahead', followed by 'rocks above the mast head'. Within minutes the bowsprit crashed into the perpendicular cliffs of Cape Frio.

Captain Burgess wrote in his narrative:

> I heard the bowsprit crash, and found all three masts fall aft, in the quickest possible succession covering the deck with masts, yards, sails, killed and wounded, and an immense black precipice (extending about half a point on the weather bow) under her lee, upon which the surf was breaking with terrific noise. The hull however, did not appear to come in contact with rocks, but, answering the helm, turned off shore. . . . The winches were manned and guns, rockets and blue lights let off in the quickest possible succession.[4]

Captain Burgess ordered the crew to clear away the boats and get ready but the cutter, jolly boat and gig on the stern and quarters were smashed by the falling masts.

> 8.20 the ship having come round with her head to the southward and westward the relieving tackles being put on, and the helm hard to starboard. The wreck of the mizzen mast hanging partly over the starboard quarter. The starboard quarter coming in contact with a part of the rock which stove in the cutter . . . spares were got over to bear the ship off the rocks. After the ship drawing ahead about her own length and not making any water, we were in hopes of her going off altogether. But soon observing that the swell was again setting her on the rocks . . . the starboard anchor was let go (the larboard one being foul by the gear of the bowsprit) 40 fms cable run out but the anchor would not hold and the ship drifted with her starboard quarter on another projecting point, and after beating there very heavy for five or ten minutes during which time about two officers and men were able to jump ashore from the quarters but several were drowned in the attempt. . . . At 8.50 the ship swung with her head to the eastward having drifted into the bottom of a small cove and striking heavy. The water was on the lower deck and filling fast. . . .[5]

As the ship was sinking, the remaining crew on board managed to secure a line to the shore and were hauled one by one through the surf to safety. At around 9.15, the *Thetis* sank in 50 feet of water; of her 300 officers and men, twenty-eight perished.

Admiral Thomas Baker, Commander-in-Chief of the British naval station at Rio de Janeiro, on being informed of the loss of the *Thetis*, sent three naval

The *Thetis* sailed from Rio de Janeiro bound for England carrying a cargo of $810,000 in gold and silver bars. On the evening of 4 December 1830 she hit the cliffs at Cape Frio in dense fog and sank to a depth of between 50 to 80 feet

vessels, *Clio*, *Algerine* and the tender, *Adelaide*, to bring relief to the stranded survivors.

Captain Thomas Dickinson

At this time HMS *Lightening*, commanded by Thomas Dickinson, was in harbour at Rio being refitted. Dickinson approached Admiral Baker and proposed his services to salvage the treasure from the *Thetis*.

Permission was granted and on 24 January 1831 Dickinson sailed in the *Lightening* for Cape Frio. On arrival, he described the area:

The coast is formed of rugged and almost perpendicular rocks, varying from 80 to 195 in height. . . . On viewing this terrific place, with the knowledge that at the time of the shipwreck the wind was from the southward, I was struck with astonishment, and it appeared quite a mystery, that so great a number of lives could have been saved. And indeed it will never cease to be so, for that part on which the crew landed, is so difficult of access, that (even in fine weather) after being placed by a boat on a rock at the base, it required considerable strength and agility.[6]

Dickinson, with the assistance of Mr Moore, a civil engineer, constructed a diving bell made from iron water tanks with a Truscott pump as a force pump to maintain a constant air pressure in the bell.

Having surveyed the cove, Dickinson decided to construct a 158-foot-long derrick whereby he could raise and lower the diving bell above the wreck. Using a small diving bell to make a preliminary investigation of the wreck site, Dickinson recorded that 'the treasure was so strewn about and mixed with pulverised granite, splinters of wood, and various materials and contents of the ship, that it was impossible to form an idea of the extent and quality of it'.[7]

Dickinson continued diving with the small bell and after two months was able to write, 'our efforts at last crowned with success.'

Dickinson recovered the first 3,000 dollars, working well into the early hours of the morning of 1 April. . . . 'Having obtained in the whole by this attempt, 6326 dollars, 36 pounds 10 ounces of plata pina, 5 pounds 4 ounces of old silver, 243 pounds 6 ounces of silver in bars and 4 pounds 8 ounces in gold.'[8]

The large diving bell was completed by 6 May and made its first descent a week later with great success. Dickinson's first shipment of recovered treasure was sent to England and amounted to ($123,995).

Over the next twelve months, Dickinson sent five other shipments to England. The total amount of treasure recovered by him was '290,805 dollars valued at $588,801, 138bs in gold, 9106bs in bar silver, 4478 plata pina, 904bs old silver'.[9]

After fourteen months of hard work, Dickinson received orders from Admiral Baker to hand over salvage operations to the commander of the *Algerine*, Captain Frederick de Loos.

Dickinson wrote in March 'On the 23rd, I made my sixth and last shipment, by His Majesty's ship *Maidstone*, of the value of about 64,000 dollars, making the whole 588,801, and the *Algerine* subsequently recovered about 161,500 making about fifteen sixteenths of the whole property sunk.'[10]

Some $50,000 in gold still lies scattered on the seabed in 'Thetis cove' at a depth of between 50 to 80 feet — it is valued at over £166,000 ($250,000).

LEXINGTON

The Lexington was a sidewheeler steamer, 205 feet long with a 22-foot beam, constructed of oak, cedar, chestnut, and yellow and white pine. Built in 1835 for passenger service between New York and Stonington, Connecticut the Lexington was first owned by Cornelius Vanderbilt then sold to the New Jersey Steam Navigation and Transportation Company. In 1839 she was converted from a wood burner to a coal-burning steamer. Elihu S. Bunker, the United States steamboat inspector, issued a certificate of safety and seaworthiness.

AREA: *Caught fire and sank off Old Field Point, Long Island Sound, New York, USA, Atlantic.*

On the morning of 13 January 1840 the *Lexington* was taking on her last remaining cargo of bales of cotton on to her top deck (as not all bales could be stored below). All 100 passengers were aboard; among them Mr Harnden of Harnden Express Company who was responsible for $60,000 in specie[1] contained in boxes and safely stored in the express car on the forward deck below the promenade deck.

The ship's Captain, George Childs, blew his whistle and cast off the ropes at the departure time of 3pm before heading down New York's East River, through Hell's Gate, into Long Island Sound.

Just after 7pm, when the ship was approximately two miles east of Eaton's Neck Light, Captain Childs was informed of a fire below deck. As a precaution the Captain changed course towards the Long Island coast and sent McCrowley, the second mate, to report on the incident. McCrowley discovered that six bales of cotton were on fire which was spreading rapidly; on deck the flames began pouring out around the woodwork at the base of the smoke stack. Captain Childs summoned all available assistance to quench the fire with buckets of water but the crew were forced back by the flames and smoke.

Several passengers and crewmen tried to launch the ship's boats but with the steamship still underway, the boats struck the paddle wheel; one capsized, the other drifted off full of passengers and was never seen again.

Captain Hillard, a passenger, later told the court of enquiry:

It was about an hour after supper that I first heard the alarm of fire. I was then on the point of turning in and had my coat and boots off. I slipped

The *Lexington* was a 205-foot sidewheeler steamboat sailing between New York and Stonington. She caught fire in Long Island Sound and sank on 13 January 1840. There were only five survivors.

them on. I then discovered the casing of the smoke pipe, and, I think, a part of the promenade deck on fire. There was a great rush of passengers and much confusion, so that I could not notice particularly. The after part of the casing was burning and the fire was making aft. I thought at the time that the fire might be subdued, but being aft at the time, could not, therefore, see distinctly. . . . I shortly after went on the promenade deck; my attention had previously been directed to the passengers who were rushing into the quarter boats, and when I went to the quarter deck, the boats were both filled. They seemed to be stupidly determined to destroy themselves, as well as the boats, which were their only means of safety. I went to the starboard boat which they were lowering away, they lowered it until she took the water, and then I saw some one cut away the forward tackle fall, it was at all events disengaged, and no one at the time could have unhooked the fall; the boat instantly filled with water, there being at the time about twenty persons in her . . . by this time the fire had got under such headway, that

I pretty much made my mind up 'it was a gone case' . . . the fire by this time began to come up around the promenade deck, and the wheel house was completely filled with smoke . . . the engine had now been stopped about five minutes. I recommended to a few passengers who remained, to throw the cotton overboard.[2]

Captain Meeker of the sloop, *Merchant*, anchored at Southport, Connecticut, sighted the burning ship but, in attempting to leave harbour, ran aground on the falling tide.

The *Lexington* stayed afloat, burning from stem to stern; at approximately 2 am the ship sank beneath the waves.

By 9am the *Merchant* freed herself with the rising tide and arrived at the scene of the disaster to search for survivors. Only three survivors were found clinging to floating bales of cotton; two others survived two days and two nights and reached shore forty miles west of the disaster. A total of 145 passengers and crew perished.

In a church sermon shortly after the disaster the Reverend S.K Lothrop said: 'The steamboats of Long Island Sound have, till recently, been in general managed with distinguished skill and care, and all necessary, nay even a scrupulous attention paid to the safety and comfort of passengers. Of late years, however, the growing competition and increased facilities for carrying freight, afforded by the railroads to Providence and Stonington, have produced unfavourable change, and taken from the boats the high character of safety and comfort that once attached to them.'[3]

In September 1841 the remains of the *Lexington* were located and a 'thirty pound lump of silver valued at $800'[4] was recovered. There is a mystery, however, attached to the *Lexington*. In the April 1961 issue of the American magazine, *Skin Diver*, Ray Wagner states that a number of divers attached to the salvage vessel, *Melta II*, found the wreck. Using a derrick they lifted the express car where Harnden stored the boxes of specie; on opening the vault the divers found it empty.

YANKEE BLADE

The Yankee Blade *was a sidewheel steamer built of pine and oak, sheathed in copper. She was 274 feet long with a 35-foot beam of 2000 tons. She was launched at the Perrine and Stack shipyard at Williamsberg, New York, on 11 November 1853. Built for the Independent Opposition Line (which later merged with the Vanderbilt Independent Line), Yankee Blade was transferred to California to sail the San Francisco Panama route under the command of Henry Randall.*

AREA: *Struck a submerged rock at Point Pedernales, California, USA, Pacific.*

Until California became a state of the Union in 1850, it was always a problem to travel from the east to the west coast.

In 1847 two shipping companies were incorporated by Congress to operate a joint service: the US Mail Steamship Company sailed between New York and Aspinwall in Panama; passengers then crossed, by mule or wagon, the fifty-two-mile stretch of land across the Isthmus of Panama from the Atlantic to the Pacific; they then transferred to the Pacific Mail Steamship Company ships and continued their journey north from Panama City to San Francisco.

It was not until 1855 that a railway was built across the Isthmus from Aspinwall to Obispo; the remaining twelve miles to Panama City were travelled by foot, mule or wagon.

When gold was first discovered in California by James N. Marshall at Coloma on the South Fork of the American River on 24 January 1848, miners came in their thousands by land and sea, all hazardous, long and difficult routes. They arrived overland from the Missouri River along the 'Oregon Trail', round Cape Horn or via the Isthmus of Panama from New York, Boston and ports south.

By the following year, over 700 ships had arrived in San Francisco Bay from all over the world. It was estimated that more than 80,000 people came to California during the first year of the gold rush.

On 5 December 1848, President Polk told Congress: 'The accounts of the abundance of gold in that territory are of such an extraordinary character as would scarcely command belief, were they not corroborated by authentic reports of officers in the public service.'[1]

The first two steamships to inaugurate the joint service were the SS *Falcon* and the SS *California* in 1848.

The *Yankee Blade* was incorporated into the Atlantic service of the Independent Opposition Line – on 15 December 1853 a notice appeared in the *New York Daily Tribune*:

For California – Independent Opposition line – the new and splendid steam ship *Yankee Blade* 2200 tons will sail for Aspinwall on Tuesday 20 December at 5pm from the foot of North Moore Street, New York to connect with the new and unrivalled Steamship *Uncle Sam* 2000 tons which will sail immediately on the arrival of the passengers at Panama for San Francisco, direct, without stopping at any of the intermediate ports. These steamers are vastly superior to any others on the route, in point of speed, ventilation and good accommodation, and it is confidently expected that the voyage to California will be made in 22 days.

Passengers procuring tickets during this month will be allowed a discount of 10 per cent from the lowest rates charged by any other line.

In 1854 the *Yankee Blade* was transferred to the Panama City–San Francisco route under the command of Captain Randall. On her first voyage to Panama City, the *Yankee Blade* carried $355,650 in gold, returning to San Francisco on 1 July.

On her arrival, three ships departed south to Panama, *The Golden Gate, Pacific* and *Uncle Sam*, carrying gold to the value of $2,067,876.

On the afternoon of 30 September 1854, 812 passengers boarded the *Yankee Blade*. The ship carried 122 officers and crew, along with an unknown number of steerage passengers and stowaways. She was also loaded with $153,000 in gold specie, contained in nine boxes, 1000 oz to each box, plus $60,000 in gold bars packed in a large wooden crate.[2] In addition, the first- and second-class passengers carried an unspecified amount in gold dust and nuggets.

The SS *Sonora* was also sailing to Panama City the same day. The day before departure, an announcement appeared in the *San Francisco Daily Alta California*:

$5,000 WAGER: Wanted to bet $5,000 that the passengers by the *Yankee Blade* will arrive at Panama in advance of those per the *Sonora*, also $2,500 that they will reach New York in advance of those by the *Sonora* on their downward trip – money deposited with Page Bacon and Co.

It was against company policy to participate in racing but it was not an uncommon occurrence for captains to challenge each other.

The *Yankee Blade* cast off from Jackson Wharf and headed towards the entrance of San Francisco Bay with the SS *Sonora* not far behind. Allowing the *Sonora* to align herself with the *Yankee Blade*, Captain Randall lowered the ship's flag, indicating the challenge for a race. The *Sonora's* captain dipped his flag in acceptance; the race was on.

The ships, on leaving the Bay area, ran into patches of fog which cleared later. Steaming south down the Californian coast Captain Randall, unable to get an accurate navigational fix, estimated his position to be about thirty to thirty-five miles off point Buchon, sailing about ten knots and ahead of the *Sonora*. Heavy patches of fog again appeared and, at around 2pm, the Captain assumed his position to be about twenty miles seaward of the coast.

He changed course southeast by south. At 3.30, in dense fog, the *Yankee Blade* struck submerged rocks at Point Pedernales, a quarter of a mile off the coast, cutting a 30-foot-long gash 6 feet below the waterline.

Mr A. J. Calvin, a passenger, wrote: 'I was at the time of the wreck in the upper steerage . . . she was about a mile from shore and her bow ran up on the rocks very high. She ran on as far back as the wheel house. The water was 90 feet deep at her stern. The anchors were immediately dropped at the bow which helped keep her from slipping off.'[3]

Captain Randall ordered a survey of the damage. He was informed that the stern section was filled with sea water and had to be abandoned. It was also reported that the vault containing the gold under the purser's cabin was covered with 5 feet of water and rising. The Captain, realizing the ship was lost but not in immediate danger of sinking, lowered the starboard quarter boat and, along with four other crew members, left the ship to search for a safe landing place on the coast.

Mr G.A. Hart, another passenger, wrote:

As soon as the ship struck, Captain Randall left, as he said, to find land. He found it and found it convenient to stay on it. The first and second mates also left, with other boats, and then we were left with no officer on board but the third mate, an old Scotchman, who did all he could to quiet the fears of the passengers, who were driven from the cabins aft, by the water, and had to all huddle forward to the number of full eleven hundred men, women and children, as thick as they could stand.

A great many, wild with alarm, thinking they were abandoned by the officers to a merciless fate, went overboard in the vain hope of being able to swim ashore. Of course, all who attempted it, were lost. The numbers that were aboard was unknown, and of course, the number that have perished, or their names, can never be ascertained.[4]

Captain Haley of the 300-ton steamship, *Goliah*, en route to San Diego and carrying 100 passengers, sighted the wreck of the *Yankee Blade* about 9am. He manoeuvred his ship as close as possible to the wreck and passed a line between his stern and the job boom of the *Yankee Blade*. By 4.30, the 600 passengers that remained on the wreck were rescued; about thirty perished.

An article appeared in the *Southern Californian* on 5 October 1854: 'The utter incompetency.... The careless villainy of the captain is to be seen in the fact that he recklessly turned his back to every advice ... was told and told the course he was pursuing would be destruction to the ship and passengers, but no matter, on he went ... unheedingly and wilfully causing the loss of lives and property ... irretrievably forging hundreds into misery and ruin.

The *Daily Alta California* published the following on 10 October:

We are informed by passengers, on whom we can rely, that captain Randall acted during the whole disaster with much coolness and bravery. He went ashore as soon as possible for the purpose of finding a place where passengers could land, and it is said that he found it impossible to get the crew to row him off again, which accounts for the otherwise singular circumstances that he was absent from the ship during the night. We cannot believe that Captain Randall is the man to desert his ship in time of danger. . . .

Steam Tug Company

By the time the first salvage attempts were made, the *Yankee Blade* had slipped off the rocks and lay in 66 feet of water.

The majority of the gold in the wreck belonged to the bank of Page, Bacon and Company which lost $153,000.

Mr Haight, representative of the bank, and Mr Green, the Lloyd's of London agent, contacted Mr Haven of the Steam Tug Company with a view to recovering the gold on the wreck. The *Caroline*, under the command of L.T. Cuyler along with Captain Randall as a senior member of the salvage team, sailed to the wreck site on 12 October 1854. Poor visibility and difficult diving conditions allowed only two dives, which recovered a suitcase containing some gold, one case of liquor and two watches. The *Caroline* returned to San Francisco on 21 October.

The Steam Tug Company organized another expedition, negotiating with Captain Randall to direct salvage operations. Randall's reward for the recovery of gold was to receive 60 per cent of the treasure as 'official' salvage officer. *The Dancing Feather* commanded by Captain Fowler and the steamer *Sierra Nevada* set sail on 26 November. An article appeared in the *Daily Alta California* newspaper: 'The pilot boat *Dancing Feather* with Captain Fowler in command, arrived from the wreck of the *Yankee Blade* with four boxes containing treasure to the value of $68,000 which had been recovered from the ill-fated vessel.'

The following year on 18 October the schooner *Ada* returned to San Francisco having salvaged a large crate containing $60,000 in gold. However, Randall's success continued, and he made numerous trips to the wreck, arriving in San Francisco with gold valued at $51,000 completing the $213,000 'official' amount of gold the *Yankee Blade* was carrying.

On 15 December 1855 the *Los Angeles Star* wrote: 'The *Yankee Blade* – the last of the treasure from the ill-fated steamer has been raised by Captain Randall, who is said to have cleared above $80,000 by his diving operations at the wreck.'

Passage fares from San Francisco to Panama were paid on board ship in the form of gold nuggets or gold dust and stored in the safe in the purser's cabin. These amount to approximately $25,000, valued at $500,000 (£333,000) by today's standard. The amount of loss from passengers' fares was estimated at $12,000 ($232,000/£155,000 today). The total treasure unaccounted for could be worth $500,000 (£333,000).[5]

At the present time, salvors must have permission from the Vandenburg Air Force Missile Range and local authorities as ammunition and unexploded shells lie buried in the sand.

CENTRAL AMERICA

The Central America *was originally named the* George Law. *She was a sidewheel steamer, 278 feet long and 40 feet in breadth, constructed of pine and oak and sheathed in copper. The* Central America *was built in New York's East River by William H. Webb & Co. and launched in October 1853 for service between New York and Panama. She was owned by the US Mail Steamship Company.*

AREA: *Sank during a hurricane 225 miles southeast of Charleston off the south Carolina coast, USA, Atlantic Ocean.*

At 4pm on 3 September 1857, the *Central America*, captained by William Herndon, with 476 passengers and 102 crew, departed Panama bound for New York via Havana. This was her forty-third bi-monthly round trip between New York and Aspinwall (now part of Colon, Panama).

The *Central America* carried an estimated 3 tons of gold; this included the monthly delivery of San Francisco mint coins and other payments to banks, 'valued at $1.25 million, and possibly $750,000 in passengers hands'.[1]

The gold had been loaded on to the SS *Sonora* at San Francisco, then sailed to Panama City and transported across the Isthmus of Panama, to be picked up by *Central America*. During her period of service, the *Central America* carried approximately one third of the total output of gold from the California gold fields.

Between 1849–68, gold coinage reported to have been shipped to New York via Panama was more than 2.9 million lbs and would be worth, at today's prices, over $15 billion (£10 billion),[2] not including individual fortunes or unregistered shipments.

The ship arrived in Havana on 7 September, departing at 9am the next day. The weather was clear, with a moderate westerly wind. By the following day, a full gale was blowing. On Friday, 11 September, the wind had increased to hurricane force with mountainous seas. Sometime during the morning, the ship sprung a leak. George Ashby, chief engineer, reported;

> At 9 am, I discovered that the ship was making considerable water, more than ordinary results from the drippings of different parts of the machinery. I reported this fact to Captain Herndon at once, and then started all hands at passing coal in to the fire room in buckets and baskets. Captain Herndon, at my request, sent down nearly all the waiters to assist in passing coal. The ship was so listed over to the starboard, that our coal barrows were useless in passing coal ... at about 12 o'clock, the water overflowed the coal bunker floors, both forward and aft, making it impossible for the men to work the steam from the water, putting out nearly all our lamps.[3]

By 5.30pm, all boiler fires were flooded, stopping the engines and bilge pumps. With the sea breaking heavily over her decks, the ship began to wallow. Captain Herndon had the crew cut away the foremast in an attempt to right the ship, but to no avail. Lt M.F. Maury later reported to the Secretary of the Navy: 'The ship was now at the mercy of the waves, and was wallowing in a trough of the sea like a log ... the storm spencer had been blown away, and the foreyard was sent down during the night. Attempts were made to get the ship before the wind, but no canvas was stout enough to withstand the raging storm ...'[4]

At dawn on Saturday, the 12th, the wind abated slightly, but the water level on board kept rising. Towards noon, a sail was sighted, distress rockets and guns were fired and a distress flag hoisted. The *Marine*, a brig sailing out of Boston bound for the West Indies, answered the ship's distress signals. Although she was badly damaged by the hurricane, Captain Burt of the *Marine* brought his vessel as close to the sinking ship as possible. A schooner, *El Dorado*, also sailed close by, but was unable to offer any assistance.

Three of the usable lifeboats from the steamship were lowered and 100 passengers, mainly women and children, were rescued by the *Marine* before darkness descended. The *Marine* then drifted away to stand by until morning. A passenger, Thomas Badger, noted the horrific turn of events:

> At 10 minutes of 8 o'clock, Captain Herndon took position on the wheel houses with his second officer, and fired rockets downwards, the usual signal to the brig and schooner, that we were sinking rapidly. ... The ship immediately after, at 8 o'clock on Saturday evening sank, going down at an angle of 45 degrees, stern foremost. The suction of the ship, drew the passengers under water for some distance, and threw them in a mass together. When they reached the surface, the struggle for life was intense with cries and shrieks for help. ... Many unable to swim, clung to those who could or laid hold of the larger pieces of the wreck, which were soon swamped. ... In ten minutes, not less probably than three hundred had sunk to rise no more. There was a larger number of passengers who had bags of gold dust, and some doubtless, perished in their efforts to save it.[5]

The *Central America* sank to a depth of 8000 feet, taking with her 426 passengers and crew, including Captain Herndon.

At 9am on Sunday the Norwegian barque, *Ellen*, rescued fifty men. Miraculously, nine days later, four men were picked up by the British brig, *Mary*, having drifted 476 miles without food or water.

Columbus-America Discovery Group

Thomas G. Thompson was an ocean engineer working with the Battelle Memorial Institute of Columbus, Ohio, which conducts studies in research for government and industry. Thompson worked on feasibility studies for deep-ocean mining of metals. Aside from his work, he became interested in

The *Central America* was sailing from Panama to New York carrying three tons of gold from the Californian gold fields when she ran into a fierce storm and sank to a depth of 8,000 feet. She took with her 425 passengers and crew, and gold to an estimated value of $1 billion

shipwrecks: 'I got interested in deep water wrecks like The *Central America*, because they were less likely to have been disturbed by other salvers, but there was no way to do this.'[6]

Taking leave of absence in 1985, Thompson founded the Columbus-America Discovery Group, along with two friends, Barry Schatz a journalist, and Bob Evans, a geologist, as fellow directors. Their project was to look for the *Central America*.

Thompson and his partners found 161 investors who raised $12.7 million to fund the project. The group bought a thirty-year-old 180-foot, 900-ton ex-Canadian icebreaker, *Arctic Discoverer*, as a diving vessel; the group's technicians also designed and built a 4-ton ROV (Remotely Operated Vehicle), *Nemo*, capable of transmitting video and picking up heavy objects or the most delicate of artifacts.

A team of historians and researchers gathered relevant information, maps, meteorological and navigational records from 1857. The data was correlated in a computer which narrowed the search to a 1400-square-mile area on what is called the Blake Ridge. 'The ridge is virtually ideal for sonar searching because it is flat and featureless, and anything like a ship will show up clearly.'[7]

Using the most sophisticated of equipment, the wreck was located in six weeks. In July 1987 the *Nemo* spotted ship's artifacts and black lumps of coal scattered over a wide area of the sea floor; *Central America* had burned anthracite coal. The artifacts and a sample of coal were brought to the surface and flown in the supply plane to the Group lawyer, Richard Robol, who rushed the samples to the US District Court in Norfolk, Virginia, to claim salvage rights. Judge Richard B. Kellam issued a temporary order giving Columbus-America exclusive salvage rights to the area where the samples were found.

Thompson knew that other groups of salvage investors, the Boston Salvage Consultants Inc. and the South Carolina Marine Archaeology Trust, were also searching for the *Central America*'s treasure.

Thompson ordered new computer software to enhance earlier sonar images; reviewing the video, the faint outline of the wreck could be seen. This was confirmed by *Nemo* bringing to the surface the ship's bronze bell inscribed, 'Morgan Iron Works, New York 1853'.

On presentation of videos, artifacts and progress reports to the court, Judge Kellam awarded the Columbus-America Group a permanent injunction against rival salvors, granting them a right to a 20-square-mile area of the ocean – the first time private individuals had been granted rights in international waters.

By the summer of 1989 *Nemo*, with its five video cameras and high-precision robotics arm, began to recover the gold. 'It was absolutely phenomenal, there was a garden of gold, a bridge of gold bars. Bars had been stacked on wood, but the wood had disintegrated and the gold remained cemented together. Gold is very bright down there. There were rivers of gold coins, carpets of gold. They were stuck together, falling off beams that had disappeared, bags that held gold dust were long gone, but the dust was stuck together. *Nemo* blew off silt, and a carpet of gold coins appeared before you.'[8]

By mid September *Nemo* had made fifteen dives and brought up a ton of gold, including one bar of gold weighing 62 lbs.

When news was released of Columbus-America's success in recovering the gold, thirty-nine claims were filed by insurance companies asserting title to the gold. Judge Kellam asked the various company lawyers how they would identify their share of the gold; they were unable to reply and he dismissed thirty-one of the thirty-nine companies.

In August 1990 a federal judge awarded the Group title to all gold and other artifacts from the *Central America*. It will take several years to recover all the gold which is estimated to be worth $1 billion (£559 million),[9] the richest sunken treasure in history.

BROTHER JONATHAN

The Brother Jonathan *was a steamship of 1181 tons. Built in New York in 1850, at 221 feet long, she was originally designed for service on Long Island Sound. In 1852 she was sold to Cornelius Vanderbilt who rebuilt her, extending her capacity from 350 to 750 passengers. Sent to the Pacific to sail the San Francisco–San Juan del Sur route, she was sold to the Nicaragua Steamship Company. The* Brother Jonathan *was again sold to Captain John T. Wright who renamed her the* Commodore, *sailing the San Francisco–Seattle run. Her name was later changed back to Brother Jonathan.*

AREA: *Wrecked during a storm on Northwest Seal Rock, part of St George's Reef off the coast of California, USA, Pacific Ocean.*

In July 1858 the *Commodore* sailed out of San Francisco, bound for Seattle, under the command of Captain George T. Staples. Two days out she encountered high winds and rough seas, and began leaking badly. With her pumps fully manned Captain Staples ordered her cargo to be jettisoned.

The *Commodore* was forced to return to San Francisco in a sinking state. Wright sold her to the Californian Steam Navigation Company. There is an old superstition that changing the name of a ship brings bad luck. The new owner therefore refitted and overhauled the *Commodore* and renamed her *Brother Jonathan*.

On 27 July 1865 the ship, under the command of Samuel de Wolf, prepared to depart Meiggs Harbour near Fisherman's Wharf in San Francisco loaded with 700 tons of mining equipment and wool-process machinery. The ship also carried a strong iron box containing $225,000 in army payroll, along with 130 passengers and a crew of eighty-four.

The steamship was now considered a very fair traveller when not overloaded. Captain de Wolf was under pressure from the agent, however, to receive more cargo even though this would overload his ship. In Lewis & Dryden's *Maritime History of the Pacific Northwest*, published in 1895, it states that the Captain: 'Endeavoured to induce the agent to stop receiving cargo, warning him that she was already as deeply laden as she could run with safety, even without the large number of passengers expected. The official, who was acting in place of Major Samuel Hensley, the regular agent and Vice President of the company, paid no attention to his remonstrances, and intimated that, if the captain did not wish to take the steamer out, he could find a man who would.'[1]

At 12 noon on 28 July the overloaded ship cast off and headed out of San Francisco Bay and into the Pacific. Two days later the *Brother Jonathan* was steaming north against strong wind and heavy seas. On the afternoon of 30 July Jacob Yates, the Quartermaster, was on watch. Later he recalled:

> I took the wheel at twelve o'clock. A north west gale was blowing, and we were four miles above Point St George. The sea was running mountain high, and the ship was not making any headway. The Captain thought it best to turn back to Crescent City and wait until the storm had ceased. He ordered the helm hard aport, I obeyed, and it steadied her. I kept due east. This was about 12.45. When she made Seal Rock, the Captain said 'Southeast by south.' It was clear where we were, but foggy and smokey inshore.[2]

Captain de Wolf kept his course until six miles from the mainland. Quartermaster Yates's account continues:

> Then she struck (the reef) with great force knocking the passengers down and starting the deck planks. The captain stopped and backed her, but could not move the vessel an inch. She rolled about five minutes, then gave a tremendous thump, and part of the keel came up alongside. By that time the wind and sea had slewed her around until her head came to the sea, and she worked off a little. Then the foremast went through the bottom until the yard rested on the deck. Captain Woolf ordered everyone to look to his own safety and that he would do the best he could for all.[3]

The passengers crowded round the six lifeboats. As harassed crewmen lowered the first boat passengers piled in but, unable to clear the ship, the lifeboat capsized. The second was swamped with the number of passengers on board. Only one lifeboat managed to get clear of the ship; holding six women, three children and ten crew members, they were the only survivors.

Regarding the army payroll,

> there have sprung a great number of wild tales of fabulous wealth supposed to have gone to the bottom with the vessel. In some cases the amount has

been stated as over a million dollars, while as a matter of fact the property lost by the wreck was only about $250,000 all told, much of it in cargo of a nature which contact with water would render worthless. Nevertheless, many expeditions have been undertaken at an expense of much time and money in the endeavour to ascertain the position of the wreck with a view to recovering the treasure, and hardly a year passes but some new story is given to the public to the effect that the long sought steamer has finally been definitely located; but up to the present time the exact resting place of the unfortunate craft still remains one of the mysteries of the deep.[4]

In 1930 a group of salvors in the salvage ship, *Janette R.*, spent several months trying to locate the wreck. The only evidence they found was the paddle wheel.

REPUBLIC

Built by Harland and Wolfe Shipyard as the Columbus *for the Dominion Line, the ship was transferred to the White Star Line and renamed the* Republic. *Launched on 26 February 1903 the 15,378-ton liner sailed between Liverpool – Boston in the summer months and New York – the Mediterranean for the rest of the year; she was commanded by Captain William Sealby.*

AREA: *Collided with the Italian emigrant steamship* Florida, *south of Nantucket Island where she was taken in tow by the US tug,* Gresham, *with the liner* Furnessia *steering her aft. The* Republic *was abandoned by the Captain and crew; she sank near Martha's Vineyard some miles south of Nantucket Island, USA, Atlantic.*

A company brochure at the time stated: 'The White Star Line services from New York and Boston to the Mediterranean prove the ideal entry into this vast treasure house of art, history and literature of untold ages.'

The *Republic* departed New York for her winter cruise to Italy on 22 January 1909 with a crew of 300 under Captain William Sealby, along with 250 wealthy first-class and 211 steerage-class passengers. Her cargo consisted of relief supplies for Italy's disastrous earthquake in Sicily and Calabria (killing over 85,000 people), and 650 tons of supplies for Rear-Admiral Sperry's American fleet stationed at Gibraltar. It was also rumoured that the *Republic* 'carried $3 million in American gold eagle coins destined for Czar Nicholas II of Russia, who was bankrupt and threatened by the Germans and the rising Bolsheviks'.[1]

Departing New York, the *Republic* sailed past the Sandy Hook Lightship and increased her speed to a maximum sixteen knots. The *Florida*, an Italian liner carrying emigrants, was thirty-six hours from New York. As the *Republic* passed the eastern end of Long Island, patches of fog appeared, causing the Captain to reduce speed and sound the whistle every two minutes. Heading towards the Nantucket Lightship which marked the trans-Atlantic sea lane the *Republic* encountered dense fog. The *Florida* had also entered the fog bank and sounded her fog whistle every ninety seconds. As she neared the Massachusetts coast the *Florida* turned southwest; trying to locate her position by the Nantucket Lightship she entered the eastbound shipping lane.

It is customary for in-bound steamers from European ports approaching the coast ... in thick weather to hunt for the 30 fathom curve, which sweeps down 40 miles from Nantucket Island, and just outside of which is anchored the Nantucket South Shoal Lightship. Vessels failing to pick up the lightship in the fog keep on sounding until they strike this 30 fathom curve.

To the westward of the lightship there is a mud bottom, and this also gives a pretty definite position for vessels trying to get their bearings.[2]

At about 5.45am the two ships collided. The *Florida's* bow hit the *Republic's* port side behind the funnel, cutting halfway through the *Republic's* 68-foot beam from the promenade deck to below the waterline. Four seamen and two passengers were killed immediately, the engine room flooded, watertight doors were closed and Captain Sealby gave orders to the radio operator to send the distress signal: 'C.Q.D *Republic* rammed by unknown steamship. Twenty-six miles south-west of Nantucket Lightship. Badly in need of immediate assistance, but no danger to life. Sealby'.[3]

Dominic Roberts, a passenger aboard the *Republic* described the moment after the collision. 'Already the steerage passengers awakened from sleep were swarming in terror to the deck. Looking down from the deck we could see them running about, some crying, while others huddled under the side of the deckhouse; others were praying. All was excitement when the ship's officers went about among the half-crazed, praying crowd and assured them that there was no danger.'[4]

The radio operator, Mr. J. Binns, continued to send the CQD distress signal – 'CQ' meaning 'All Stations, Attention' plus 'D' indicating 'Urgency'.[5] This was the first radio distress signal ever made by a sinking ship. The signal was picked up at Siasconset Radio Station and relayed to ships in the area.

At 7 am Captain Sealby addressed the passengers from the bridge:

Passengers of the *Republic*: I want to advise you that the steamer has been injured in a collision. We are in no immediate danger, but I want to ask you to stand by me and act with coolness and judgement. There is, I repeat, no immediate danger; but to be on the safe side it is necessary for you to be transferred to the *Florida* as soon as possible. It will take some time, and I expect that you will be cool and not excited. Take your time getting into the lifeboats. Remember, the women and children go first, the first cabin next, and then the others. The crew will be the last to leave this vessel.[6]

The *Florida* backed away and stood by. Guided by signals she made her way back to the *Republic* where all the passengers were ferried by lifeboat and trans-ferred from the *Republic*, leaving Captain Sealby and thirty of the crew on board.

A passenger wrote of the conditions on the *Florida*: 'They covered every deck of the smaller steamship so thickly that there was no room to move about. Here the passengers huddled together for fifteen hours, suffering from cold, hunger and thirst. The *Florida*'s officers did the best they could to give assistance, but they were carrying a large list of immigrants, and as the vessel was in the condition you might expect from that fact, they could do but little for the comfort of the *Republic*'s passengers.'[7]

Sixty-four miles from New York the White Star liner *Baltic* promptly turned back to search for the stricken vessel. Fog persisted throughout the day, making it difficult for the *Baltic* to locate the *Republic*. Binns recorded:

A little later we heard the *Baltic*'s fog horn blowing faintly and this increased in volume as she lessened the distance between us. Occasionally we fired rockets but they could not be seen through the fog, although a little later the *Baltic*'s siren was heard so plainly that we knew the ship was close by. Realising this, Captain Sealby issued orders that the *Baltic* be told to proceed as carefully as possible, as she was now too close on our port side to be safe. I had just communicated this message when I heard a cheer, and I at once realised that these sounds of rejoicing could not come from our men, as only Captain Sealby, the officers, myself and the crew were aboard, and they were all busily engaged in standing by the boats. Looking aft through my splintered cabin I made out the *Baltic* quite near to the stern of our ship. . . . She was a blaze of light and as I sat there in my little cabin, the thought occurred to me that the most beautiful sight in the world is a ship at sea, especially when that ship is needed to supply a link between life and death.[8]

The *Baltic* was joined by two other ships and the liner, *Furnessia*, and two tugs, the *Gresham* and *Seneca*. The *Gresham* attached hawsers to the *Republic*'s bow and the two tugs began to tow the ship with *Furnessia* acting as a rudder. Towing at about two knots the *Republic* was now half submerged. Captain Perry of the *Gresham* realized the task was impossible as the ship was sinking; the remaining crew abandoned ship and the *Furnessia* stood by as the *Republic* began to sink, stern first, along with her $3,000,000.

Sub Ocean Salvors International

Martin Bayerle has spent fifteen years, as vice-president of Sub Ocean Salvors, a Florida-based salvage company, in studying the history and the wreck of the *Republic*. In 1981 Bayerle and his team of seven divers located the *Republic* in 260 feet of water, fifty-five miles south of Nantucket. He stated to the *New York Times* that 'he was convinced from his study of shipping records and the United States Treasury reports that the gold was placed aboard the ship secretly as a security measure'.[9]

Bayerle believes that the gold was stored in the second-class baggage section, and that 'there has been an International cover-up. . . . He said all blueprints of the ship have disappeared and that all records relating to the purchase of gold coins by a group of French Banks are missing'.[10]

In June 1987 the salvage vessel, *Sosi Inspector*, with thirty-five crew and divers set sail from New York for a three-month expedition to search for the gold bullion, now estimated to be worth $1.2 billion (£800 million). Ending their expedition in September Mike Gerber, the Sub Ocean Salvors spokesman, stated: 'We would have been happier if we'd found gold. . . . But the more we got into the ship the more we realised what terrible shape it was in . . . and our plans were not as complete as we'd hoped. In the last month, we realised we'd have to do more research. But we're still confident the gold is there.'[11]

ANDREA DORIA

The Italian luxury liner, Andrea Doria, was named after a distinguished sixteenth-century Genoese admiral. The liner was built in 1953 by Ansaldo Spa of Genoa. She weighed 2083 tons, was 700 feet long and 90 feet wide, with accommodation for 1241 passengers and a crew of 572, commanded by Captain Piero Calamai.

AREA: *Collided in dense fog with the 11,000-ton Swedish ship* Stockholm. *The* Andrea Doria *sank forty-five miles southeast of Nantucket Island, Massachusetts, USA, Atlantic.*

On 17 July 1956 the *Andrea Doria* departed Genoa on her fifty-first trans-Atlantic voyage bound for New York via Cannes, Naples and Gibraltar. She carried 1134 passengers, many of them wealthy and travelling first-class. The ship had several well-stocked jewellery shops, a casino and two banks, one situated on the foyer deck. The estimated value of American and Italian currency, jewellery and other valuables on board was $4 million.[1]

The voyage out from Gibraltar was uneventful with fine summer weather and Captain Piero Calamai expected his ship to dock in New York on time at 9am on the 26 July.

On the 25th at 3pm the *Andrea Doria*, sailing at her maximum speed of twenty-three knots, encountered fog just off the Massachusetts coast. Captain Calamai ordered speed to be reduced to twenty-one knots with the foghorn sounding for six seconds every minute and fifty seconds.

By the late afternoon, the fog thickened, cutting visibility down to half a mile. At 10.40pm a bleep was picked up on the ship's radar screen, four degrees on the starboard bow, at a distance of seventeen miles, moving east directly in line to the *Andrea Doria*'s course. The senior Second Officer estimated that the ship would pass a mile to starboard; Captain Calamai gave orders to 'steer four degrees to port'. A few minutes after 11pm, the ship's lights were sighted through a patch of fog about a mile to starboard. As the two ships neared each other, the oncoming ship slowly turned towards the *Andrea Doria*. At 11.10 the 11,000-ton Swedish ship *Stockholm*, sailing at a speed of nineteen knots, sliced into the starboard side of the Italian ship just forward of the bridge. Within minutes the liner took on an 18-degree list. Immediate orders were given to the radio operator to send out the ship's call signal:

'SOS DE ICEH – SOS Here at 0320 GMT. Lat 40.30 N 69.53 W. Need immediate assistance.'[2]

The message was picked up by a number of ships in the area. Captain de Beaudean of the 44,500-ton French liner, *Ile de France*, radioed to the liner: 'Captain Andrea Doria – I am going to assist you. Will reach your position 5.35 GMT (1.35am) are you sinking? What kind of assistance do you need?'[3]

Captain Calamai replied: 'SOS DE ICEH – Danger immediate. Need boats to evacuate, 1000 passengers and 500 crew. We need boats.'[4]

The freighter *Cape Ann*, the US destroyer *Allen*, the US Navy transport *William H. Thomas* and the tanker *Hopkins* sped to the rescue of the stricken liner. On arrival they rescued all the remaining passengers and crew. At 10.09am on 26 July the *Andrea Doria* slipped beneath the waves. Forty-five passengers on the liner had died on impact, five crew members of the *Stockholm* also died.

Jacques Cousteau

The year of the collision Jacques Cousteau, the under water explorer, dived to the wreck, but he and his crew concluded the waters were too deep and shark infested and the currents too tricky to attempt salvage operations.[5]

Solomon and Garvin

In 1964 Robert Solomon and Glenn Garvin converted a coast cutter into a salvage ship and invested $300,000 in a twenty-man salvage operation; the crew included nine US Navy divers. The divers blasted two 8-foot by 5-foot holes through the outer and inner bulkheads to reach the main salon. Diving proved more difficult than Solomon and Garvin calculated and, as time slipped away, operations had to be abandoned. The only result of months of salvage operations was the recovery of the bronze statue of Admiral Andrea Doria which now stands in the lobby of a Florida motel.

Saturation Systems

Two divers, Don Rodocker and Chris DeLucchi, founded Saturation Systems Inc. in San Diego, California. Rodocker was a Navy-trained diver and expert mechanic who had been consultant to Oceaneering International Inc., a large deep-diving company. DeLucchi was also an ex Navy diver who, in 1972, established a world record saturation of 945 feet.[6] (Saturation diving is a method whereby divers live under water day and night in a pressurized compartment, without coming to the surface.)

In the summer of 1973, Rodocker and DeLucchi organized a twenty-six-man diving expedition to salvage the 'treasures' from the *Andrea Doria*. They established a supply base at Fair Haven and arrived over the wreck the next day. Using a 12-foot by 5-foot steel cylinder-diving bell, nicknamed *Mother*, three divers could live for a period of twenty-one days, being self-sustained for five to six days at a maximum depth of 600 feet. After many problems *Mother* was moored next to the wreck at a depth of 150 feet.

The divers cut an entrance hole into the liner's hull; according to the liner's manual the bulkheads were made of steel but, in a statement to the *New York Times*, Rodocker said: 'The whole interior is false bulkheads made out of wood, and it's all collapsed ... we didn't expect that at all ... we expected metal bulkheads covered with wood. That's how they are described in the manuals.'[7]

On clearing a way through a mass of tangled metal, cables and debris to the upper deck they were able to announce: 'We have reached a point in the ship where the purser's office, the jewellery store and the bank were supposed to be, but they just weren't there ... that section of the ship had collapsed into a 20-foot deep pile of rubble in the bottom of the vessel.'[8]

After spending $250,000 searching for the 'treasure', Saturation Systems gave up the project. They had recovered four silver plates and a crystal bottle of perfume. One of the divers stated: 'That ship is a hazard and anyone who values his life won't go down there.'[9]

Peter Gimbel

Peter Gimbel, the New York department-store heir and film director, led a salvage filming expedition to the wreck in 1981. Gimbel approached the salvage company, Oceaneering International, for assistance and an agreement was made to use its diving vessel *Sea Level II*. After thirty-three days above the wreck Gimbel and his divers located one of the bank's safes. Miss Lillian Pickard, spokesman for the expedition, said: 'The bank of Rome's safe was located in the debris-strewn lounge of the ship's foyer deck. Divers were continuing their search for the purser's safe.'[10]

Unable to locate the purser's safe, the expedition ended in September with a statement by Gimbel's wife: 'We know we are close to that other safe, but I think it takes guts to quit when you are so close. We said all along that it wasn't a treasure hunt. We are tired and I think the important thing now is to get everybody back to port, nice and safe. It is time to say goodbye to the *Andrea Doria* . . .'[11]

Four years later, on 17 August 1984, custom officials opened the safe. Mr Kaufman of the US customs, said: 'It's all paper money . . . it's dirty, murky, soggy currency – $1 bills, $10 bills, $20 bills and Italian lire.'[12]

Kaufman estimated there were only fifteen bundles of bills. No further salvage attempts have been made to locate the rest of the treasure. Gimbel spent over $2 million on his efforts and produced a film of his dives on the *Andrea Doria*.

AUSTRALASIA
AND
THE FAR EAST

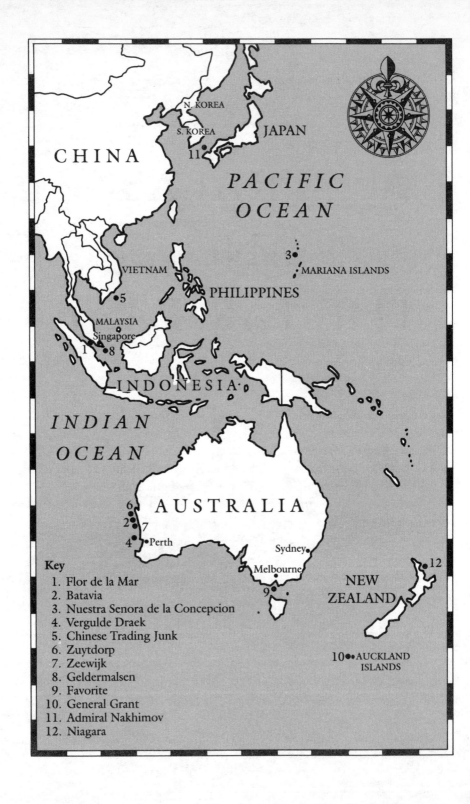

CHINA

N. KOREA

S. KOREA   JAPAN

11

PACIFIC

OCEAN

VIETNAM

3

MARIANA ISLANDS

5

PHILIPPINES

MALAYSIA
Singapore

1 8

INDONESIA

INDIAN

OCEAN

AUSTRALIA

6

2 7

4   Perth

Sydney

Melbourne

NEW
ZEALAND

9

12

Key
 1. Flor de la Mar
 2. Batavia
 3. Nuestra Senora de la Concepcion
 4. Vergulde Draek
 5. Chinese Trading Junk
 6. Zuytdorp
 7. Zeewijk
 8. Geldermalsen
 9. Favorite
10. General Grant
11. Admiral Nakhimov
12. Niagara

10   AUCKLAND
      ISLANDS

FLOR DE LA MAR

The galleon, Flor de la Mar, was the flagship of a small sixteenth-century fleet under the command of Admiral Alfonso de Albuquerque.
   AREA: *Wrecked during a storm in the Malacca Straits between Malaysia and Indonesia.*

Alfonso de Albuquerque was a Portuguese soldier sent to the East Indies by the King of Portugal in 1506 to establish Portuguese settlements and gain control of the main sea routes of the East Indies.

In 1509, Albuquerque became Governor of all Portuguese possessions in India. With a fleet of twenty-three ships, he plundered and captured the ports of Mozambique and occupied Goa in India. Continuing his success, in 1511 he embarked on a conquest of Malacca (now Melaka) on the Malay Peninsula. The port of Malacca was the richest city in the east, trading in gold, exotic and luxury goods and spices in Japan, China, Arabia, India and Africa. Albuquerque and his soldiers laid siege to Malacca and, after twelve days of much bloodshed and fierce fighting, the Malays surrendered.

The wealth of Malacca and the treasures of the Sultan's palace were immense. Albuquerque loaded his flagship with '20 tons of life-size solid gold statues of baby elephants, monkeys and tigers, many studded with jewels, gold plated palanquins, chests full of diamonds, rubies and other precious stones, and tons of Arabic and Chinese coins.'[1]

Having secured the city and built a garrison fort for his soldiers, Albuquerque set sail with his fleet for Spain in 1512. Two days out from Malacca, the fleet encountered a storm, nearing the entrance to the Strait of Malacca; the *Flor de la Mar* was driven on to a reef off the northeastern tip of the island of Sumatra.

Albuquerque lowered the longboat and, with five officers, sailed for Malacca to obtain help. Later, they were picked up by one of the fleet's ships but, instead of returning to his ship, Albuquerque returned to Portugal.

Pounded by the surf the *Flor de la Mar* broke up and sank, slipping to a depth of 120 feet. Of her 400 crew and soldiers, only three of those on board survived.

Bruno de Vincentiis

Bruno de Vincentiis was a wealthy Italian diamond miner with a serious interest in shipwrecks. De Vincentiis teamed up with Dr Paul Andel, an Australian professor of maritime history who had spent a number of years researching the *Flor de la Mar*. De Vincentiis and Andel stated that, with documentary evidence from one of the survivors and the latest infrared satellite technology, they had located parts of the wreck in an area a few hundred yards square. De Vincentiis began negotiations with the Malaysian and Indonesian governments in April 1988, proposing the treasure be shared in three ways. Meetings were held but, when the two governments realized the value of the treasure, each claimed it. De Vincentiis's negotiations collapsed.

According to a *Sunday Times* newspaper article, De Vincentiis encountered harassment and Dr Andel received a number of death threats and threatening visits which so alarmed him he locked away in a bank vault all research concerning the *Flor de la Mar*.[2]

President Suharto of Indonesia then granted a licence to PT Jayatama Istika Cipta, a family company run by a stepbrother of the president. Jayatama Istika Cipta hired Paul Martino, an Australian who had been under arrest in 1988 for illegal salvage operations in Indonesia, to organize a team of divers and to assist with the search.

Martino began to search for the wreck in the summer of 1989 but, a number of months later, a diving colleague stated: 'They were diving into a very silty area, a lot of gunge. They found the odd Chinese junk and the odd anchor, but nothing that indicated the *Flor de la Mar*. . . . They came back to the shore and the Indonesians began playing around with their percentages. Martino had just had enough and quit'[3] He took most of the crew with him.

Since 1989 Jayatama Istika Cipta has spent over $20 million searching for the wreck and has approached the Malaysian government to share expenses; so far nothing has transpired from these negotiations. In 1990 the Malaysian and Portuguese governments contested Indonesia's claim to the *Flor de la Mar*.

Controversy began in September 1991 when southeast Asian banking sources revealed large financial transactions on behalf of a group of Indonesian businessmen; these indicated that some of the gold from the wreck had been found, melted down and sold. A spokesman for Jayatama Istika Cipta denied these rumours, saying only coins, ballast stones, pieces of pottery and iron nails had been found.

The question of ownership of the wreck is at present being considered by the International Court in the Hague.

Robert Marx

Robert Marx applied with no success for a permit to locate the wreck but, in 1989, the Indonesian company hired Marx as a consultant. Marx claims he found the wreck from an obscure map drawn by Albuquerque's son which marked the spot where the ship had gone down, 'five miles north of a point off Jambu Air [Diamond Point] on the Northeast coast of Sumatra'.[4] Marx claims he recovered several gold figurines and Ming dynasty porcelain. The wreck lies scattered over a wide area under fifty feet of mud.

The *Sunday Times* reported on 29 September 1991 that experts had estimated the value of the treasure to be worth at least $1 billion; some put it closer to $9 billion.

BATAVIA

The Batavia *was a Dutch East India Company merchantman of 600 tons, 150 feet long and armed with twenty-four guns. She was captained by Ariaen Jacobsz and carried 318 passengers and crew.*

AREA: *Wrecked on the Houtman Abrolhos Islands near Morning Reef, part of the Wallabi Group, Western Australia, Indian Ocean.*

On 27 October 1628 seven Dutch East India Company ships bound for Java left Texel Island for the East Indies. Francisco Pelsaert, Fleet President, sailed on the merchantman *Batavia*. She was carrying a cargo of cochineal and general merchandise, plus an additional cargo of £25,000 in Dutch florins packed in wooden chests, and a casket of jewels containing the 'Cameo of Gaspar Boudaen', an agate brooch carved in AD 312 which was to be sold to the Moghul Emperor Jehangir. It has been described as follows: 'It is a larger agate of two layers of grey and brown and shows an Emperor and his family on a chariot drawn by two centaurs trampling on fallen enemies while a flying Victory holds a wreath ... Constantine the Great is pictured with his spouse Fausta, his son Crispus and his mother Helena. ... this work of art ... served as a present on the occasion of the tenth anniversary of the Emperor's accession, in 315.'[1] Also on board was the 'Rubens Vase', considered one of the world's masterpieces of gem carving.[2]

Pelsaert carried his own private trade goods which consisted of gold and silver dinner services valued at £6000.

On a previous voyage in 1620 Jacobsz met Pelsaert in Surat on the west coast of India and the two men quarrelled violently. Eight years later the enmity between the two was very much still in evidence. Jacobsz was now captain of the *Batavia*, but he was still an antagonistic and arrogant man, especially towards Pelsaert and his private trade deals which threatened Jacobsz's opportunities to make lucrative cargo dealings of his own. This general resentment was to have serious consequences for the future of the *Batavia*'s voyage.

The fleet arrived at the Cape of Good Hope where the ships took on fresh water and meat supplied by the natives. Indications of trouble emerged when Pelsaert, returning from the mainland, accused Jacobsz of being drunk and molesting Lucretia Janst, a passenger travelling to Java to join her husband. Pelsaert's severe reprimand to Jacobsz is recorded in the former's journal:

> Next morning in the cabin in the presence of Jeronimus and many others, I spoke to the skipper about this evil-provoking which he had begun, with admonishing and threatening, and said that if he did not cease, should have to take other measures even before we arrived at Batavia ... The skipper had also take a great hatred to a woman named Lucretia whom he had tried to seduce for a long time and had not succeeded, and therefore he was very embittered towards her. And had chosen her servant Zwaantie Hendrix with whom to spend his time and do his will, who readily accepted the caresses of the skipper with great willingness and refused him nothing whatsoever he desired; through which the love on both sides became so intense that without taking any thought of his honour or the reputation of his office he had sworn that if anyone made so much as a sour face at Zwaantie he would not leave it unrevenged. At last when they were away from the Cabo, he took from her the name and yoke of servant and promised her that she should see the destruction of her Mistress and others, and that he would make her a Great Lady.[3]

This reprimand served to increase Jacobsz's bitterness towards Pelsaert. Jacobsz fell in with a passenger, Jeronimus Cornelisz, a company merchant; these two began to conspire with other malcontents. The plan was to mutiny and to sail the *Batavia* away from the other ships. Pelsaert further notes:

> Jeronimus Cornelisz, having made himself a great friend and highly familiar with the skipper Ariaen Jacobsz, moulded their similar intelligence and feel-

A 17th-century engraving of Batavia (present-day Djakarta), the headquarters of the Dutch East India Company

ings into one; the skipper being innate with prideful conceit and ambition so that he could not endure the authority of any over him. Moreover he was mocking and contemptuous of all people in-so-far-as it did not concern sea-faring. . . . But Jeronimus on the contrary was well-spoken and usually knew how to give the polish of Truth to his lying words; he was far more sly and skilled at getting-on with people.[4]

Dutch East India Company ships were ordered to sail a specific course once they had navigated past the Cape of Good Hope. This route was: 'S. Lat 36' to 42' on an easterly course approximately 2,400 to 3,000 miles';[5] then steer north via the Sunda Straits to the company's headquarters at Batavia (Djakarta) on the north coast of Java.

As the fleet left Table Bay and sailed past Cape Agulhas Jacobsz's plans were inadvertently realized: a severe storm blew up and the ships were separated. Thus began the headlong series of events leading to a complete breakdown of discipline and behaviour amongst crew and passengers aboard the *Batavia*.

It was later recorded:

Very great insolences, yea, monstrous actions, have been committed on the mentioned ship (Batavia) before her wrecking, wherefore amongst other things the Highboatswain of the ship (Jan Evertsz) has been punished here with death, having confessed to being the principal culprit when a certain woman named Lucretia Jans was dragged by the legs along the ship and maltreated very indecently on her body, as cannot be imagined by Christian people, as Your Hon. will be able to see from the enclosed declarations and statements of the (legal) processes, the skipper scp. 'Batta' (sic) was very much suspected that the previous had happened with his knowledge, yea, even with his aid and at his instigation. . . .[6]

A few days later, after the storm, Pelsaert fell ill. During his stay in India he had contracted malaria and had suffered several periods of recurring illness. When he had recovered from this particular bout, he was unable to take the necessary actions to establish and to maintain discipline amongst the already troublesome crew and passengers.

On the evening of 3 June, the sky was clear with a full moon and the seas were moderate; by first light Jacobsz sighted spray and surf ahead. He thought it was the moon on the water and, continuing on course, sailed on to the outer reefs of the Houtman Abrolhos Islands. Suddenly, there was only shallow

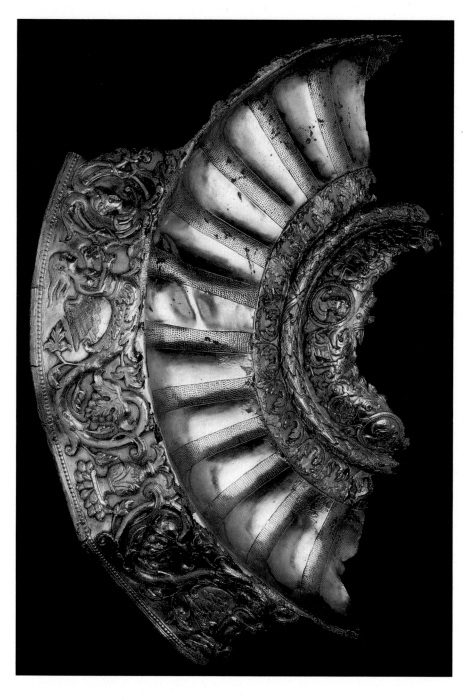

A part of a silver-gilt dish which was recovered in 1985 from the wreck of the *Nuestra Señora de Atocha* off Key West, Florida. The *Atocha* was lost when the Tierra Firma treasure fleet was hit by a hurricane in 1622

Christie's, New York held an auction of treasures from the *Atocha* and *Santa Margarita* in June 1988. This beautiful silver-gilt two-handled cup recovered from the *Atocha* raised $165,000 (£110,000)

A coral and gold rosary recovered from the wreck of the *Atocha* in 1973. As well
as the vast amount of treasure carried as cargo, the *Atocha* had on board many
wealthy Spanish officials and religious dignitaries with their own personal jewels
and valuable religious artefacts

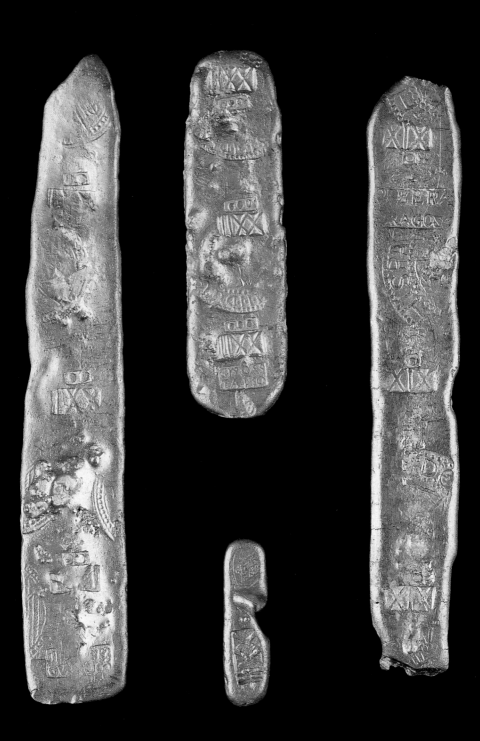

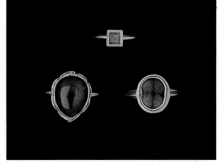

Above left A fine Renaissance gold chain recovered from the *Santa Margarita*
by Mel Fisher in 1980 during his search for her sister ship, the *Atocha.*
Chains of this type were worn by both sexes throughout the sixteenth and
seventeenth centuries

Left and above right Treasure recovered from the *Nuestra Señora de las Maravillas,*
a Spanish treasure galleon which sank off the Bahamas in 1656. Since it was
first discovered by Robert Marx and his company Seafinders Inc., in 1972,
the wreck has yielded millions of dollars' worth of treasure, including gold bars
(left) and jewellery (above right). The gold pectoral cross (top right) studded
with 66 flawless Colombian emeralds was sold at auction in London in 1992
for a record-breaking £231,000 ($346,500)

Above One of a pair of blue and gilt dishes from the Nanking Cargo,
a collection of near-perfect eighteenth-century porcelain recovered in 1985
from the Dutch East Indiaman *Geldermalsen*, wrecked in the South China Seas.
When the porcelain was auctioned at Christie's Amsterdam in April 1986,
it raised over £10 million ($15 million)

Right 4 Fujian *blanc-de-chine* figures, from the Vung Tau Cargo. The wreck
from which this cargo was taken was discovered off the south coast of Vietnam
in 1989 by a fisherman; the name of the ship and the exact date of its sinking
are unknown

A selection of Chinese export porcelain from the Vung Tau Cargo. In total, the cargo consisted of 28,000 pieces of porcelain. A few coins were also discovered but no other artefacts

water; realizing that the tide was now ebbing, Jacobsz ordered the mainmast to be cut away and cannons to be thrown overboard to lighten the ship. As the *Batavia* floundered in the shallow water she was unable to make way and struck the reef.

Pelsaert wrote:

Fourth of June being Monday morning, on the 2nd day of Whitsuntide, with a clear full moon about 2 hours before daybreak during the watch of the skipper (Ariaen Jacobsz), I was lying in my bunk feeling ill when felt suddenly, with a rough, terrible movement, the bumping of the ship's rudder, and immediately after that I felt the ship held up in her course against the rocks, so that I fell out of my bunk. Whereon I ran up and discovered that all the sails were in Top, the wind South west, that during the night the course had been north east by North, and that lay right in the middle of thick spray. Round the ship there was only a little surf, but shortly after that heard the Sea breaking hard round about. I said 'Skipper, what have you done through your reckless carelessness you have run this noose round our necks?' He answered, 'How could I do better? I did not sleep, but watched out very well, for when I saw the spray in the distance I asked Hans the gunner, What can that be? Whereupon he said, Skipper, it is the shine of the Moon, upon which I trusted.' I asked him 'What counsel now? Where about do you think we are?' He said, 'God knows; this is a shallow that must be lying quite a distance from the unknown Land, and I think we are just on the tail of it. We must see now to putting out an anchor astern, perhaps it is low tide, so that it will be possible to wind it from it.' I asked him how deep it was there. He answered that he did not know. I ordered the lead to be fetched, which was in the cabin of the steersman, and I found that astern there was only 17 to 18 feet of water, but at the fore part of the ship still less. At the moment, I did not know any better than that it was an unknown shallow in the Sea as the skipper said. – So we started to throw all our cannons overboard in order to make it lighter, and the yawls with the boat was put out, and I ordered them to sound round about, and found at an arrow's shot at the back of the Ship, 7 fathoms of Water. But forwards very dry; we made a kedge anchor ready, to put out at the stern. Meanwhile it began to blow harder with showers, and the boat was smitten overboard by a gush, so that it floated quickly away and we had to send the yawl to help it row up. But before it could be put aboard again, it had become daylight and we found ourselves then amongst rocks and shallows on every side, and very suddenly through the fall of the waters (for we had sailed there by high tide) it began to surf and foam around the ship, so that through the bumping of the ship, could not stand or walk. Therefore we decided, to put overboard the main mast, in order that it would not immediately push into the ground. But when it was cut down we found that it caused much damage, for we could not get it from aboard, so that we could not get the boat aboard through the big surf. I saw no Land that I thought would remain above at high water except an island that by guessing lay at least 3 miles from the ship.[7]

Pelsaert realized the seriousness of the situation and ordered Jacobsz to take the 20-foot yawl and reconnoitre the nearest islands with the intention of landing some of the survivors.

Therefore I sent the skipper to 2 small islands or rocks not so far from the ship in order to see if the people and some of the goods could be saved there. About the 9th hour the skipper returned because it was nigh impossible to get there through the stones and rocks, for at one spot one could not get over with the yawl, whilst at another it would be several fathoms deep. He reported that the Islands would not be flooded so far as he could see. Because of the great Yammer [sic] that there was in the ship, of Women, Children, Sick and poor-hearted men, we decided to put most of the people on land first and meanwhile to get ready on deck the money and the most precious goods, for which I did my utmost. But God the Lord chastised us with many rods for in spite of all the duty we made to cant the ship to leeward or to land, it turned out exactly the opposite because of the uneven rocks upon which it was set, which so caused it that the people could only come out of the ship very slowly. Secondly, the ship had already burst at the 10 hour, and all speed and skill had to be used to get some bread out of the bread cabin. Of water we hoped to get enough but our goodwill and diligence were impeded by the godless unruly troops of soldiers, as well as crew, and their women whom I could not keep in the hold on account of the liquor or wine, so that one could not get there [to the bread cabin] and in the meantime the entire hold started to float, so that hardly 1½ leggers were filled with tankards and buckets and lay ready on the deck of the ship. So that day went by and the boat had only done three trips with folks, with which we had put on land 180 Souls, 20 Casks of bread and some small barrels of water. – About Sunset the skipper came aboard with the sloop which had taken to land a Casket of Jewels and some people, and said to me, 'It won't help at all that we save water and bread, for everyone on land drinks as much as he can, and to forbid this has no result unless you order it otherwise.' Whereupon on account of our water the which, as far as I could see, would be very little available, moreover there was such a great number of people that it had to be better used, I jumped into the yawl, with the intention of returning immediately in order to get the money from the ship with the next boat, according to our resolution. But by God's Truth, I was scarcely from aboard than it began to blow so hard that it was outside Human power to reach the ship with the boat. Yea, we could hardly prevent it from drifting away. In the morning before daylight, the 5th, we put some folks, with some bread and water, on the largest of the islets. . . .

In the afternoon it started to blow very hard out of the North-west and the ship was pounded very much that day by the waves, so that one could hardly see it and it was a miracle that it remained together. In the evening we calculated our water which we had in the small barrels and we found ourselves, on the smallest islet where we were with the folks of the boat and the yawl, with about 80 kannen of water, where we were about 40 people, and on the largest island, where there were 180 Souls, was still less.[8]

These islands offered a safe refuge. The yawl's first three trips were responsible for the saving of 180 persons. On the following day the remaining survivors were rescued from the ship along with thirteen barrels of sea biscuits, some small barrels of water, and all else that could be salvaged from the wreck. Pelsaert prudently saved the casket of jewels.

On 6 June Pelsaert, along with Jacobsz, decided to try to land passengers on the mainland to search for food and water.

On 15 June they reached the coast.

In the morning we found ourselves at the point where a large reef stretched about one mile to Sea then we ran between the land reef and the sea reef, which we guessed to be at 23 degrees, and sailed thus along the Coast, alongside which stretches a reef where between the land [and the reef] appears to be very smooth and still water, we did our best to get into it, but found no opening till nearly noon, when we found an opening where there was no surf; ran into that, but it was very rocky and sometimes not more than 2 feet of water. – This coast had a dune fore land of about one mile width before one comes to the High Land, therefore began to dig in this place; there was salt water, a party of folk therefore went to the High land where they found by chance some small holes in a rock that were full of fresh water that the rain had left there. It seemed that the blacks had been there a little time before, for there lay bones of Crabs and ashes of fires. We quenched our great thirst a little for we hardly were able to do more, for since the wrecking of the ship we had been without wine or other drink except for one or two small mugs of water. Also collected a fair provision, about 80 kannen of water, and remained there the whole night until the 16th of do. In the morning we continued to see whether there were more such holes in the range. But our search was vain, it appeared it had not rained there for a long time, nor was there any sign of running water, for beyond the heights the country was flat again, without trees, foliage or grass, except for high anthills thrown up of earth, which in the distance were not unlike the huts of people. Was also such a host of flies, which came to sit in the mouth and the eyes, that they couldn't be beaten off. – Towards noon, seeing that there was no more water to be come by, set sail, and ran through another opening of the reef which lay a little more to the North.[9]

Having failed to find food or water Pelsaert made the decision to head for Java some 1000 miles to the west. 'Therefore we were forced to take a resolution, because we were more than 100 miles away from the People left by us and had up to now not found water to assist them, as for ourselves only [enough] that we might have the benefit of 2 mugs daily; to do our utmost in the name of God to further our journey to Batavia as quickly as possible in order that through the Hon. Lord Gov. Gen. some order or means might be set to work towards succour.'[10]

Four weeks later they were picked up by the Dutch ship *Sardam* also bound for Java. They then transferred to the *Fredrick Hendrick*

on which was the Heer Raemborch, Councillor of India. Therefore I sailed immediately to him, where I told his Hon. with heart's grief of our sad disaster. He showed me much friendship and permitted that I should stay on the ship with him until we reached Batavia. The other ships were Brouwers Hauen and Weesp, with which was the Commander Grijph coming in company of the Heer Commandeur Pieter van den Broeck from Suratte, but had been parted from each other.

On 4 do. the ship Batavia sailing from Suratte, also came by us, saying that still some ships had been seen outside the Straits [of Sunda], but not knowing whether they were English or our own ship. On 7 do. we arrived towards evening in the roads of Batavia. God be praised and thanked.[11]

On arrival Pelsaert immediately reported to the Dutch Council and accused Jacobsz of neglect of duty and public assault. He had Jacobsz arrested.

Because Adriaen [sic] Jacobsz, skipper of the wrecked ship *Batavia* is notorious through allowing himself to be blown away by pure neglect; and also because through his doings a gross evil and public assault has taken place on the same ship, on the widow of the late Boudewijn van der Mijl, in his life under merchant, it has been decided by His Hon. and the Council to arrest the mentioned skipper and to bring him to trial here in order that he may answer those accusations made to his detriment.[12]

With the departure of Jacobsz and Pelsaert from the islands, Cornelisz became the self-acclaimed leader of the survivors. Not much is known about Cornelisz's early life. He was aged about thirty and a native of Haarlem, and was an avid disciple of Torrentius Van Der Beeke, a sixteenth century religious fanatic and printer of obscene subjects. Cornelisz combined these beliefs with those of the Adamites, a religious sect who stripped and prayed naked in their places of worship, known as Paradise. On the island, Cornelisz wore a scarlet cloak, adorned himself with gold braid and wore silk stockings. He formed a council of seven chosen men and, using the devotion of the castaways, instigated dogmas that allowed and encouraged acts of murder and rape.

His followers signed an oath of allegiance to

'accept as our chief and Captain General, Jeronimus Cornelisz whom we with one accord and each separately swear as God shall help us, and in so far as the contrary happens we shall be the Devil's own . . .'.[13]

On 15 July Pelsaert sailed on the *Sardam* to rescue the survivors who had remained on the Abrolhos reef; and he was given instructions by the Company's Council to salvage any gold from the *Batavia*.

On 13 September *Sardam* arrived at Abrolhos. Pelsaert continued in his journal:

Before noon, approaching the island, we saw smoke on a long island 2 miles West of the Wreck, also on another small island close by the Wreck, about which we were all very glad, hoping to find great numbers, or rather all people alive. Therefore, as soon as the anchor was dropped, I sailed with the boat to the highest island, which was the nearest, taking with me a barrel of water, ditto bread, and a keg of wine; coming there, I saw no one, at which we wondered. . . . hoping to find a large party of people, alive, had to learn with hearts' grief that more than 120 persons, Men, Women, and Children, had been Miserably murdered, by drowning as well as by Strangling, Hacking and Throat-cutting; and also had in mind to do still more, which they would have put into action if Almighty God had not been aggrieved and thwarted their plan and all their intentions.[14]

Along with officers from the *Sardam*, Pelsaert set up a council on 17 September. The council examined, tortured and tried those involved in the killings.

The Commandeur and we the undersigned persons of the council of the ship Sardam, having given the matter our utmost consideration after long examinations and much searching, and after much discussion and weighing, in order to turn from us the wrath of God and to cleanse the name of Christianity from such an unheard of villain – have sentenced the foresaid Jeronimus Cornelisz of Haarlem.—Thus we sentence him hereby, that on Monday being the first of October, Anno 1629, as he requests to be baptised, he shall be taken to Seals Island to the place prepared for that, to execute Justice; and there first to cut off both his hands and after that punish him on the gallows with the Cord till death follows – with confiscation of all his goods, Moneys, Gold, Silver, monthly wages and all that he may have to claim here in India against the General East India Company, our Lord Masters.—Thus done and attested on the Island named Batavia's Graveyard, this 28 Sept. 1629.[15]

In the days following, seven others were hanged and two were castaway on Southland (Australia). Seventy-four survivors were brought back to Java on board the *Sardam*. Before departure *Sardam* anchored near the wreck. Four divers brought up a total of fourteen chests of gold, some loose gold and silver coins and a few silver dishes. As the days passed it became apparent that little else of value was to be salvaged. Pelsaert gave up further search and returned to Java.

Abel Tasman

Thirteen years after the wreck Abel Tasman, the Dutch navigator, was instructed by the Dutch East India Company to

further continue your course along the land of d'Eendracht as far as Houtmans Abrolhos, and come to anchor there at the most convenient place, in order to make efforts to bring up from the bottom the chest with eight-thousand rixdollars, sunk with the lost ship Batavia in 1629, owing to a brass half cannon having fallen upon it, and which the men of the Yacht Sardam dived for without success, and so save the same together with the said gun, which would be good service done to the Company, on which account you will not fail diligently to attend to this business. You will likewise make search on the mainland to ascertain whether the two Nether- landers who, having forfeited their lives, were put ashore here by the Commander Francisco Pelsert [sic] at the same period, are still alive, in which case you will from them ask information touching the country, and if they should wish it, allow them to take passage hither with you.[16]

Tasman did not reach the Abrolhos Islands. The two castaways, Wouter Loos and Jan Pelgrom De Bye, either died or managed to survive by living with the aborigines. These two men were, in actual fact, the first white men to live on the mainland of Australia.

Edwards and Cramer

In 1963 a salvage operation was organized by two Australians, Hugh Edwards and Max Cramer. After they had located the wreck they recovered four bronze cannons, a number of artifacts and several human skeletons. The Western Australian Museum launched a programme of excavation in 1972. A few gold coins and some silverware were recovered.

There is no record of the actual chest of gold or Pelsaert's gold and silver dinner services being found. Somewhere near Morning Reef lies a small fortune.

NUESTRA SENORA DE LA CONCEPCION

The Nuestra Senora de la Concepcion was one of the largest Manila galleons of her time, and was probably built at Cavite on Manila Bay. Her length was between 140 and 160 feet, and she displaced 2,000 tons. She was armed with thirty-six cannons.

AREA: *Wrecked in the Saipan Channel on a reef off Agingan Beach, southwestern tip of Saipan Island, Mariana Islands, Pacific Ocean.*

The first Manila galleon sailed from the Moluccas Islands to Mexico in 1565, carrying Chinese silks, porcelain and spices. By the mid-sixteenth century the Spanish viewed the Philippines as a base to the wealth of trade from China and the Spice Islands. In 1571 the city of Manila was founded by the Basque sailor Miguel Lopez De Lagazpi who wrote: 'We shall gain the commerce with China, whence come silks, porcelains, benzoin, musk and other articles'.[1]

The eastbound galleons usually left Manila by July each year, sailing north-wards to the latitude of Japan and picking up the prevailing westerly winds between the 30th and 40th parallels, before crossing El Mar del Sur, which was the Spanish name for the Pacific Ocean. The voyage was long, 9000 miles lasting between four to six months, making landfall at Cape Mendocinco on the coast of California and sailing south to Acapulco. The cargoes were then transported to the warehouses at Veracruz and shipped to Spain.

The voyage from Acapulco to Manila normally lasted two and a half or three months with the advantage of the winds and currents between the 10th and 14th parallels.

In August 1638 the *Nuestra Senora de la Concepcion* was loaded at the port of Cavite on Manila Bay; she was heavily laden with spices, silks, porcelain, gemstones and jewellery.

The Governor of Manila, Hurtado de Corcuero, was a man of greed and corruption, procuring bribes and bestowing appointments in return for gold. Corcuero appointed his nephew, Don Juan Francisco, as commander of the *Concepcion*, mainly in order to safeguard a large consignment of his private trade goods. Don Juan refused to submit a registered manifest of the *Concepcion*'s cargo to the custom agent. Charges of corruption and incompetence levelled against him later, in 1644, stated that he was

> . . . at most 22 or 24 years of age . . . of little age or experience in military or naval matters. For this reason a few days . . . out . . . the officers of the Concepcion lost respect and obedience for him, each one seeking to give orders and be obeyed, splitting into factions and attacking each other, in which mutiny men were killed and wounded. While they were obstructing each other, and not attending to navigation, the ship broached to and the wind seizing it thus broke the masts up to the bowsprit, which all went into the sea in an instant, leaving the ship without control at the mercy of wind and currents which carried it to run aground on a reef . . . [2]

With mutiny and bad weather the voyage proved to be the ship's last. Sailing towards the Mariana Islands the wind increased to gale force, the *Concepcion* was unable to weather the storm, cleared Agingan Point but was driven on to a reef between the islands of Tinan and Saipan; her hull was torn open below the waterline. Waves continually smashed against the hull and she quickly broke up half a mile off shore. Of her 400 passengers and crew few survivors reached the shore; of those that did, all but six were killed by the Chamorro Indians.

William Mathers

William Mathers studied Asian history at Yale University and then became a US Army salvage officer in Vietnam. After this he worked as a marine construction manager in Asia and developed a keen interest in the history of the Manila galleons, and especially in the *Concepcion*.

For two years Mathers studied documents at the Archivo General de Indias in Seville and early Spanish papers in Mexico City and Guam. He discovered that some of the *Concepcion*'s cargo had been salvaged by local fishermen and divers, and in 1684 the Spanish had recovered thirty-five cannons and seven anchors, but much of the treasure was still unrecovered.

According to Mathers's research, Spanish officials charged Governor Corcuero with appropriating a 'solid gold plate and a ewer set thought to be a gift from the King of Spain to the Emperor of Japan'.[3] The Governor was returning them to Spain as personal cargo in the *Concepcion*.

In March 1987 Mathers assembled a team of thirty divers, archaeologists and conservationists and, with the salvage ship *Tengar*, began a half-square-mile search southeast of Agingan Point on the southwestern tip of Saipan Island.

Over a two-year period Mathers and his divers found the remains of the *Concepcion* scattered over a wide area at depths of 2 to 400 feet. During the first few weeks of diving, ceramic sherds and ballast stones were found. In a ten-month period between 1987 and 1988 the divers brought to the surface '1300 pieces of 22.5 karat gold jewellery . . . crucifixes, beads, buckles . . . rings and brooches set with precious stones. . . . A mass of 32 gold chains each about five feet long . . . 997 gold buttons.'[4]

As no manifest was recorded it is impossible to know the complete value of the treasure, or what she was carrying, but other documents indicated she was a richly loaded Manila galleon. Mathers estimated the *Concepcion*'s cargo would be worth 'tens of millions of dollars today.'[5]

Although Mathers recovered a major portion of the treasure, some jewellery and valuables may still lie on the seabed.

VERGULDE DRAECK

The Vergulde Draeck *(meaning the 'gilt' or 'golden dragon') was purchased by the Amsterdam Chamber of the Dutch East India Company, before being overhauled and refitted for service between Holland and the East Indies. The* Draeck *was approximately 140 feet long with a beam of 35 feet. Her Captain was Pieter Ambertsz and 193 crew plus three women sailed on board during the voyage of 1655–6 to Indonesia.*

AREA: *Struck a reef about three to four miles off Ledge Point, near Cape Leschenault, seventy miles north of Fremantle, Western Australia, Indian Ocean.*

The *Vergulde Draeck* sailed from Texel, Holland, to Batavia (Djakarta) on 4 October 1655. She carried a cargo of general merchandise as well as a valuable consignment of eight chests containing 45,950 coins, valued at 78,600 guilders, mostly in pieces-of-eight.

The voyage from Holland to the Cape of Good Hope was uneventful. The *Draeck* made landfall on 9 March 1656 and stayed only two days at the Cape before continuing on to Batavia, sailing the 'Brouwer Route' which took her directly east across the Indian Ocean.

At 4 o'clock on the morning of 28 April, under full sail with a following wind, she smashed into submerged reefs near Cape Leschenault on the western coast of Australia.

The log of the *Vergulde Draeck* survived, with this entry: 'The Vergulde Draeck ... was wrecked very suddenly on the 28 of April at night at the beginning of the first dog-watch on the coast of Southland on a reef out to sea about a mile and a half, latitude 30⅔ degrees ... nothing was saved from the ship, which foundered and sank at once, except a small quantity of provisions washed on the shore by the waves.'[1]

Only her stern was left above the water. Many of those on board were trapped below deck and drowned before they managed to reach the upper decks. 'Of the 193 heads, only 75 landed safely, amongst whom the skipper Pieter Albertsz and the mentioned under-steersman. From the ship, which immediately burst open when touching ground, nothing was saved and only very few provisions were thrown on the beach by the waves.'[2]

The captain proposed that the surviving longboat be used to sail to Batavia to get help; the pilot and six crew members volunteered to make the voyage.

At the beginning of May the seven set sail, carrying as much food and water as could be spared. On 7 June, the seven men, exhausted and starving, arrived in Batavia. The Council of the Indies recorded: 'Today, shortly after midday, the schuyt³ of the yacht *Draeck* arrived after one month wandering around with the under-steersman and six sailors. They brought the sorrowful news that the above mentioned fine yacht had run aground on the coast of Southland on 28 April during the night, in the middle of the morning watch, on a reef stretching out in the sea for about 1½ miles at a latitude of 30⅔ degrees.'⁴

Rescue Attempts

The Governor-General Joan Maetsuyker, and the Council of the Indies agreed to send two ships, the *Witte Valck* (White Falcon) and the *Goede Hoop* (Good Hope), to rescue the survivors and to recover the chests of treasure.

In the southern hemisphere June marks the beginning of the winter months with weather conditions becoming severe – storms and rough seas are common. The rescue ships set sail under threat of imminent winter weather.

The Captains were instructed to

> sail together out of Sunda Strait and steer immediately southward, until the latitude of 32 degrees to 33 degrees or until they get a steady westerly trade wind. From there they will steer for the coast of the Southland and having arrived with God's help, at the people of the *Draeck*, they will distribute them over the two ships (which must do their utmost to stay constantly together). Further they will try to recover, in the most careful way, whether diving or otherwise, if it is possible, firstly the cash and then as much as is possible and practicable of the cargo, the guns and what else is particularly valuable.⁵

The weather, as predicted, was stormy and caused the two ships to separate. Northeasterly gales, winds, rough seas and heavy surf along the Western Australia coast, made a search of the coastline extremely hazardous.

> Having arrived at the coast of Southland, [*Witte Valck*] met such storms and high running seas that she did not dare come close to it, but thanked God that she could stay clear. The 'yacht' [*Goede Hoop*] endured the same heavy storms but managed to land with the boat on the mentioned latitude, and they have been several miles inland. They had sailed a long way along the coast but have seen neither wreck or people. Instead they have lost eleven

Mid-seventeenth-century engraving of a Dutch East Indiaman

of their own men. Firstly, three, who seemed to have lost their way in the bush, and after the other eight, who, having been sent ashore with the boat to look for them, having never appeared again. The boat was found smashed to pieces on the beach with which the crew is probably lost.[6]

The two ships abandoned the search, the *Witte Valck* arriving back in Batavia on 12 September and the *Goede Hoop* a month later. The Governor-General wrote a report on 28 November to the company directors in Amsterdam, stating,

> . . . to our great regret and the Company's great concern, the *Goede Hoop* even having lost 11 men instead of bringing any of the *Draeck*'s crew or goods (as we had hoped) and as it has not been a good enough time nor have we had any able ships to take us upon a second mission thither. So now it is thought best and agreed, to notify Commander Jan van Riebeeck at the Cape of Good Hope of this and to command him that he will (as is his and our Christian duty) do his utmost for the saving of so many miserable people and our Gentlemen's goods which maybe are still there.[7]

The Dutch had established a colony at the Cape of Good Hope in 1652 under the command of Jan van Riebeeck. In 1657 the Governor-General made recommendations to van Riebeeck to organize a search for survivors. Van Riebeeck sent two ships, the *Veenenburgh* and the *de Vincq* departing from the Cape on 27 April with the following orders: 'You will visit the aforementioned Southland at about 32⅔ degrees ... you will keep a close watch for any signs of fires for such from these poor, miserable people (also for any remains of the wreck) in order to release them from their misery, and bring them back to Batavia. You will also bring back the cash and unspoiled cargo as much as you can salvage.'[8] The *de Vincq* searched along the Southland coast but saw neither signs of survivors nor wreckage; the two ships arrived back in Batavia on 7 July.

One final attempt was made to find survivors: the Councillors in Batavia agreed in late 1657 to send another two ships to Southland. On 1 January 1658 the *Waeckende Boey* and the *Emerloort* set sail; on board were provisions to last for a six-month expedition. Upon arrival at the site of the wreck, the captain of the *Waeckende Boey* sent his upper-steersman, Abraham Leeman, with a small party, to search the shoreline. Leeman later made a report that was entered in the ship's log:

> ... they had been on land and observed many signs of the wrecked ship *Draeck*, but no footprints nor any place where people had lived, although they had gone far and wide, both inland and along the beach.
>
> The signs of the ship on the coast which they had observed are as follows: A heavy beam, a piece of oak planking, a small keg, buckets, thwarts of the boat (probably cross-pieces from the *Vergulde Draeck*'s second boat, the one that the seven survivors at Batavia had said was damaged when landing at the beach), pieces of chest, staves and other similar rubbish.
>
> It was noteworthy that a number of pieces of planking had been put up in a circle with their end upwards.[9]

They continued to search but found no other signs either of castaways or the vessel. The ships returned to Batavia and, on 1 August 1660, the Governor-General decided to discontinue further rescue attempts and wrote to the directors on 14 December 1658: 'we assume that the poor people of the ship, the *Draeck*, no one will be present any longer since otherwise it would be diffi-cult to explain, as they would have shown themselves by means of fires or other signs here and along the beach.' In reply the directors wrote: 'Now that all missions have been fruitless, we will have to give up, to our distress, the people of *Draeck*, who have found refuge on the Southland.'[10]

Western Australian Museum

In 1931 a young boy playing in the sand dunes near Cape Leschenault found forty silver coins which were possibly associated with the *Draeck*.

Further discoveries were made in April 1963 when a group of skindivers anchored their boat about eight miles south of Ledge Point. The diving party consisted of five men: J. Henderson and his two sons, Alan and Graeme, E.A. Robertson and J. Cowan.

After a few dives Graeme Henderson found a pinkish brick, identified as a ballast brick. Further dives indicated evidence of an old wreck. On later visits the divers found a bronze mortar bearing the inscription: 'amor vincit omnia' (love conquers all) and 231 silver coins; they also raised an iron cannon inscribed with the Dutch East India Company monogram 'AVOC'. These finds were presented to the Western Australian Museum where it was verified that they originated from the wreck of the *Vergulde Draeck*.

In 1968 investigations of the wreck were made by three of the museum divers, headed by Jeremy Green. Dr Jack Hinton describes the site: 'The Gilt Dragon site ... is a craggy undulating mass of what appears at first sight to be nothing but reef formation with considerable variation in depth, valleys, pockets and holes, arches and grottoes. Although a certain amount of material lies around in an immediately moveable form, with varying amounts of encrustation or conglomeration, the greater part of the wreck must lie ... within a thick encrustation of marine growth.'[11]

The wreck site covers an area approximately 150 feet in length by 120 feet wide. The wreck lies on a limestone and coral reef seven miles south-south-west of the small fishing village of Ledge Point.

On investigation of the wreck it seemed the *Draeck* broke up almost immediately. The main structure of the gun-deck and the upper deck were cast on to the reef and the Captain's cabin (where the treasure chests would have been kept) and the main cargo area fell into deeper water on the west of the reef.

Nineteen cannons and five anchors were found, along with 7881 coins ranging from 1590 in date to 1654, mostly silver pieces-of-eight from Spanish colonial, Dutch and Spanish mints. An estimated 21,905 coins have been recovered over the years from the wreck site leaving 24,045 silver coins still missing.[12]

In 1972 the Dutch Government signed an agreement relinquishing all rights of ownership of all Dutch East India Company ships that were purported to lie off the coast of Western Australia. All salvage from all said shipwrecks would now be owned by the State Government and the responsibility of excavating and protection was given to the museum.

CHINESE TRADING JUNK

This seventeenth century Chinese trading junk, 110 feet long and 33 feet wide, was possibly sailing from Hsiamen, China, bound for the northwestern islands of Indonesia, probably Batavia, (now Djakarta).

AREA: *Sank a few miles from Con Mau Island, which lies approximately 100 nautical miles south of Vung Tau on the southern coast of the Republic of Vietnam, South China Sea.*

Nothing is known about the exact date or sinking of this junk but, from evidence found by divers, the vessel burned to the waterline and sank in 120 feet of water.

It was first located by a Vietnamese fisherman who snagged his nets on the wreck when trawling for shellfish in 1989. The wreck was brought to the attention of the director of the Vietnam Salvage Corporation, Mr Le Minh

Chinese junks. The classic Chinese sailing vessel, high-sterned with a projecting bow, usually carried five masts on which were set square sails consisting of panels of linen or matting flattened by bamboo strips. By the fifteenth century junks had developed into the largest, strongest and most seaworthy ships in the world

Cong, who combined salvage operations with a Swedish Singapore company, Hallstrom Oceanics.

Vietnam Salvage Corporation

The recovered cargo became known as the Vung Tau Cargo; this consisted of 28,000 pieces of porcelain from Fujian Province and from the famed centre of Imperial Court Kilns at Jingdelhen in Jianxi Province. According to Hetti Jongsma, Director of Oriental Art at Christie's in Amsterdam, 'The cargo contains an astonishing variety of shapes, recalling western glass, metal and wooden vessels. . . . We have seen individual examples of these types before. But such a large quantity suggests that Chinese manufacturers of export porcelain, were tailoring their production specifically to western demand at such an early date and that is a remarkable discovery.'[1]

The Dutch, as we know, had settled in Batavia in 1619; this became a major trading centre for European and South-East Asian goods. A few coins from the reign of the Chinese Emperor Kangi (1662-1722) were recovered, but no other artifacts were located.[2]

The sales at Christie's of the Vung Tau porcelain totalled £4,165,667 ($7,370,000).

ZUYTDORP

The Zuytdorp was built in 1701 by the Dutch shipwright, Penne, for the Zeeland Chamber of the Dutch East India Company. She weighed about 400 tons and measured 178 feet by 44 feet. She was armed with forty cannons.

   AREA: *Wrecked off the Western Australian coast forty miles north of the mouth of the Murchinson River at the base of the Zuytrop Cliffs, Australia, Indian Ocean.*

The *Zuytdorp* made her maiden voyage from Holland to Java in 1702. Her third, and last, voyage, begun on 27 July 1711, took her from the port of Vlissingen, Holland, bound for Batavia (Djakarta) Java. Her captain was Marinus Wysvliet and she carried a crew of 286. The ship's manifest has never been located but it is known from various papers held in the Company's archives, under Zeeland Chamber, that in 1711 the Dutch East India Company sent a total of 3,700,000 guilders to the Indies in order to finance their eastern trade activities. 925,000 of these guilders are known to have been transported by five ships including the *Zuytdorp*. It is believed that she carried 248,886 guilders, as well as undisclosed numbers of gold and silver bars.[1]

The *Zuytdorp* sailed from Holland in company with the *Belvliet*. They called at the island of Sao Tome and Cape de Lopez Gonsales off the African coast before arriving at the Cape of Good Hope within days of each other. On this first leg of the eastward voyage 112 of the *Zuytdorp*'s crew had died of scurvy and a further twenty-two were seriously ill. Aboard the *Belvliet* sixty of the crew of 164, along with the captain, died at sea. The long voyage from Holland to South Africa usually resulted in 20 to 50 per cent of ships' crews dying or being incapacitated due to scurvy.

In late March 1712 the captain followed the usual pattern of the times by taking on resident or recovered seamen at the Cape. The *Zuytdorp* took on extra crew but the *Belvliet* was delayed as she was unable to find additional men.

On 22 April the *Zuytdorp* set sail for Batavia in the company of another Dutch ship, the *Kockenge*. Dutch East India Company ships normally sailed from Holland between August and January, arriving in Batavia during July to September of the following year. In 1611 the Dutch navigator, Hendrick Brouwer, discovered that the quickest way to the East Indies was to sail directly east from the Cape of Good Hope, thus following the prevailing winds known as the 'roaring forties' for 4000 miles, and then turn north and make for Java. Although this route was to become a Company directive it was a difficult course to follow; longitude could not be determined accurately and the pilots and navigators had to rely on dead reckoning. Ships that followed Brouwer's route sailed to within sight of 'Southland' or the 'Land of Eendracht' (Australia).

The *Kockenge* arrived in Batavia on 4 July with the news that she and the *Zuytdorp* had been separated during the arduous voyage. The *Zuytdorp* was never heard of again; no report or other evidence as to her loss was ever recorded or passed down by the Dutch East India Company's archivists.

P.E. Playford

In 1927 an Australian bushman named Tom Pepper reported finding relics of an eighteenth-century ship at the base of a limestone cliff. Could this be the long-missing *Zuytdorp*? Scattered around the rocks, forty miles from the

Murchinson River, were large pieces of ship's timbers, an old carved sternpost, ships artifacts, and a number of silver coins. A Mr P.E. Playford, a geologist who also worked for the West Australian Petroleum Company, met Tom Pepper in 1954 and learnt of the wreck site. Playford visited the area, accompanied by a few fellow explorers, in 1958. For the first three weeks, diving was not possible due to bad weather, so Playford conducted searches both at the foot of the cliff as well as on the top of the cliff. At the base he found over 200 coins lodged in rock crevices and reef ledges: 'The findings at the wreck-site of numerous schellingen and dubbele stuivers, dated 1711, with the name "Zeeland" and the mint mark of the Middelburg Mint is clear evidence that the wreck is that of the *Zuytdorp*. It is known that the entire minting of these coins was sent to the Indies in the *Zuytdorp* and perhaps the *Belvliet*, and as the *Belvliet* reached its destination safely, this wreck must be that of the *Zuytdorp*.'[2]

As he explored the top of the cliff Playford discovered two pairs of nautical dividers, fragments of clay pipes, nails, barrel hoops and broken glass bottles. These finds seemed to indicate that a number of the crew had survived the probable sinking. Evidence that some crew lived for a while near the wreck site was substantiated by the finding of a thick layer of ash lying a few inches below the ground; Playford supposed that this could have been a huge fire lit as a signal fire for the *Kockenge* to be seen from the top of the cliff.

There is no permanent supply of drinking water in the area, but, on the other hand, no human remains have ever been discovered. The aborigines, who once inhabited the area (the Nanda and the Mulgana tribes), have become extinct. There are no native stories to support Dutch seamen appearing in the area. It is doubtful that the true fate of the survivors will ever be known. The area south of Murchinson River is inhospitable, the country inland is extremely barren.

Geraldton Divers

A small salvage operation was launched in 1964 by a group of divers from Geraldton. They made four dives on the site and managed to retrieve four small brass cannons, along with some artifacts and coins.

Western Australian Museum

Another salvage attempt was made by divers working for the Western Australian Museum in 1971. The divers recovered '3,500 coins, a bronze

Cape Town, called 'Kaapstad' in Afrikaans. In 1652 Jan van Riebeeck was sent to the Cape of Good Hope by the Dutch East India Company to build a fort and establish a provisioning station for Dutch ships sailing to the East Indies

cannon, a ship's bell and a navigator's divider'.[3] Strong currents make diving dangerous and the wreck site is difficult to reach. In the rock crevices at the base of the imposing cliffs there must still remain large numbers of the missing currency.

ZEEWIJK

The Zeewijk was built in Middelburg, Holland in 1725 for the Zeeland Chamber of the Dutch East India Company. She was 145 feet long and had a 40-foot beam. Armed with thirty-six guns, the Zeewijk was commanded by Captain Jan Steyns.

AREA: *Wrecked off the coast of Western Australia in the Houtman Abrolhos Islands, on the western side of the Pelsart Group, on Gun Island (previously known as Half-Moon Reef), Indian Ocean.*

The *Zeewijk*, an East Indiaman, with a crew of 170 and 38 military personnel, sailed from Vlissingen on 7 November 1726, bound for Batavia (Djakarta) in Java via Cape Town. Her cargo was mainly ironwork, liquor, cheese and military supplies. Listed on her manifest was also a valuable shipment of 3 tons of treasure contained in ten boxes: 'Each box weighed about 600 pounds, and was made of wood, bound with metal bands, and with three locks. The money was in gold and silver ingots in pieces of eight from Mexico, in Ducatons, and "payments" – small change coins.'[1]

On 26 March 1727 the *Zeewijk* dropped anchor in Table Bay at the Cape of Good Hope.

The Portuguese navigator Bartolomeu Dias de Novias sailed round the tip of South Africa in 1488, naming the promontory 'Cabo da Boa Esperanca' the Cape of Good Hope. In 1620, a commander of an English East Indiaman planted the Cross of St. George at the Cape in the name of James I, but the king neglected the proclamation; thus there was no official recognition of English sovereignty. In 1652 Jan van Riebeeck raised the Dutch flag on behalf of the Dutch East India Company, thus the first Dutch settlement was established.[2] By the end of the seventeenth century, the Cape had become an important half-way port of call for trading ships sailing between Europe and Asia. Carl Thunberg, the Swedish traveller, described Cape Town in 1772: 'An inn for travellers to and from the East Indies, who after several months' sail may here get refreshments of all kinds, and are then about half-way to the place of their destination, whether homeward or out-ward bound.'[3]

Whilst at the Cape, the *Zeewijk* offloaded some of her general merchandise and transferred many of those suffering from scurvy. Fresh crew, water and provisions were taken on. On 21 April she departed Table Bay. As the *Zeewijk* left the South African coast she followed the Company's instructions for setting a course for the Indies:

> Observe that the distance between the Cape and the Land of Eendracht[4] is in reality much shorter than the chart shows, and it may happen by the aid of currents that the route may be found even shorter than it really is. So that the Land may be reached in much less time than we are led to expect. Remember that the Land of Eendracht S. of 27 deg. Lat. has many perilous sandbanks and that the soundings are of sharp rocks, consequently EXTREME CAUTION and the constant use of the lead at night and in stormy weather is indispensably necessary.[5]

The *Zeewijk* crossed the Indian Ocean and, for whatever reason, contrary to

Company policy, Captain Steyns changed course to east-northeast. His log entry for 21 May states: 'This day it was decided that we should turn our course E.N.E., and anchor off the coast of Endracht's land; occasion permitting.'[6]

On 8 June the *Zeewijk* was on an east-northeast course, 29 degrees latitude. The captain was unaware that his longitudinal position was soon to place him seven to eight miles south of the notorious Houtman Abrolhos Reef. In 1619, the Dutch navigator Frederick Houtman discovered and charted what were to become known as the Houtman Abrolhos Reefs. The name Abrolhos was a corruption of the Portuguese 'Abri Vosso Olhos' meaning 'open your eyes'. This term became an accepted international navigational term for hazardous reefs or shoals. Houtman wrote of these particular reefs: ' . . . at night, about three hours before daybreak we came unexpectedly upon a low lying coast. A level country with reefs all around it. We saw no high land or mainland, so that this shoal is to be very carefully avoided as it is very dangerous to ships that wish to touch at this coast.'[7]

As the *Zeewijk* kept to her erroneous course, she sailed closer and closer to the Pelsart Group that was part of the Abrolhos Islands. At 7 o'clock on the evening of the 9 June, with a southwesterly wind, surf was suddenly sighted ahead. It was too late to brace foresails into the wind; the *Zeewijk* ran starboard against a low flat reef. Her head swung into the wind and the rudder, catching on the reef, was knocked from its fitting. The second mate, Adriaan Van Der Graeff, was ordered aft to report on the damage. He later wrote:

> The Skipper ordered me to go aft, and I found eight feet of water in the hold: and we cut the mainmast and threw it overboard. We resolved also to cut the fore and the mizzen masts when we found ten or eleven feet of water in the ship.
>
> . . . We prayed the Almighty to deliver us. Every minute the surf came over us, and we did out utmost to get rid of all rigging and the masts. When the foremast and the bowsprit went over the side a sailor, Jurysan Roefran, was also swept overboard. We could only look at each other with weeping eyes and pray the Almighty that he would take us away from the heavy punishment He had sent us. We could see nothing but surf, which came over in a terrible manner.[8]

The *Zeewijk's* perilous position was made worse by the fact that a severe storm was brewing. All day the surf continued to rise, breaking over the decks and making it impossible safely to abandon ship. To the lee side of the reef, a number of small islands, lying some two miles distant, could be made out. On the third day the seas abated somewhat, and an attempt was made to launch the yawl. The hoisting tackle broke and the small ship plunged, bow first, into the stormy sea and rapidly filled with water, drifting uselessly away. The captain, not wishing to risk losing the longboat, ordered that a flat-bottomed scow (or raft) be constructed. His plan was to transfer survivors to the calmer part of the reef that lay 100 yards away.

On the first attempt thirteen men scrambled aboard. As the scow cleared the ship it capsized and eight men drowned; the remaining five managed to swim to the reef. Meanwhile, the *Zeewijk*, still being pounded by the seas, was slowly moving on to her beam. The captain, realizing that he might soon have to abandon ship, decided to launch the longboat and to construct more scows.

On the following day the weather cleared, and men and supplies were moved on to the reef. The good weather continued, permitting the crew to salvage great quantities of goods from the shipwreck. Canvas sails, rigging, spars (all useful for building shelter), barrels of fresh water, bread, wine, casks of butter and meat were all rescued.

The chosen 'island' was four miles long, with small rocky enclosed beaches. A few clusters of mangroves and salt bushes grew between the rocks. The cast-aways built shelters from the salvaged timbers. But, as the days passed into weeks, despair and desperation set in; they began to realize the hopelessness of their plight and the unlikelihood of being rescued.

On 1 July some of the officers approached the captain and demanded: 'We want it that a boat shall go to Batavia: and we shall appoint the first mate as skipper, and no one else.'[9]

It was agreed that ten of the best seamen be picked along with the first mate, Pieter Langeweg, who was to be their leader. Nine days later the long-boat had been provisioned for the 1700-mile voyage and, on 10 July, ' . . . at sunset the longboat set sail for Batavia. May God guide her.'[10]

The men were never heard from again.

The weeks passed on the island; discipline collapsed, groups formed with demands for extra wine and brandy, fights broke out, men died of sickness, men died of despair. Food was in short supply, and the senior officers were finding it more and more difficult to control the crew and the soldiers. At the end of September a scouting party found the yawl washed up on a small sandy beach; it was damaged but repairable. As Captain Steyns realized that Pieter Langeweg and his crew were most probably lost, he decided to build a boat large enough to accommodate all the remaining survivors and to then make a desperate attempt to reach Batavia. Using the yawl, the *Zeewijk* was stripped of her timbers and the ten chests of treasure were transported, in two careful trips, to the island. 'From the wreck we have despatched a good deal of victuals to those who came daily to the reef, as well as timber, rope, and iron fittings. Everything, in short, which could serve for the building of a new vessel for our rescue. We have also continued demolishing the fore castle on which a start had been made, as well as the cabin and master's cabin and have made of the planks a large new scow to sail to the reef sending the remainder of the timber to the reef as rafts.[11]

By early November the keel had been laid for a boat large enough for the all-important three tons of treasure, provisions, and the remaining survivors. At the very end of November an incident occurred that served to show the cruel standards under which these men all lived:

> December 1st, 1727: At 8 o'clock in the morning the Petty Officers enter our tent and ask to see the Skipper, and inform him that two hands named Adriaen Spoor, from St Maertensdyck, and Pieter Engels, from Ghent, both boys, were found yesterday committing together the abominable sins, of Sodom and Gomorrah. Which fact cries greatly to Heaven and distresses the Skipper and other members of the Ship's Council.[12]

The boys were brought before the captain and senior officers:

> It has appeared to us clearly and truthfully that the persons mentioned, on 30 November, 1727, at about 3 o'clock in the afternoon, committed in the island the abominable and God-forsaken deeds of Sodom and Gomorrah, to the great sorrow of the officers, distress of the crew, and general peril of our island. Through which deed terrible plagues may strike our people, or discord may occur among us, with the loss of all that is good.
>
> . . . where justice prevails ought to be punished by death for the prevention of further evil.
>
> . . . Whereupon we have resolved in council to place them apart from each other on the remotest islands.
>
> . . . This verdict has been passed, sentenced, announced, and executed by us at Fredrik Houtmann on December 2nd 1727.[13]

The two boys were each marooned separately on small coral cays and left to die of starvation, thirst or madness.

The carpenter and his mates took a further four months to complete the boat that was to take the survivors to Batavia. She was around 45 feet long with a 20-foot beam. On 19 February the hull was caulked and eight days later *Sloepie* (Little Sloop) was launched. The castaways '... brought her on rollers and launched her. We found that she was water-tight.'[14]

By mid-March *Sloepie* was ready; she had been rigged and provisioned. The all-important ten chests of treasure had been safely loaded.

Of the original 208 crew and passengers only eighty-eight remained alive to board *Sloepie*. She sailed from the desolate shore on 26 March 1728, ten months after the *Zeewijk* was wrecked.

Sloepie reached the Sunda Straits on 21 April and anchored at Batavia on 30 April with eighty-two survivors. Steyns reported to the Company officials and was charged:

> ... Jan Steyns had not only run too near the Southland, contrary to his orders, and in opposition to the protests of the steersmen, and thereby caused that disaster: but had also contemplated deceiving the government by altered and falsified journals in order to hide as much as possible his indefensible conduct. Whereupon, on 17th August, it was determined to indict the said Jan Steyns before the Court of Justice, and he has since been placed under arrest.[15]

In the trial that followed, on 17 December, he was found guilty and sentence was passed in May 1729. The Company showed little mercy to employees who lied or disobeyed orders. Even though Steyns brought the treasure, intact, to Batavia, this had no bearing on his actual sentencing:

> In consequence of the malicious and irresponsible mis-sailing of the ship Zeewyk (sic) by the accused he shall be marched to the place where criminals are usually executed and handed over to the executioner to be tied to a pole and flagellated severely with rods. Forced to labour in chains and without wages for fifteen years at the Company's common works. Remain banished, wherever it pleased the Honourable High Government. And be responsible for the costs of the Court proceedings.[16]

GELDERMALSEN

The Geldermalsen was built in Middelburg, Holland, in 1746, commissioned by the Zeeland Chamber of the Dutch East India Company. She was an impressive ship of 1100 tons with a 42-foot beam and an overall length of 150 feet. Armed with twenty-four iron cannons and two cannons of bronze, she carried 112 crew and passengers. Her captain was Jan Diederik Morel.

AREA: *Sank on the Admiral Stellingwerf Reef, approximately twelve miles south of the island of Bintan, Indonesia, South China Sea.*

The Dutch East India Company took delivery of its new ship *Geldermalsen*, named after the family estate belonging to one of the Zeeland directors, on 10 July 1747. A year later, on 16 August 1748 she made her maiden voyage to the company headquarters at Batavia in Java and, from 1749 to 1751, the ship was employed on the eastern trade routes between India, Batavia and China. Canton was China's major southern port and the main trade outlet for silk, spices, tea, porcelain and other exotic goods.

At the end of 1751 the *Geldermalsen* was given instructions from the company directors to sail to Canton to pick up her cargo. The company appointed a new captain along with a fresh crew. As the *Geldermalsen* lay in harbour she was loaded with 686,000 lbs of various grades of tea, 225,300 pieces of porcelain and fifty dinner sets consisting of 161 pieces packed in standard crates measuring 6 feet square and 18 inches high. Included in the cargo were 147 gold bars packed in a wooden chest.[1]

There was also an undisclosed, but probably quite valuable, quantity of 'private trade goods'; this personal merchandise belonged to company officials and senior merchants indulging in private enterprise. The *Geldermalsen* departed Canton on 18 December 1751 bound for Amsterdam.

On Monday, 3 January she was sixteen days out from Canton, the weather was clear and fine with a slight northerly wind. At 4 pm the Captain came on deck to consult the boatswain (Christoffel Van Dijk) and the Third Watch. They were concerned as to the ship's position with regard to the Geldrias Reefs; the boatswain reported that these very reefs had to be passed to the northwest and Captain Morel then ordered a change of course to south. No land was in sight and the sea was calm. Three-and-a-half hours later, at sunset, the helmsman saw surf ahead. It was too late to steer the laden ship away; she crashed on to the reef. Morel gave orders to slacken the mizzen sheet and to haul in the mainsheet and the starboard sheets; the ship loosened herself from the reef but, in the confusion, she drifted back and broke her rudder. She was badly holed and taking on water rapidly, the pumps were unable to stop the rising water. Captain Morel ordered the longboat and the barge to be lowered. A statement made later to Company directors by the boatswain said that, in the darkness and confusion, the boats drifted away from the ship. Only twenty men were able to board the barge with twelve more survivors reaching the longboat. The *Geldermalsen* capsized and sank in 25 fathoms. Ten days later the two boats with thirty-two survivors reached the island of Edam; the following day they arrived at Batavia.

Mike Hatcher and Max De Rham

Mike Hatcher was born in York, England and spent his childhood in a Dr Barnardo's orphanage. At thirteen he was sent to farm school in Australia's outback and, in his early twenties, he left farming and worked in Sydney, building swimming pools. Hatcher joined a surf club and was active in scuba diving and yacht racing; by the age of twenty-seven he had saved enough money to buy his own boat with plans to sail around the world. He sailed as far as Singapore where he started working in underwater salvage recovering scrap metal and cargo from sunken Second World War wrecks. In the early 1970s he bought another boat and began to work for himself, salvaging the odd wreck here and there.

Max De Rham studied marine geophysics at Lausanne University. After graduating he joined a French oil company. Unhappy in his work, he decided to start his own business in marine engineering and surveying, working out of Singapore. By 1971 he was well established in the fields of undersea mineral exploration and oceanographic diving.

Hatcher and De Rham first met in the 1970s, but it was not until early in 1985 that they formed a business partnership. Hatcher had the boat and salvage experience and De Rham the equipment and survey knowledge.

In Singapore they met Henri Bescancon, a Dutch ex-naval officer and historian, who proposed a search for the *Geldermalsen*. In his research Bescancon was convinced that the eighteenth-century records were inaccurate and that there was confusion over the name of the reefs where the *Geldermalsen* was thought to be located. Bescancon believed the most likely location of the wreck was on the Admiral Stellingwerf Reef. The reef takes its name from a Dutch ship which was wrecked there in the nineteenth century. Ships sailing from China to Europe sailed south and turned northwest into the Straits of Malacca.

In March 1983 Hatcher sailed from Singapore for the Admiral Stellingwerf reef in the converted trawler, the *Restless M.* After many months of searching and diving, Hatcher discovered a seventeenth-century Chinese trading junk in 130 feet of water. Excavating the wreck for the next two years, Hatcher recovered over 25,000 pieces of Ming porcelain, which was sold at Christie's, Amsterdam in two auctions for a total of over £1,500,000.

After salvaging the Chinese junk Hatcher and De Rham began to search for the *Geldermalsen* in February 1985. Using a sidescan sonar and a magneto-meter, they picked up an interesting anomaly on the sonar at 130 feet below sea level. Two divers were sent down and located a large anchor and a number of cannons; digging around the cannons the divers found a Ming porcelain coffee cup. The *Restless M.* returned to Singapore for supplies and for Hatcher and De Rham to organize salvage operations. Returning to the site in May 1985 with additional divers and a modern equipped support barge, the *Costay Nile*, the divers began to search the area, clearing away sand and coral with an airlift. They exposed ship's timbers and nineteen cannons. About 9 feet of the hull remained and the basic outline of the ship could be measured. Using the airlift inside the hull section, the divers located broken wooden chests filled with a variety of porcelain, plates, tea pots, bowls and mugs in large quantities. Chests upon chests, filled with blue and white Ming porce-lain (most of it in perfect condition), were loaded into buckets and brought to the surface.

At the centre of the wreck the divers found the 'private trade goods' lost by the officials and wealthy passengers. These crates were found to contain the more expensive and individual pieces of porcelain. By 22 June 170,000 perfect pieces of porcelain had been brought to the surface. On the last few days of diving it was agreed that the final excavation should be made outside the hull. Using the airlift two divers discovered the *Geldermalsen*'s consign-ment of gold bars. These gold ingots were of two types 'shoes' or cup shaped ingots which symbolized wealth and small rectangular ingots, 4 inches long. Of the 147 gold bars 126 were recovered.[2] It was only when the divers found the ship's bell, and – the final clue – the surgeon's seal with the initials 'F.B.' for Frederick Beckenhouwer, that the wreck was formally identified as that of the *Geldermalsen*. On 28 April 1986 Christie's saleroom in Amsterdam sold

160,000 pieces of porcelain in 2746 lots for over £10 million ($15 million), a magnificent find known as the 'Nanking Cargo'. Somewhere on Admiral Stellingwerf Reef lie twenty-one remaining gold bars valued at about £500,000 ($750,000).

FAVORITE

The Favorite *was a 96-ton schooner built in 1849. She was 84-foot long and had a beam of 19 feet. Thomas Chowne of Melbourne was part owner, along with Thomas Steriker who was also her captain. She had a crew of eight.*

   AREA: *Possibly wrecked near Cape Liptrap, southeast of Melbourne, Australia, Bass Strait.*

The *Favorite* departed Port Philip, Melbourne, bound for Sydney on 9 May 1852. She had thirteen passengers and a consignment of 2000 oz of gold, 'besides a large amount belonging to Captain Kersopp, Mr. Smith and Mr.

The *Favorite*, a 96-ton schooner lost on a voyage between Melbourne and Sydney in 1852, carrying over 2000 oz of gold

Pepper'.[1] The proposed journey was approximately 450 miles. She was last seen by the *Randol* on 15 June and by two other ships on the 17th. Her reported position was west of Cape Howe. As she was seen carrying reduced sail and making poor headway it was assumed that she had been damaged by bad weather. The *Favorite* was never seen again. 'The government sent out a steamer, the *Acheron* in a search for her as many circumstances warrent (sic) a belief that she was driven ashore on Ninety Mile Beach. During our passage a careful lookout has been kept and I am perfectly convinced that had any vessel been lost on the beach, no vestige would have remained on account of the heavy surf breaking on the beach.'[2]

A year later it was reported in the *Melbourne Argus*: 'A seaman belonging to the *Duke of Wellington*, recently wrecked near Cape Liptrap, reports having seen a head-board, carved with the name 'Favorite' in gilt letters on a blue banner, in the possession of some settlers about three miles from the wreck, who report having picked it up with a portion of kaurie deck ten months ago.'[3]

No other information is available.

GENERAL GRANT

The General Grant *was built in 1864 on the Kennebec River, Bath, Maine, USA. She was named in honour of Ulysses S. Grant, then Commander of the Union Army, who was to become President of the United States after the Civil War.* General Grant *was described by the American Lloyd's register as a 'class A-1 ship: well built of oak, fastened with copper bolts and nails below the water-line; iron-fastened above'. She was triple-masted with an overall length of 179 feet. Her registered weight was 1103 tons.*

AREA: *Sank in a cliff cavern off Beerocks on the west coast of Auckland Islands, 350 miles south of New Zealand, Pacific.*

The *General Grant* was sold to the Australian Shipping Line Company in 1865 and sailed from Boston to Melbourne for service between Liverpool and Melbourne. She arrived in Australia in March 1866 to begin transporting cargoes of general merchandise.

On 1 May Captain Henry Loughlin supervised the loading of a cargo of wool, skins, leather and general cargo bound for Liverpool. Special attention was given to 'two boxes containing (2,576 ounces 6dwt) and nine tons of spelter (crude zinc)'.[1] The ship also took on extra cargo that had been bound for Liverpool aboard another ship, the *London*, which had sunk in the early spring in the Bay of Biscay with great loss of life. It was reported by the Melbourne Bank of New South Wales that 9000 ounces of gold destined for the *London* could possibly have been transferred to the *General Grant*, but no firm evidence of this transaction supports this report. The *General Grant* left Melbourne on 3 May carrying a crew of twenty-four and fifty-six passengers, many of whom were gold miners returning home from the Victoria gold fields carrying their own personal fortunes. The ship passed Port Phillip and turned into the Southern Ocean, heading east, taking the Great Circle Route then making south to catch the prevailing westerlies. The *General Grant* passed New Zealand and the Auckland Islands with her course set for Cape Horn.

During the first week the weather was fine with a cold westerly. The glass began to fall on 11 May and the wind veered southwest, bringing with it thick patches of fog. For the following two days, Captain Loughlin was unable to check his position. He doubled the lookouts. On 13 May at 10pm land was sighted off the port bow. Loughlin, thinking that the land was the most northerly group of the Auckland Islands, immediately tacked to the north. This was to prove a grave error, for the land was actually Disappointment Island lying to the west of the Aucklands. By 11pm the wind had dropped to a dead calm; the lookout again sighted land three to four miles eastward. The captain ordered more sail and the crew stood by as the *General Grant* began to drift. To catch what little wind there was, every sail was vainly set, 'anything which might catch a wisp of wind and give some grip to the rudder ... a breeze, though ever so slight, might save the ship and allow her to run between the islands'.[2]

But the tide and currents took the ship slowly towards the towering cliffs and jagged rocks of the main island. An attempt was made to anchor the ship, but no bottom could be found. At 1am on the morning of 14 May the ship swung into an eddy and struck the rocks with such force that her rudder was shattered. The spanker boom broke, fell to the deck and crushed the helmsman. As the ship scraped along the rock face, the cliffs gave way to a narrow cavern-like cove. The swell of the sea pushed the ship into the cavern entrance; her foremast broke; her remaining spars came down along with her rigging; the mast struck the roof of the cavern, rock debris and rubble crashed down on to the upper deck and the starboard deck house. By dawn the sea swell had increased and the ship was battered against the serrated rocks. The hull was further ground against the rocky cavern face; with the sea washing over the remaining decks, the ship slowly sank.

The *General Grant* carried one longboat and two quarterboats, insufficient for eighty passengers and crew. Forty passengers squeezed into the longboat, but the swells caught the tiny vessel and she capsized. Three surviving passengers managed to reach the quarterboat. Billy Sanguilly, one of the crew, later recorded:

> The scene at this moment was one of such misery as few men ever see, and fewer still survive to tell of. Every sea washed over the stern and swept the deck. The longboat was crammed with all who could gain a foothold. It was partly filled with water and several poor creatures lying in the bilge were crowded down and drowned before she was clear of the ship. Women clinging to their children and crazy men to their gold, were seen washing to and fro as the water invaded the upper decks of the General Grant.
>
> One wretch saw his wife and two children driven by him in this way without making an effort to save them, whilst the last man who got aboard the longboat nearly lost his life trying to persuade the mother to be saved without her children. . . . I found myself suddenly struggling in the water for life, diving beneath the struggling crowd I swam as far as I could under water, and on coming to the surface found myself free to make my way to the other boats. Only three of forty-odd were able to reach them. The rest struggled for a few moments, and all was over.[3]

As the *General Grant* went down sixty-five persons drowned. Many of the gold miners wrapped their gold dust and nuggets in makeshift bags tied round their waists; the weight of their treasures only hastened their drowning. The women, in the style of the day, wore voluminous skirts and petticoats; these they refused to remove. The sea water saturated the fabric and the unfortunate women were sucked down by the great weight of their soaked skirts. The final survivors numbered fifteen, in two small quarterboats. There was one woman amongst the lot. Captain Loughlin went down with his ship.

As the two boats fled the cavern, the steep rock cliffs of the island, stretching forbiddingly north and south, were seen to offer neither landfall nor shelter. It was agreed that the boats should make for Disappointment Island, some fifteen miles to the northwest. After twelve hours of rowing they were exhausted and decided to stop at a rocky islet and to rest overnight. The following morning the sea was calm and they rowed around the northern tip of the main islands towards landfall at Sarah's Bosom, named after *Sarah,* the ship belonging to the island's 1806 discoverer, Captain Abraham. This was Auckland Island.

The survivors managed to construct shelters from brushwood and grass. Seals and seabirds were plentiful and provided fresh meat. One of the crew had a few matches; only one match proved to be dry enough to ignite tinder. Once the castaways had eaten hot food they felt better about their chances of survival. After a few months Bartholomew Brown, Chief Officer of the *General Grant*, decided to attempt to reach New Zealand, a 300-mile sail to the north. He took three other men with him and they sailed away, provisioned with smoked seal meat, birds' eggs, water stored in seals' bladders and powered by sails made from seals' skins. As no navigational instruments or charts were available they knew that they would have to steer by dead-reckoning. On 22 January 1867 the four men left Sarah's Bosom and were never heard from again. Brown had not realized how the prevailing winds, the tides and the currents would all serve to carry their little boat into the empty regions of the Southern Ocean. David Ashworth, one of the survivors, was to write later to one of the lost crew's family telling of their brave departure:

> We were bound together by ties which only those who have suffered together can realise. Our only method of rescue by God's providence lay in the little boat and the four brave-hearted men that volunteered to go in her. The scene is almost beyond description. Your dear brother was quite confident in starting, more than any other, setting an example to all of faith and courage and patience under trial which God in His wisdom had seen fit to place us. . . . We were a few ragged, helpless creatures, the remnants of a fine ship's company, with dangers staring us in the face on every side.[4]

As the weeks moved into months the islanders began to suffer from scurvy and David McLelland, the oldest seaman and a former rigger, cut his hand and died of the resulting blood poisoning. On 21 November 1867 a sail was sighted and signal fires were lit. Captain Gilroy of the *Amherst*, on his first voyage to the Auckland Islands was searching for an anchorage. He was seal hunting and discovered the ten remaining survivors. It was eighteen months after the sinking of the *General Grant*.

James Teer

James Teer was one of the ten survivors. Born in Ireland in 1827, he was an adventurer with a strong mind and a strong body, and had spent twenty years in the goldfields of New Zealand and Australia with little success. When the *Amherst* picked up Teer and his companions they were taken to Invercargill on New Zealand's South Island. It was here that they all recovered and then went their separate ways. A few months after his rescue Teer described the area, where the *General Grant* was lost, as 'forming a deep indentation in the cliffs . . . about 300 yards wide at the mouth, then gradually slopes until it forms a large cavern underneath the cliffs . . . where the ship entered the sides are perpendicular. The bows of the vessel only entered the cave, but the rocks overhung the vessel's stern high enough to keep clear of the mizzen topmasthead. She was in that state when she went down . . . distance of some eight miles.'[5]

James Teer chartered a steam tug, *Southland*, commanded by Captain Kirkpatrick. Teer's plan was to return to the cavern with the hope of salvaging the *General Grant's* gold. *Southland* located the cavern and Kirkpatrick noted in his log:

> *Sunday, March 29*: At 11am the steamer was abreast of the place indicated by Mr. Teer as where the General Grant was wrecked. The lifeboat was got out and Mr. Putwain, the diver, and Mr. Teer made an attempt to reach the spot, but owing to the heavy seas running and the wind increasing, they did not succeed. The boat was taken on board and the steamer put astern on to the shore and backed slowly and carefully, taking soundings as she approached the shore, the water gradually shoaling from 25 fathoms to 15 fathoms (which was the least water obtained). The steamer being about 40 yards from the rocks and 200 yards from where the vessel sank, and as the rebound of the waves against the rocks began to wash over the stern, it was not deemed prudent to venture any further in.[6]

No sign of the wreck was visible, the weather continued to be stormy and further investigation of the cavern was abandoned.

Captain Wallace and David Ashworth

In 1870 Captain Wallace of the 48-ton schooner, *Daphne*, approached David Ashworth, one of the survivors, to accompany him in a search for the *General Grant* and to salvage her gold. Ashworth agreed and the *Daphne* sailed to Invercargill where they picked up extra crew and continued to Port Ross where they set up a base camp. Wallace and Ashworth decided to take a 28-foot whaleboat (with provisions and a crew of six) to inspect the cavern where the ship had been wrecked. As the days passed the three men remaining at base

camp became concerned and set out to search along the rugged and inhospitable coastline but found no sign of their companions. Five weeks later they
returned to Invercargill. Two ships, including the *Daphne*, were sent to investigate Ashworth's and Wallace's disappearance, but no trace of the men or their
whaleboat was ever discovered.

Cornelius Drew

An Australian syndicate involving a third survivor, Cornelius Drew, was
mounted in 1876. This third salvage attempt was aided by the 130-ton
schooner, *Flora*. Although well financed and equipped this expedition was
completely unsuccessful and found no evidence of the wreck.

Captain McConville

In July 1877 Captain McConville set out from Invercargill in the 47-ton
schooner, *Gazelle*, with a crew of six and G. Sherwill, a professional diver. The
expedition based its camp to the south of the island with the intention of
offsetting the costs of the expedition with a bit of sealing. Bearings were taken
from Disappointment Island and Sherwill was able to make several trips to
the cavern with the steward. He describes one visit: '. . . there is no trace of
the wreck in the cave, as the two men and myself saw the bottom as clear as
day. It is a rough, stony bottom where a ship would not last 24 hours in a
gale of wind. The walls of the cave are about perpendicular at the entrance,
and about 152 feet high by 64 feet wide for a distance of about 100 feet or
more in, and then they close in to about 26 feet wide by 70 feet high. After
this they open out to a great extent.'[7]

Sherwill was bitterly disillusioned and wrote: 'Some people may say I write
these lines because I am a disappointed man in not getting the gold out of
the *General Grant* . . . but let me tell them that the ship *General Grant* never was
looked for excepting the first time we went on the coast when the steward,
Jim White, and myself left the steamer in the whaleboat to sound for the
wreck . . . the other boat went ashore to catch seals.'

The *Gazelle* departed the island in November with a large number of seal
skins.

A number of further attempts were made in the area of the wreck. In 1911
Captain Sonerson formed a syndicate with a capital of $100,000 which came

to nothing. In 1915 Captain Catling explored the cavern in his vessel *Enterprise*. He wrote:

> The only indication of a wreck I could find in the cavern was two pieces of timber jammed fast beneath some large boulders. The rest of the wreck had completely disappeared. ... I have no doubt whatsoever that the seas which come in with the north west gales would in a short time smash any vessel into fragments. I closely examined the bottom of the cavern, searching in between the crevices for any sign of gold. If the *General Grant* gold was not in dust but in bars, I am satisfied it must still have been there – that is, if it had not been recovered by someone else.[8]

Bill Havens received a permit from the New Zealand government in 1954 to salvage the gold in his vessel, *Absit Amen* (let no evil befall), but he never sailed to the island. On 31 December 1959 his licence expired. Kevin Tarlton, one of the divers who salvaged gold and silver from the SS *Elingamite* searched the wreck site and reported:

> We have searched the cave very thoroughly and all the surrounding area within half a mile ... plus every other cave to the north and south, and did not find a single nail or other trace of the *General Grant*. We went on our 96 foot steel twin motor boat the *Hamutana*. The weather was bad but not unworkable with aqualung gear. The bottom of the cave is loose rock, but I am sure that if that is where the *Grant* went we would have found some trace – unless she drifted out in one piece again. We found a 150 pound anchor outside and to one side of the cave which we think was probably from a previous salvage attempt. Anyway, we had no joy.[9]

ADMIRAL NAKHIMOV

The Admiral Nakhimov was a heavily armed Russian cruiser of 8524 tons, built in 1888. She was a unit of the second division of the Baltic Fleet, officially known as the Second Pacific Squadron.

AREA: Torpedoed off the Island of Tsushima in the Korea Strait. She was badly crippled and sank later when the Captain ordered her sea-valves opened.

During the nineteenth century Tsarist Russia began to expand its empire into the Far East. In 1891 Russia started construction of the Trans-Siberian railway, connecting Moscow with Vladivostock, the Russian port on the Sea of Japan. The Tsar signed a treaty with China in 1896, allowing Russia to build the Chinese eastern railway and to construct the naval base at Lushun (Port Arthur).

These Russian moves and influences caused the Japanese to break off diplomatic relations on 6 February 1904. On 8 February the Japanese fleet attacked a number of Russian ships at Lushun, and war was declared on 10 February.

The Russian Admirals sent the Baltic Fleet, consisting of thirty-eight ships including the cruiser *Admiral Nakhimov* under the command of Vice-Admiral Sinoh Rozhestvenski, to Vladivostock. When the cruiser left European waters she was believed to have carried on board over $50,000,000 in British gold sovereigns.[1] On entering Japanese waters at the Straits of Tsushima, the Russian ships were attacked by the Japanese Fleet under Vice-Admiral Heihachiro Togo and were severely defeated.

The *Admiral Nakhimov*, commanded by Rear-Admiral Nebogatoff, was badly damaged and her speed had to be reduced. During the night she was attacked by a Japanese destroyer and was hit by a torpedo on her starboard side. Collision mats were placed over the hole but, by daybreak, she had begun to sink. Captain Nebogatoff ordered her sea-valves to be opened to hasten her end. Her crew was rescued by the Japanese destroyer, *Shiranui* and the cruiser *Sado Maru*. In a report published by the New York-World-Telegram, it states: 'May 28, 1905 – Russian battle cruiser, *Admiral Nachimov* (*Nakhimoff*), sank in fight with Japan's fleet in Bay of Tsushima; loss of life unknown. The vessel carried $53,000,000 in gold.'[2]

Shintiki Deep Diving Research Institute

Professor Akiyuki Susuki, President of the Shintiki Deep Diving Research Institute of Japan, started diving to the *Admiral Nakhimov* in 1938. Diving operations were stopped during the Second World War but started again in late 1953.

In the Institute's prospectus it states:

Effective diving operations commenced during the summer of 1954, and have been concentrated in cutting away the third deck in the after part of the vessel, the first and second decks having been cut away during the previous year's operations. ... The vessel lies just over 300 feet below the

The Russo-Japanese war began when Japan launched a surprise attack on Russian forces at Port Arthur (Lushun) on 8 February 1904. The *Admiral Nakhimov* was badly damaged at the Battle of Tsushima Straits (pictured above) in which the Russian Baltic fleet was heavily defeated

surface at an angle of about 50 degrees to starboard on a generally even longitudinal keel, in open water where fast currents are wont to run. . . . While the two upper decks were lighter construction made of iron and easier to cut, the third deck is of semi-armoured steel which is very difficult to cut, particularly at these depths. Mr Susuki's divers, with the exception of two helmet divers, are skin divers who wear a mask with a simple air supply. They remain on the bottom for a maximum of about four minutes. Most of the demolition is done by planting fairly small charges of explosives, the size of which has been increased during the year at the recommendation of the company's observers. Because of the condition of the vessel, the use of large charges of explosives is precluded. Qualified American divers engaged by the company . . . to observe and report were impressed with the work being done by the Japanese divers and with the efforts being made . . .

During the 1954 season . . . a passage had been blasted up to about four feet from the base of the after gun turret. . . . It is hoped that the treasure is located in the magazine situated below the after turret.[3]

It seems salvage operations were discontinued due to lack of financial support.

Nippon Marine Development

In 1980, Mr Ryoichi Sasakawa, President of the Japan Shipbuilding Foundation and wealthy businessman, financed the salvage company, Nippon Marine Development. Its main project was to recover the treasure which the *Admiral Nakhimov* was thought to be carrying. This consisted of '5,500 boxes of gold coins, 48 gold ingots and 16 platinum ingots'.[4] The total value was estimated to be between '20 to 32 million pounds'.

Three rumours circulated concerning the treasure:

1. That the Admiral Nakhimov was the pay-master mother ship of the Baltic Fleet and that it used its stores of gold and other precious metals to pay for provisions when the fleet was in distant waters.
2. The cruiser was loaded with gold towards the development of the military port of Vladivostock into an ice-free port.
3. The Czarist government had sent out a high treasure trove out of the country for imperial refugees, as the country had become fearful of its downfall.[5]

On hearing of the Japanese attempt to recover the treasure the Russians publicly stated that salvage attempts by Mr Sasakawa were 'illegal' and formally filed an ownership claim to the wreck. On 23 October *The Times* reported that 'A Japanese official, Mr Nago Hyodo, on Monday told Mr Georgi Komarovski, a Soviet diplomat, that under international law, captured enemy warships and their contents remain the property of the victor.'[6]

In reply to Mr Hyodo's statement, the news agency Tass put forward the following arguments, repeated by the Soviet Embassy in Tokyo, which were rejected by the Japanese:

That the ship did not surrender to the enemy, but was sunk at its commander's order. All the markings showed it belonged to the Russian navy.

Japan's attempt to consider the ship a war trophy was 'not only illegal but contradicts common sense', Tass said.

The cruiser *Admiral Nakhimov* was not captured by the Japanese navy and could not be considered a trophy ... 'It is not the practice of sea powers to connive in the plunder of property aboard a sunken warship of another state.'[7]

The Japanese Government and the Nippon Marine Development Company brushed aside Soviet objections and sent out the salvage barge *Ten Oh* (Heavenly Response) to search for the *Admiral Nakhimov*. After months of searching the *Ten Oh* located the cruiser at a depth of 310 feet, resting at an angle of 80 degrees from the seabed, three miles off Tsushima island.

At a news conference on 17 September 1981 Mr Tamanai, President of the salvage company, held up a 22-lb platinum ingot with Cyrillic characters; he stated that the first platinum ingot was found in the officers' quarters, but the bulk of the treasure was stored in the strongroom.

According to Mr Sasakawa: 'At the present rate of salvaging, it will take another eight years to raise the rest of the fortune.'[8]

NIAGARA

The Niagara *was built in Scotland by John Brown & Co. in 1913 and was the first large passenger liner to use fuel oil as certified by the Board of Trade. She was 13,415 gross tons, 543 feet in length and had a beam of 66 feet, her speed was seventeen knots and she had accommodation for 701 passengers. The first owners, Union Steamship Company, sold her in 1932 to the Canadian Australasian Line for service between Sydney and Vancouver.*

AREA: *Ran into a German minefield and sank in Hauraki Gulf about 100 miles from Auckland, New Zealand, Pacific.*

At the beginning of the Second World War, Australia and New Zealand, as Commonwealth countries, sent troops and supplies to aid Britain in the war effort. The Germans were quick to realize the importance of this supply-line, and the German minelayer, *Orion*, laid over 150 mines in the Hauraki Gulf of North Island, New Zealand, in an effort to stop the convoys.

In May 1940, the *Niagara* sailed from Sydney to Vancouver, via Auckland, carrying 148 passengers and a crew of 203. At Sydney, Captain Martin signed a receipt for a secret consignment of gold bullion that had arrived from Johannesburg. This consignment consisted of 590 gold ingots packed in 295 pine boxes with a total weight of over 8 tons, valued at £2,500,000.[1] The gold was stored in the strongroom on D deck.

Officially the gold was bound for New Zealand but, in reality, it was being sent from South Africa by Great Britain to the United States as payment for pre-lendlease contracts for vital war materials.[2]

On 18 June 1940 the *Niagara* departed Waitemata Harbour. She sailed down the Gulf of Hauraki and passed the Maro Tiri light. On the morning of the 19th at 3.45am, cruising at seventeen knots, the *Niagara* ran into a German mine. The impact of the explosion was in the No. 2 hold, forward of the bridge; as the ship quickly began to list to port Captain Martin sent out an SOS and gave orders to abandon ship. Lifeboats were launched and all passengers and crew were later successfully picked up by rescue boats from Whangarei. By 4.45am the list had increased to 25 degrees and the foredeck was awash. The captain accepted that the *Niagara* was sinking and he, along with the remainder of the crew, abandoned ship. At 5.30am she slipped bow first below the surface and rested on the seabed at a depth of 438 feet.

United Salvage Syndicate

When the loss of the *Niagara* became known the British Government and the Bank of England approached the Admiralty to salvage the gold; there was neither ship nor manpower available.

In Melbourne, the Bank of England discreetly contracted four Australian companies: Macdonald Hamilton & Co., Gibbs Bright & Co., William Crosby & Co., and United Salvage Proprietary, Ltd of Melbourne;[3] they formed a consortium under the United Salvage Syndicate.

P. Williams was to be captain of the salvage vessel and in charge of salvage operations, and J. Johnstone was chief diver along with his brother, William.

In October 1940 Captain Williams visited New Zealand to supervise the refitting of a 118-ton, forty-year-old Scottish coastal steamer, the *Claymore*. She had been used in 1908 to salvage specie from the *SS Elingamite* sunk off Northland, New Zealand, in 1903. By December, *Claymore* was declared seaworthy and equipped with powerful winches, derricks, an explosive store and diving apparatus. An improved diving bell, based on a design used in salvaging *Egypt* (1922) by the Sorima Salvage Company, 'a great improvement on the bell used by the Italians',[4] was to be employed in the operation. An Australian consulting engineer, David Isaacs, made the modifications and the new bell was manufactured by Thompson Castlemaine Ltd:

> The bell looks like something imagined by Jules Verne, though really it is no more than a huge domed cylinder in which one man can stand in comfort and

two just squeeze. In the dome are fourteen circular windows of quartz glass, some for observation and others on top to admit light. Designed by David Isaacs, a consulting engineer in Melbourne, it stands nine feet six inches high, and weighs nearly three tons. It is made of specially cast manganese bronze and mild steel, strong enough to resist a pressure of 350-pounds to the square inch at 750 feet. We will enter through a circular hole in the dome over which a lid will then be clamped by four large holding-down bolts. The idea is that the diver, wearing a shock helmet, oxygen mask, telephone headpiece and the warmest clothing he can lay hands on, will enter the bell in the hold As soon as the lid has been fastened down the bell will be hoisted by a steel holding wire wound by a winch (also in the hold), and swung over the side. There's nothing much to it in theory, but we can't help wondering how it will all work out in practice.[5]

Although there was no record of the actual position of the *Niagara* when she was mined, it was decided to concentrate on an area of nine square miles, 112 miles northwest off Auckland and about twenty-two miles east of Whangarei. *Claymore* left Whangarei in early 1941 accompanied by a small support ship, the *Betsey*. They trawled the seabed 'with a 1¼ inch trawl wire that was kept down on the bottom by two otter boards angled fan wise from the stern of the two vessels. Starting from a given point they moved out from it in spreading concentric circles at three knots, each sweep clearing a lane five hundred feet wide.'[6]

During this process several German mines were snagged, causing a serious risk to the ships.

On 31 January 1941 (Lat. 36°S/Long.175°E) the cable hooked on to a massive object; engines were stopped and a marker buoy was placed over the position. Two days later Jack Johnstone was lowered, in the diving bell, to 70 fathoms. His brother, William, kept a diary, recording Jack's impressions:

Here and there I could see vague objects on the sea-bed, but it was too soupy to make out what they were. I was thinking all the time of mine-anchors and wasn't game to ask the skipper to move me over towards them. The bell was suspended about ten feet from the bottom and was moving slowly with the drift of the Claymore. Intent on what was below me, I did not see the wreck till the bell actually collided with it, knocking me off my feet. Then I yelled, 'Up the bell!' for it continued to knock against the hull structure. I passed a porthole. Then more portholes. Them some davits. After that I lost sight of her. But I had seen enough to convince me that we had found the Niagara for sure. I think it was the davits which clinched the matter. They were definitely of the Niagara type.[7]

The *Niagara* was lying on a mud bed at an angle of 75 degrees; the strongroom was on D deck, on the 'high' side of the ship so it was relatively accessible. Even so, three decks had to be blasted with a series of explosive charges. Work began on 5 April and continued until 25 September; 113 gelignite explosions were used, some containing as much as 144 lbs of gelignite in order to penetrate the steel structures of B, C and D decks. A grab was then used to remove the metal debris and, by the time the excavations reached the area of the strongroom, a tapered hole, 60 feet at the top and 9 by 5 feet at the bottom, had been blasted. Small charges were then used to prise open the door and a specially-designed grab (directed by the diver in the bell) was guided into the strongroom to extract the boxes of gold. William Johnstone's diary describes the operations:

> . . . in the afternoon Jack (i.e. Johnno) and I took turns in the bell. Visibility was good for a while, but every time the grab bumped amongst the wreckage it raised a cloud of mud and blacked out our view. We plumbed the bullion room several times with no result. The opening was too small for the grab to go in with its jaws open, as it should, and repeatedly it fouled the doorway. This made it fall over and put it temporarily out of action. My nerves frayed with the strain of watching and waiting and shouting into the telephone. To make matters worse, more and more debris began to slide into the strongroom, burying the gold still deeper. I can see a big job of clearing up ahead of us. But there is always tomorrow.[8]

The following day operations had to be suspended due to poor visibility. Work was resumed the day after. The grab was eventually better managed and brought its first find to the *Claymore*'s deck: 'In a mash of decaying sawdust lay two massive ingots, so shiny they might have come from the mint. Each was about a foot long, four inches broad, an inch and a half thick, and 34 lbs. in weight.'[9]

By mid December the divers had recovered 555 ingots, 277½ boxes of the total amount listed as having been on board the *Niagara*; the remaining thirty-five ingots could not be located. Captain Williams decided to halt the Syndicate's operations.

A secret document, number 340 and sent in code from the Bank of England on 12 December 1941 to the Commonwealth Bank of Australia in Sydney, stated: 'We have read the reports of the salvage operations of S.S. Niagara forwarded with your letter September 30. Since that date Captain Williams has achieved recovery of approximately 94% of the gold. I now learn from your letter No.329 that the operation is finished and the salvage party has returned.'[10]

The salvaging of the gold was of particular political concern to the British Government. The Treasury Department was trying to suppress the circumstances and any publicity surrounding the recovery because the gold had been 'officially' on its way from South Africa to America, not New Zealand. Another secret cablegram was sent to the Reserve Bank of New Zealand on 24 December:

> 1) Whitehall have made arrangements to prevent publication of the Niagara story here and will see that no messages giving the story are cabled abroad. 2) They foresee difficulties in imposing a ban in the U.S.A. as the censorship is not yet properly established. I presume, however that your authorities will prevent any messages being sent to U.S.A.[11]

A British Parliamentary Document states: 'Mr Curtin recently gave details to the press much to the indignation both of the New Zealand Government and ourselves as we thought it a grave mistake to publish anything, at any rate until the gold had safely been moved away from Australia where it now is.'[12]

As news of the recovery appeared in the Australian press a further secret telegram was sent from the New Zealand Government to the Australian Government:

> ... in view of the wide publicity accorded the statement regarding Niagara we have felt obliged to release in New Zealand despite vehement protests by authorities responsible for the disposal of the gold ... It had been generally understood between ourselves, London and Canberra that no publicity was to be given to this incident until the appropriate moment.[13]

The salvage contractors were allowed 2½ per cent: 'The bank got £2,360,000 at a cost, without the 2½ per cent, of £26,700; the salvors got £59,000 and paid 70 per cent of it back in income tax; and out of what remained they had to pay for the whole of their equipment.'[14]

In 1952 the Risdom Beazley Company, out of Southampton, took their salvage ship, *Foremost 17*, and recovered thirty of the remaining ingots; five ingots are still unaccounted for.

EUROPE

Key
1. San Juan de Sicilia
2. Girona
3. Cinque Chagas
4. Lastdrager
5. Kronan
6. De Liefde
7. Slot Ter Hooge
8. Hollandia
9. Lutine
10. Colossus
11. Earl of Abergavenny
12. Royal Charter
13. Lusitania
14. Hampshire
15. Laurentic
16. Egypt
17. Edinburgh

17
Murmansk

NORWAY

SWEDEN

BALTIC SEA

Shetland Islands
6
4
Orkney Islands
14

Hebrides

1

NORTH
SEA

SCOTLAND

15
2
NORTHERN
IRELAND

IRELAND

12
ENGLAND

NETHER-
LANDS

9

13

London
Isles of
Scilly
8
11
10
ENGLISH CHANNEL

16

FRANCE

AZORES
3 ATLANTIC

PORTUGAL

SPAIN

OCEAN

MADEIRA 7

SAN JUAN DE SICILIA

The details of this Spanish galleon are unknown and her name has never been confirmed; she may also have been known as the Duque De Florencia. *She was of the Squadron of Castile, 750 tons, twenty-four guns, and carried 297 soldiers and 136 marines, under the command of Don Diego Manrique'.*[1]

AREA: *Blown up in Stroms Hellier, a narrow inlet in Tobermory Bay on the Isle of Mull, Inner Hebrides, Scotland, Atlantic Ocean.*

On 22 July 1588 the Spanish Armada, consisting of 130 ships carrying 28,000 soldiers and seamen, set sail under the command of the Duke of Medina Sidonia to rendezvous with the Duke of Parma's army at Calais and invade England. Medina Sidonia's instructions were: 'You will sail up the channel as far as Cape Margate, where you will rendezvous with my nephew the Duke of Parma and Piacenza, in order to cover his crossing.'[2]

The English fleet of eighty ships was led by Lord Howard of Effingham, Lord High Admiral of England, who divided his ships into two columns. Sir Francis Drake, his second-in-command, harried the Spanish ships from the rear with Effingham attacking windward of the forward ships. The English ships manoeuvred with greater advantage, hunting stragglers from the slow-moving Armada.

After the sea battle at the Calais Roads, the Armada was defeated and its ships scattered. Medina Sidonia and his remaining ships, unable to return home through the English Channel, fled north round the northern coast of Scotland and south along the west coast of Ireland. Of the 130 ships of the Armada only 'sixty-six returned to Spain'.[3]

In a document in the Archbishop's Library in Lambeth Palace in London, dated 22 September 1588, the Lord Deputy Fitzwilliam writes to Sir Thomas Morris, Sir George Boucher and Sir George Carew:

Whereas the distressed fleet of the Spaniards, by tempest and contrary winds, through the providence of God, have been driven upon this coast and many of them wrecked in several places in the province of Munster, where it is to be thought hath not only been much treasure cast away, now subject to the spoil of the country people, but also great store of ordnance, munitions, armours, and other goods of several kinds, which ought to be

The English navy finally defeated the Spanish Armada in a battle at Gravelines, east
of Calais. The Duke of Medina Sidonia and his surviving ships were forced to
escape by sailing into the North Sea and returned to Spain via the perilous route
round the north coast of Scotland

preserved for and to the use of her Majesty ... we authorise you to make
inquiry both by oaths and otherwise, to take all hulls of ships, stores, treasures, etc., into your hands; and to apprehend and execute all Spaniards
found there of what quality soever. Torture may be used in prosecuting the
inquiry.[4]

Information from Spanish spies in the English Court was communicated
to King Philip: 'A fresh report has just come from Ireland saying that many
ships of the Spanish Armada have been lost on that coast, and that many
persons have been beheaded and others taken prisoner. I send a list of them,
furnished by a friend, which makes me believe what I have hitherto doubted.
The ships lost there, they say, amount to sixteen or more.'[5]

Many of the Spanish ships disappeared without trace around Scotland or
Ireland. The *San Juan De Sicilia*, however, accompanied by a few other galleons,
safely sailed round the north of Scotland and down through the Western Isles.

Badly in need of repairs to her hull, spars and canvas, and unable to keep up with the other ships, she sailed into the Sound of Mull, passed Ardmore Point and anchored in Tobermory Bay. Throughout September the Spaniards repaired the ship as best they could.

The Isle of Mull was the domain of the Clan MacLean of Duart. Lachlan Mclean, Chief of the Clan, sent word to the Scottish Court in Edinburgh informing it of the arrival of a Spanish galleon. The English Ambassador to Scotland reported in a letter to Sir Francis Walsingham, Queen Elizabeth's Secretary of State:

> This 6 weeks on the [west coast] of Scotland a great ship of Spaigne about the Ile of Mula in MacLanes countrie, which thei here report cannot go from thence; those irishe people releave them with victell, but are not able to possess her, for she is well furnished both with shott and men; if there be anie shipes of war in Ireland thei might have a great praie of this ship for she is thought to be verie riche.[6]

Although it has been suggested by numerous writers that the ship carried a considerable quantity of specie, it is doubtful if she was a treasure galleon. However, she did carry a certain amount of gold, silver plate and valuables belonging to the Duke of Medina Sidonia's brother, the Marquis de Vallanueva, and other notable Spaniards.

Don Diego Manrique and his men established a cordial but uneasy relationship with the MacLeans. The Spaniards, not trusting the MacLeans, continued to live in the safety of their cramped conditions on board ship.

On 13 November the English Ambassador in Edinburgh wrote to Walsingham: 'The Spannishe shipe i mencioned in my Last, which was driven by tempest to the west part of Scotland to the Isle called Mula in MacLanes countrie is burnt ... and almost all the men within is consumed with fire; it is thought to be one of the principalle shippes, and some one of great accompt within; for he was alwais, as thei saie, served in sylver.'[7]

In another letter, dated 18 November, written by William Asheby, an English agent to Lord Burghley, Elizabeth's personal advisor, states that the ship was blown up by John Smollet, or Smallet, a spy in the pay of Walsingham: 'A man that has grett trust among the Spagniardes entered the ship and cast into the pow roome a pese of lyntt and so departed within a shortt tyme after the lyntt toke fire ... whither this be true or not I am not sure, but so his Majesty is informed.'[8]

James Mauld

The eighth Earl of Argyll, as Admiral of the Western Isles, had by the King's
authority all legal salvage rights of wrecks on the Western Islands.

In 1660 the Earl was convicted of treason against Charles II and detained
in the Tower of London; he was executed on Tower Green in 1661. The King
now believed that any treasure recovered from the Spanish wreck belonged to
the Crown but he was forced by the Scottish Courts to give the legal right of
salvage to the ninth Earl of Argyll. In 1665 the Earl made an agreement with
James Maulde of Melgund to salvage the wreck at Tobermory. The agreement
stated that

> the hail ornaments and furniture therof, and the hail ammunition, guns,
> gold, silver, metal, goods &c. therein, with power to said James Maulde, his
> dowcars [divers], seamen, craftsmen and others, at their own charges to
> search, recover and intromit the same, and to apply the same to their own
> profit. And, inter alia, the said Earl binds in his work, and that his workmen,
> &c. shall have peaceable living in those parts during their stay, and travel-
> ling through the Highlands and Isles, and shall be free from all robberies,
> thefts &c. so far as the said Earl can prevent the same.[9]

After three months using a primitive diving bell Maulde recovered two brass
cannons and one large iron cannon. He made a visit to England and, in his
absence, the Marquis cancelled the contract and later wrote: 'He wrought only
three months and most of the time was spent mending his bell and sending
for materials he needed.'[10]

The political situation in Scotland forced the Earl to flee to Holland; he
was dispossessed of his property and all rights to the wreck. James, Duke of
York, took over supervision of the salvage operations, offering 50 per cent to
anyone who would salvage the wreck.

Archibald Miller

Archibald Miller, a salvor from Greenock, offered his services to the Duke of
York in 1680. Using his modified diving bell he worked for three years without
any success before giving up activities at Tobermory. In an extract from a deposition by Miller, dated 12 November 1683, he states

> ... the shippe lyes sunck off the shore, about one-fingerstone east, her
> sterne lyes into the shore norwest, and her head to the southwest; she lyes

under ye water at ye deepest nine fatham at a low water and twelve fathom at a full sea on high water. There is no deck upon her except in ye hinder part. In the forepart of ye shippe lyes many great ballast stones and some shot among them, and there I found I silver bell about 4 li (pounds weight); I got within ye shippe at a pretty distance the said gun with other two, all brass, the great gun is eleaven feet length and seaven inches and one fourth part of measure in ye bore; the other two were minions (4-pounders), two slings, all brass. We lifted three anchors, whereof one was eighteen feet of length, the other was fifteen and the third was ten. I lifted the kemp stone (capstan) of curious work, pauled with a spring every inches-end; I cannot tell ye bigness, the thing I found would have been about two feet in the diamiter. I saw something like a coat of armes, but could not reach it, being entangled.[11]

Miller continues:

I saw one paper of Lattin Extractes out of the Spanish records that there were thirty millions of Cash on board the said ship, and it tells it lay under ye Sell of the Gunroome. The Lieftenant of the Ship reports the same to the Earle of Argile I mean the Marques's father & which paper holds good of the Lieftenant's report.[12]

Jacob Rowe

Jacob Rowe, a contemporary and rival of John Lethbridge (pp. 13 and 187), was an engineer and inventor, and patented a diving-engine in 1720. In 1728 Rowe successfully recovered a large amount of treasure from the Dutch ship, *Adelaar*, lost off the Island of Barra, in the Outer Hebrides. John Campbell, the second Earl of Argyll, on hearing of Rowe's success, agreed to finance salvage operations, along with Alexander Mackenzie, Robert Graham and Duncan Forbes, Lord Advocate of Scotland, to recover the Tobermory 'treasure'. Working from his salvage vessel, *Princess Mary*, Rowe began his operations. He later wrote to Robert Graham in October 1729:

Typpermorry. . . . since my Last to You we have been Very Busie . . . at Work and Under ye Ballast of ye Wreck we have discovered a Large Platform Covered with Boards Under which we Discovered a Great Number of Casks and Chists but they being semented hard together we have not as yet been Able to take up a Specimen to prove whether ye Same be Treasures.[13]

Rowe wrote again to Graham in November:

We have had very few opportunities for Diving since my last, but we have
been making as large a progress by way of Dragging or Clearing the Wreck
as if it had been Summer Season, so that in the Spring Season when the
Water is most clear and Fittest for Diving we shall have nothing more to
do than clearing Wood and taking up Guns and Treasure. The Draggs
under the Platform of which I acquainted you in my Last hath broken off
considerable quantities of semented Cakes of Ballast, the under part of
which bears the likely impression of Iron hoops of Casks and Chists, which
I really judge to be Treasure, but by the hardness and smoothness thereof
we have not been able to penetrate the same so far as to take up a Specimen
... But after Breaking a very hard semented crust of Ballast ... we found
what lay under the same to be nothing but shot ... Meeting with a disappointment I made a further Dilligent Search upon the outsides of the
Wreck, being the more Induced so to doe by the Quantities of Crushed
Matters taken up by the Drydges, which did plainly appear to have been
broken off from Casks and Chests, and in Searching on the Said Sides of
the Wreck, the Divers have discovered severall Banks of hard semented
matters that hath been blowen out of the Wreck. We have lately broken off
some crusted matter bearing the impression of hoops from an Iron-bound
Chist, as also the Impressions from a fine-wrought Cabinet, also a Buro,
and likewise the divers have seen the Shape of appearance of Severall Guns.
... proved to be Iorn, being one of her upper Deck Guns on the fore part
of the Ship where she was said to have mounted 24 of that Brank and 66
more of brass which latter are the largest of her Guns and are distinguished
even under water by the different Colour of the Crust that grows thereon
which appears white and on the Iorn red, which former colour appears on
the rest that are now seen. Banks suspected to contain Treasure and have
begun to break the same with our Loaded Steel Dart which in four Days
did effectually perform its office on a heap lying close to the Sternpost of
the Wreck, whereby next week I shall be able to give you an Account of
what it contains, which if of any value I shall immediately send you an
Express.[14]

Three years later the backers became disillusioned with Rowe and his lack
of finds. Mackenzie and the Earl of Argyll withdrew further finance. Rowe
and his men suspended further efforts and he left Tobermory with his diving-
engine to find an easier and more profitable wreck.

Between 1909 and 1950 at least six expeditions were involved in the search and salvage of the galleon: West of Scotland Syndicate, Pieces of Eight Syndicate, Tobermory Galleon Salvage Company, Mull Syndicate, Armada Galleon Salvage Company Ltd, Armada Ltd.

All their efforts offered little proof that they had located the site of the *San Juan De Sicilia* or found any evidence of objects of value.

Royal Navy

In 1950 the Duke of Argyll approached the Admiralty and it was agreed that the Royal Navy would send a team of divers under the Command of Lieutenant R. Parkinson. The understanding was that the Navy divers would locate the galleon and a private company would salvage the wreck.

In April two Navy salvage vessels arrived at Tobermory Bay and the divers began to survey the seabed and establish a search area. The weather proved a major problem, the divers only being able to work twenty days over a period of two months. They only found a leather dagger-sheath and fragments of old oak timbers.

Up to the present time the only finds over the years have been fragments of human bones, cannons, anchors, pewter plates and a few silver pieces-of-eight. But the legend of the treasure of the galleon of Tobermory lives on.

GIRONA

The Girona *was a sixteenth-century Spanish three-masted galleass,[1] probably of between 700 and 800 tons, 150 feet long with both a high stern and bow castle. She had eighteen oars on each side and was pulled by 244 men; she carried 102 sailors, 196 soldiers, sixty-eight volunteers, plus clerics and servants to make a total of 550 men[2] under the command of Fabricio Spinola.*

AREA: *Wrecked on the rocks at Port Na Spaniagh near Lacada Point, about two miles east of Bush River on the coast of County Antrim, Northern Ireland, Atlantic Ocean.*

The Spanish Armada was the largest fleet of ships ever to be assembled by Spain – 130 ships carrying over 28,000 men. Under the command of the Duke of Medina Sidonia the Armada was ordered by Philip to invade England in July 1588.

Since victories are in the hands of God, to give and to take away as he sees fit, and since your cause is so peculiarly His as to assure you of His help and favour, if this is not undeserved by sinfulness, great care must be taken that none is committed in this fleet, and in particular that no blasphemy is uttered, under pain of the most severe punishment to be carried out publicly, in order that the chastisement for having tolerated such blasphemy may not descend upon all. On receipt of my orders, you will leave immediately for the English Channel. You will sail up the Channel as far as Cape Margate, where you will rendezvous with my nephew, the Duke of Parma and Piacenza, in order to cover his crossing.

You will send him regular reports of your progress. You will prearrange certain meeting points in the event of the Armada's being scattered by a storm, say Vigo, Corunna and the Scilly Islands. Once in the Channel you will not seek battle with Drake, unless you find his forces divided and are able to get the weather gauge of him ... rather, you will sail on in good order to your rendezvous with Parma. Do not fail to let every man know that the enemy has the advantage in artillery and with his superior firepower will try to fight at long range. The aim of our men must, on the contrary, be to bring the enemy to close quarters and grapple with him. . . . You will also be sure that following the victory our fleet does not scatter in pursuit of booty ... and you will have to economise as best you can all the money there is in the Armada.

Once the troops carried by the Armada have been landed, they will be entrusted to Don Alonzo de Leiva, my Captain General of the Milanese Light Cavalry, who will command them until the arrival of the Duke, my nephew, to whom he will then turn over his command.

(Done at Madrid, April 1st, 1588, I, the King.)[3]

No ships were actually listed as 'treasure ships' in the Armada; however, many of the large galleons carried gold and silver coins to pay soldiers and seamen. The *Nuestra Del Rosario*, the flagship of Don Pedro De Valdez, who later surrendered to Drake, carried over 50,000 gold and silver coins. The total amount of specie carried by the fleet was estimated to be 600,000 ducats, about £150,000.[4]

One month's pay was paid to the troops before they sailed, with the balance to be paid as the ships departed. 'One pay for the entire Armada ... mariners and soldiers. . . . amounts to 116,000 ducats of ten reals a month two pays to 232,000 ducats. . . . The Paymaster has in his possession 433,878 ducats

A map showing the route of the Spanish Armada 'and the places where several of
the Spanish Ships were destroyed in their return to Spain'. While none of the
Armada ships were listed as treasure ships, the fleet carried large amounts of gold
and silver coins to pay the soldiers and seamen, as well as personal treasures and
gifts with which to bribe the English

of ten reals, which leaves 200,000 to take with you in the Armada. You will
permit no one to touch this sum for any reason whatsoever, but will make
sure that it is taken on board intact.'[5]

Other valuable 'presents' and specie were on board to be used as bribes to
buy English cooperation. Other personal treasures that were carried on board
showed the great wealth and status of the ships' aristocracy.

The Armada left Spain on 28 May 1588 and approached the 'Spanish Sea',
a sixteenth-century Spanish term for the waters at the mouth of the English
Channel.[6]

The Duke of Medina Sidonia, under strict orders from the King to avoid any decisive action, was nevertheless attacked by English ships under the command of Charles Howard of Effingham and Sir Francis Drake as Vice-Admiral. Three battles followed: off Plymouth on 31 July, off Portland Bill on 2 August and off the Isle of Wight on 4 August. Howard and Drake could not break the Armada's defensive formation and, on 6 August, the Armada reached Calais with the English ships anchored to windward. The Duke of Medina Sidonia was in difficulties as the wind and the English prevented retreat to the west.

At midnight on 7 August the English launched eight fire ships which created havoc and confusion among the Spanish ships. The Spanish cut their cables and, with their formation broken, the English were able to sail headlong into the Armada and cause heavy damage to many of the Spanish ships. Medina Sidonia regrouped his ships and the final battle was fought at Gravelines, east of Calais, where the Armada was finally defeated and fled into the North Sea.

Lord Howard and his commanders signed a resolution which stated:

> We whose names are hereunder written have determined and agreed in Council to follow and pursue the Spanish fleet until we have cleared our own coast and brought the Firth [of Forth] west of us: and then to return back again, as well to revictual our ships, which stand in extreme scarcity, as also to guard and defend our coast at home: with further protestation that, if our wants of victuals and munition were supplied, we would pursue them to the furthest that they durst have gone.[7]

Medina Sidonia gathered the remnants of his fleet and held a council of war on his flagship, *San Martin*, where twenty captains were executed for cowardice. The council

> decided on a return to Spain and when Captain Alonso de Benavides and Captain Vasco de Carbajal asked him what the route was like, he replied that there would be no want of intolerable hardship, because to get back to Corunna we would have to pass by England, Scotland, Ireland and the Isles about them, across seven hundred and fifty leagues of wild seas, little known to us. And then he made a test of samples of the biscuit and water he had on board, for everything else was in short supply, and more particularly on his hulk than in the rest of the fleet.[8]

Medina Sidonia gave the final sailing orders to his commanders:

The course that is first to be held is to the north-north-east until you be found under 61 degrees-and-a-half; and then to take great heed lest you fall upon the island of Ireland for the fear of the harm that may happen unto you on that coast. Then parting from those islands, and doubling the Cape in 60 degrees-and-a-half, you shall run west-south-west until you found under 58 degrees, and from thence to the south-west making to the Cape Finisterre and so to procure your entrance to the Groyne (Corunna) or to Ferol or to any other port of the coast of Galicia.[9]

The Spanish ships sailed north, passing the Firth of Forth on 12 August.

We continued our voyage through that sea by Norway, Denmark, Scotland. We sailed as far as the sixty-second parallel, where, in the height of summer, we encountered days so dark, fogs so weird, that our senses were all obliterated. It rained every day, often with downpours that left us sodden. There were chills so cold that they made it seem like Christmas time. No man was willing to go aloft where the pilot was, for all sought a place of shelter. With all this, there was great hunger and great thirst, for our only rations were a pint of water and half a pint of wine and half a pound of putrid biscuit. We were awash with water and it rained down on our heads. Our ship was leaking and we had men dying of thirst. The storms were very violent, for that is a most troubled sea that is always in uproar, and there was no human frame that could endure it. Tempests and heavy seas were so common that scarcely a night went by without wild lurching of the ships. And the nearer we got to home, the worse were the tempests – so much so that many times not I alone but all of us lost all hopes that we would ever see land again. We waited only for the ship to be capsized, for there was one time when the foremast was plunged below the water to two yards depth. Blessed be God who delivered us from such great adversity.[10]

Medina Sidonia tried to keep the remains of his Armada grouped together but, as they neared the north of Scotland, some ships sailed between the Fair Isles and the Orkneys, others sailed north around Shetland. The flagship of Gomez De Medina, *El Gran Grifon*, was wrecked on the Fair Isles. Others simply disappeared without trace. Medina Sidonia wrote:

The wind has lengthened, more favourably, for the west-north-west. But the winds in these parts are so violent and stormy, and tend to prevail from

the south, so that there can be little certainty that the present wind
will last. May Our Lord in his goodness give us fair weather so that
this Armada can reach port soon, for we are running so short of victuals
that if this voyage is much prolonged for our sins, everything will be lost
irremediably.

The ships sailed into the open Atlantic then headed southwest. In the
second week in September severe storms dispersed the ships into small groups,
solitary ships struggled to keep afloat, the Captains forever mindful of Sidonia's
final orders 'to take great heed lest you fall upon the island of Ireland for fear
of the harm that may happen unto you on the coast.'[11]

But desperately short of food and water many of the Captains headed for
the Irish coast. Between 15–28 September twenty-seven ships were wrecked
on the Irish coast.

Many Spanish sailors who survived the wrecks were given refuge and food
but, in contrast, one survivor of a wreck off Sligo was to write: 'Whenever
one of our men set foot on the shore, two hundred savages and other enemies
surrounded him, stripped him naked, ill-treated him and wounded him without
pity. . . . I passed many Spaniards stark naked and shivering with cold . . . there
is neither order nor justice in this country.'[12]

The *Rata Encoronada* (holding over 400 men and commanded by Don Alonso
De Leiva) and the *Duquesa Santa Ana* anchored at Blacksod Bay north of Achill
Island in County Mayo. De Leiva sought supplies and shelter from the local
inhabitants and stationed his men at the castle in Elly Cove. A few weeks later
the *Encoronada* dragged her anchor and ground on the rocks; unable to get off
she was stripped and burned.

De Leiva decided to leave Blacksod Bay for neutral Scotland, where he reckoned his men had a better chance both of survival and of being shipped back
to Spain. 'Don Alonso and all his company were received into the hulk of St
Ann with all the goods they had in the ship of any value, as plate, apparel,
money, jewels, weapons and armour.'[13]

Two days out the *Duquesa* ran into shifting winds and rough seas; seeking
shelter she anchored on the north coast of Ireland at Loughross More Bay
where her cables broke and the currents drove the vessel aground. All the crew
survived and set up camp on the shore. The local chieftain, McSweeney Ne
Doe, welcomed them and told De Leiva that three Spanish ships had landed
at Killybegs a few miles to the south. Three of the Spanish ships coming into
the harbour of the Killibeggs in McSweeny's country, one of them was cast

away a little without the harbour, another running aground on the shore brake
to pieces. The third being a gally, and sore bruised with the seas, was repaired
in the said harbour with some of the planks of the second ship, and planks
of a pinnace which they had of McSweeny.'[14] The third vessel was the *Girona*,
part of Don Hugo De Mocada's four-galleass squadron of Naples.

De Leiva marched his 600 men to Killybegs and joined forces with the
1000 survivors from the *Girona* and the two other ships. In three weeks the
Girona was seaworthy, her rudder repaired, sails stitched and her leaks caulked.

De Leiva intended to sail to Scotland and 1300 men were crammed into
the *Girona*, leaving over 200 men behind. On 26 October the *Girona* departed
Killybegs on the ebb tide and, heading for the open, she turned north.

There is no record of the voyage or whether the *Girona* passed inside or
outside the isolated isle near Malin Head, but she must have been sailing close
to the northern coast of Ireland. The makeshift repairs were not strong enough
to hold her rudder which broke loose from the sternpost. Unable to manoeuvre
to open sea, the *Girona* was driven by wind and tide on to the rocky coast of
County Antrim near Lacada Point.

Robert Stenuit, the Belgian archaeologist who excavated the wreck in the
late sixties, describes the wreck site:

> I watched the waves breaking off Lacada Point, fifty yards to the north-
> west. They catch on a reef there, a submerged mound, rising up in some
> forty feet of water. At low tide, the top of it is only about twelve feet below
> the surface. . . . *Girona* struck the top of the reef, or maybe she just rolled
> over it, caught athwartships by a breaker. As soon as the Spanish realised
> that they were about to go on the rocks they dropped anchor . . . the vessel
> had begun to turn round on herself, but the next moment she was broken
> apart on Lacada Point . . . the after castle broke away from the shattered
> hull and drifted eastwards . . . Another part of the *Girona* was carried along
> the west side of Lacada Point . . . from their the swirling currents drove it
> onto a reef to the west of Spaniard Cave . . . this was almost certainly part
> of the prow, containing the crew's quarters.[15]

On 28 October the *Girona* struck the rock at Lacada Point and washed on
to Port Na Spaniagh. Of the 1300 men only nine survived the ordeal; many
others were battered against the rocks or swept out to sea.

Robert Stenuit

Robert Stenuit and a fellow diver began preliminary investigations of the *Girona* wreck site in June 1967. On the following two diving seasons the divers surveyed the area from the two rock reefs at Port Na Spaniagh to Lacada Point. On the east face of Lacada Point Stenuit found the first piece of evidence of a ship – a lead ballast ingot; during further searches in the area the divers located two cannons, numerous cannon balls, more lead ingots and a copper coin. From the layout of the lead ballast and other ship's artifacts Stenuit believed that the aftercastle broke away from the hull and drifted east of Lacada Point, the prow resting to the west.

Unable to locate more cannons, Stenuit hypothesised that, with the large number of men aboard the *Girona*, the cannons were left behind at Killybegs.

The area around the wreck site is covered in boulders, pebbles and gravel on a rock surface. Crevices and long gullys, covered in kelp and algae, made excavation of the area extremely difficult; however, Stenuit did find a number of valuable items: 405 gold coins, 756 silver coins, gold chains (one of which was 8 feet long and weighed over 64 oz) and forty-five pieces of gold jewellery. Two gold rings were found: one inscribed Madam De Champagney MDXXIII was worn by her grandson, Don Thomas De Perrenoto, who perished on board; the other gold ring was inscribed, 'No Tengo Mas Que Dar Te' (I have nothing more to give thee).

On 22 June 1972 the Northern Ireland National Museum opened the Girona Rooms to house the collection of jewellery and over 12,000 artifacts.

CINQUE CHAGAS

Las Cinque Chagas *(meaning 'five wounds')* was an armed Portuguese merchant's ship of 2000 tons. Approximately 150 feet long and 45 feet wide she carried thirty-two cannons and had a heavily fortified forecastle. Her captain was Francisco De Mello.

AREA: *Southeast of Punta Negra, a few miles off the western tip of Fayal Island, Azores, Atlantic Ocean.*

The *Cinque Chagas*[1] set sail from Goa, India in late 1593, homeward bound for Lisbon with 500 passengers and crew, and carrying a large amount of treasure. Listed on her manifest were oriental pearls, rubies and other precious stones, along with gold ingots, coin and silver ingots. The Venetian Ambassador, Francisco Vendramin wrote: 'She was one of the richest ships ever to have sailed from the East Indies. Her worth was estimated at 2 million ducats.'[2]

Las Cinque Chagas called in at Mozambique, and spent the winter months in Lourenço Marques avoiding the contrary winds and seasonal storms that were so common around the Cape of Good Hope. Before departure she took on an extra consignment of gold and silver; this additional cargo came from the merchant ship *Nazareth* which was beached and in need of repairs to badly leaking seams.

At the beginning of April 1594 the *Cinque Chagas* rounded the Cape and continued to Luanda, Angola, where she picked up 400 slaves (to be sold in Spain) and was provisioned with water and supplies.

A week out of Lunada, many of the crew and passengers became ill with a fever caused by contaminated drinking water. As the days passed more and more people fell ill. The death toll rose as the fatal outbreak spread throughout the ship; hundreds died. In desperation, De Mello changed course and made for the Portuguese colony at Terceira in the Azores.

On 13 June 1594 their position was eighteen miles south of the channel between Fayal and Pico Islands when three English privateering ships sighted the *Cinque Chagas*. Captain Downton of the *Sampson* describes the first engagement:

> The 13 of June we met with a mighty carrack of the East Indies called Las Cinque Chagas or The Five Wounds. The Mayflower[3] was in fight with her before night. I, in the Sampson, fetched her up in the evening, and commanded to give her the broadside, as we term it. At the very first shot she discharged at us, I was shot in a little above the belly, whereby I was made unserviceable for a good while after. Yet by means of an honest truehearted man which I had with me, one Captain Grant, nothing was neglected: until midnight when the admiral came up, the Mayflower and the Sampson never left by turns to ply her with their great ordnance.[4]

The *Mayflower* attempted to board abaft her beam with the *Sampson* attacking her bow, but their efforts were repulsed due to the *Chagas's* high bulwarks, towering poop deck and her firepower. Captain Anthony was killed and the *Sampson* disengaged. The *Sampson* rounded to begin a second attack with the *Royal Exchange* drawing fire from the starboard side. Casualties were heavy on both sides. Captain Cave of the *Royal Exchange* was shot in both legs and died

soon after. The *Sampson* set a mat of inflammable material on fire and landed
it on the *Chagas*'s beakhead. The fire soon spread from the bowsprit to the
topsail yard; flaming spars and canvas fell to the decks below. The main deck
and the forecastle were soon ablaze and the nearby *Sampson* also caught fire.
'Desired to be off from here, but had little hope to obtain our desire; nevertheless we plied water very much to keep our ship well. By God's providence
only, by the burning asunder of our sprit-yard of the carrack, whereby we were
fast intangled, we fell apart, with burning of some of our sails which we had
then on board. The *Exchange* also being farther from fire, afterward was more
easily cleared, and fell off from abaft.'[5]

The *Chagas* burned all through the night and when, in the early morning, the
flames reached the sixty barrels of powder in her hold she blew up.[6]

Those who survived jumped overboard. They were given no quarter by the
English who systematically shot or lanced them from launches. Of over 1000
passengers, crew and slaves who had sailed from Luanda, only thirteen were
to survive.

It was noted on 28 July 1594:

The trouble caused by the English is felt more acutely every day at Lisbon.
A ship, the richest that ever sailed from an East India port, was lost the
other day. . . . This ship, the largest of the four or five that were expected
from the East Indies, and also the best armed, was laden with a cargo worth
upwards of two millions in gold, not only in pepper and drugs, but in a
large quantity of oriental pearls and jewels and other precious goods. . . .
The captain, tempted by greed, took on board four hundred blacks, whom
he intended to sell in Spain. The heat and overcrowding brought on the
plague, of which upwards of five hundred persons died in ten days. Besides
the blacks there were on board three hundred passengers, chiefly Italian and
Portuguese merchants.

After this terrible mortality, the ship began to draw near the Azores, where
she was exposed to the fire of three English corsairs, who followed her up
for two whole days with a heavy cannonade. The English drew close and
managed to board her with twenty-five men, but these were all cut to bits.

Seeing there was no hope of capturing her, as she was now in sight of
the Azores, the English resolved to fire her with Greek fire[7] which was
applied to many parts of the ship at once, and then uniting made a tremendous flame, in the midst of which she went down with crew and cargo, and
not a thing fell into the hands of the English. I hear that the loss among

only four of the merchants amounts to six hundred thousand ducats, and the total reaches two millions.[8]

No record exists giving the precise position of *Las Cinque Chagas* but, accounting for tides and currents, she probably drifted in a westerly direction towards Punta Negra. Somewhere off the western tip of Fayal Island lies the massive treasure that was on board the fated *Cinque Chagas*.

LASTDRAGER

The Lastdrager *(meaning 'loadcarrier' or 'porter') was a Dutch East Indiaman of 640 tons, built in the typical Dutch style of the mid-seventeenth century. She was purchased for the Amsterdam Chamber of the Dutch East India Company in 1648. Her appointed Captain was Jacob Struijck and she carried a crew of 120.*

AREA: *Wrecked in the Shetland Islands on the northeast coast of the island of Yell, near the tip of Cryssa Ness, Scotland, Atlantic Ocean.*

On 28 September 1652 the Heren XVII (the seventeen representatives of the Board of Directors of the Dutch East India Company) decided to send a fleet of seventeen ships to the Dutch East Indies; they were to carry a variety of trade goods and specie. During the Dutch-English war naval hostilities in the English Channel posed a threat to the continued trade of the Company's ships. New routes from Holland to the East Indies were ordered; one of these was a route north around the Shetland Islands and past the west coast of Scotland, avoiding the English Channel and the hostile English ports.

The *Lastdrager* was loaded at Texel with a cargo containing '6 chests of gold and silver, containing 42,000 ducats in gold and 24,000 guilders in money; 300 pieces of Broadcloth; 300 pieces of serge; 40 tuns of brandy; 10 tuns of sack; 10 tuns of French wine; 2 chests of quick silver . . .'.[1] In early November, with 206 passengers and crew, she set sail, accompanied by two other Company ships, the *Diamant* and the *Windhond*. In the Maas Estuary they joined the other fourteen merchantships, commanded by Admiral Tromp aboard the *Brederode*, and, on 6 December, the fleet departed from the Goeree Roadstead.

Three days out a gale blew up and the fleet was dispersed. The *Windhond* was wrecked on a sandbank off Schouwen; the *Diamant* lost her rudder and sank on the Schotse Banken; the *Lastdrager* ran aground and severely damaged her hull – she then returned to Texel for repairs. Work was completed by the

end of December. 'On 23 December Herr Cruijsvoet ... made his report
... and it appearing that the said ship is already so repaired and refitted that,
in the opinion of the captain and officers, she is in a proper condition again
to resume her voyage.'[2]

Twenty of the crew refused to sign back on, claiming that the *Lastdrager* was
unseaworthy. Johanne Camphuijs, a Company bookkeeper, recorded in his
diary: '... The sailors had left the ship and did not want to sail on her anymore
because, so they said, she was not fit and the trip on top of that, was to sail
via Hitland (Shetland). New hands were hired but few of them knew about
the dangerous seas.'[3]

On 9 February *Lastdrager* departed from Texel, accompanied by *Avenhoorn* and
bound for Batavia (Djakarta) in the East Indies. On 13 February two incoming
ships reported sighting the two outward-bound ships under full sail near
Shetland.

Camphuijs gives a horrifying account of the events that took place in
February and March:

'... a favourable wind blew on February 9 ... we sailed so swiftly that on
the 6th day we passed the snow-capped, inhospitable isle of Tairil [Fair Isle]
... but a fierce storm sprang up ... the intense cold and frightful gales
made all inexperienced sailors tumble below deck ... much against our will,
the terrifying tempest took us, all masts bare of sail near the bare isle of
Fero [Faroe Islands] where ... the ship filled with so much water ... and
so heeled ... that we should have perished there and then ... the pilots
who had seen neither sun nor stars for so long ... were so confused in
their esteem that they could not make sense of the chart any more. They
headed one way, then another, hoping to keep away from land until a
favourable wind would push us away from that dark climate, when ... on
March 2 one of the pilots ran aghast, to the aft cabin to tell us we were
but half a mile from the cliffs ... the rudder which had been made fast
for many days was freed, we hoisted our main sail to try and give a wide
berth to this still unidentified land ... but the wind ripped away the canvas
... the rudder pintle gave and we saw one of the helmsmen being thrown
by the whipstaff onto the ship's rails where he lay, bathed in his blood ..
. meanwhile our Lastdrager was pushed on the rocks by the rollers ... the
stern half of the ship was first severed by the seas and taken away from the
bow part that was jammed on the rocks. This happened at dusk as the tide
went down so that the bow half which could not now be attacked with so

much strength by the seas remained some more time on the rocks ... we all congregated in the fore-castle ... the night had fallen ... and as the tide raised again ... the half ship began to float ... and the pounding waves with full strength soon broke it to splinters ... I held on as long as I could to the broken wreckage ... a wave tore me from it ... I held to a beam ... I could hear the screams of the dying ... I was finally thrown onto a rock with my spar.[4]

A letter from the Dutch East India Company to the Governor of the Cape of Good Hope, dated 31 May 1653, stated: 'The Lastdrager is sunk and lost in Hitland, only 26 people were saved as well as some money and a little gold.'[5]

Camphuijs survived the sinking and wrote: 'The inhabitants having learned that such a richly laden ship had been wrecked, came from all places pretexting to help us salvage the goods and so over-loaded their boats with iron works and mercury, that two of them sank to the bottom with nine men, thus chastised by their own cupidity.'[6]

William Irvine

William Irvine, a wrackman (an eighteenth-century term for salvors who salvaged wrecks using hook grabs and dragging cables) and customs officer from Lerwick, agreed with Colonel George Douglas, Admiral of Shetland, that Irvine be allowed free salvage of all wrecks in Shetland. On 2 February 1736 he carried out a salvage attempt on the *Lastdrager*. Irvine stated in his later report to the Admiral: '... My pitiful purchase at Cullavoe of ye: assendragher. ... I have recovered one ducatoon and one sixpence more off the wreck at Cullavoe in the north part of this country lost in the year 1653.'[7]

Robert Stenuit

In the early 1970s a salvage contract was signed between the Dutch Government and Robert Stenuit, a well-known and experienced Belgian diver. He was given exclusive rights to scientific excavation by his sponsor, Henry DeLauze of COMEX, Marseilles, to recover artifacts and anything of value.

Stenuit took five deep-sea divers and began to search on 20 May 1971. The seabed around the wreck site was composed of rock covered with vast quantities of kelp. Deep gullies and holes, coupled with strong currents and tides, made for difficult and dangerous diving conditions. The initial months were spent surveying and charting the area. A few sherds of pottery, glass bottle fragments, copper nails and lead strips (later identified as hull sheeting) were all found over the course of the summer dives. The following year a magnetometer was used and twelve iron cannons and a ton of cannon balls were located. Over 500 Dutch and Spanish silver coins of varying denominations were also recovered as were small concentrations of mercury in the rock hollows and crevices. As the ship had broken amidship, the majority of the finds indicated that the bow section was being dived upon. The stern half, where the treasure would be located, was never found. The bulk of the treasure from the *Lastdrager* still lies unsalvaged off the island of Yell.

KRONAN

The Kronan, *meaning 'crown', was the flagship of the Royal Swedish Fleet and the pride of King Karl XI. She was designed by Francis Sheldon, an Englishman brought to Sweden by the King with the purpose of introducing English naval construction to the Swedes. The* Kronan *was the largest ship of the period, weighing 2350 tons and carrying 126 guns. Her construction took seven years and she was launched in Stockholm during October 1665.*

AREA: *Capsized and sank off the coast of Sweden near the island of Oland, Baltic Sea.*

In 1675 Sweden was at war with both Germany and Holland; the latter was joined by Denmark in an attempt to reclaim her Baltic Provinces that had been seized by Sweden some twenty years earlier. The King appointed Lorentz Creutz as Commander-in-Chief of the thirty-two strong Swedish fleet.

In early 1676 Holland and Denmark sent an allied fleet against Sweden. The Swedes placed their Commander-in-Chief aboard the *Kronan*; under him were 550 battle crew and 300 troops. She left the port of Dalaro ahead of the rest of the fleet. Between the islands of Bornholm and Rugen the enemy fleets met and engaged in battle on 25 and 26 May. Fighting continued on 1 June off the southern tip of Oland.

As the *Kronan* came about to port across a southwesterly wind, having all cannon-ports open in readiness for offensive action, a freak squall caught her and she keeled right over on to her port beam. Before she could take corrective action, water rushed in through the open ports and a massive explosion blew up her powder magazine. She vanished below the surface, taking her crew and soldiers with her.

Anders Franzen

Nearly 300 years later, in 1950, Anders Franzen became interested in the *Kronan*. But it was not until 1979 that he began to search the waters off the eastern tip of Oland. The last battle had taken place a few miles east of the village of Hulterstad where many of the bodies washed ashore.

Franzen took a small team of divers and equipped a research vessel with sidescan sonar, searching an area of thirteen square miles without success. The following year they continued their operations, but moved slightly more to the east of Hulterstad. As they towed the magnetometer over the seabed they noted that, at one particular spot, there was a reading that indicated a large deposit of iron. Lowering a television camera they filmed a mass of shattered ship's timbers and cannons scattered across the seabed. As they dived on the wreck, they realized that only her starboard hull remained above the seabed; the port-side section lay buried in the sand. Over the following dives an abundance of artifacts was brought to the surface. Forty bronze cannons were recovered and 255 gold coins, some very rare specimens, were found and identified. The gold coins were noted as the largest hoard ever found in Sweden.

King Carl XVI, the then King of Sweden, and also the patron of the recovery operation, stated: 'The recovery of *Kronan* off Hulterstad . . . is a major event and one of great significance even far outside the realm of marine archae-ology . . . this work and these fateful human events will remind us . . . despite everything . . . our close contact with times past.'[1]

DE LIEFDE

The De Liefde *(meaning 'Love') was the third ship of that name to be owned by the Dutch East India Company. She was commissioned by the Amsterdam Chamber and built in 1698 with an overall length of 166 feet, a beam of 44 feet, and a capacity of 500 tons. She was armed with forty cannons.* De Liefde *was commanded by Captain Barent Muijkens, there were 200 crew and 100 Company soldiers.*

AREA: *Wrecked on the rocks of Mio Ness, a headland on the Island of Housay, western tip of the Outer Skerries, Shetland Islands, Scotland, North Sea.*

At the end of October, 1711 *De Liefde* sailed from Amsterdam and made her way down the Zuider Zee to Texel in order to pick up her cargo of general goods and an estimated '227,000 to 700,000 guilders'[1] in the form of newly minted gold ducats, silver ducatoon and copper coins. In addition, there was an unspecified amount of gold and silver ingots. *De Liefde* departed Texel on 3 November in the company of two smaller ships, the *Mossell* and the *Kockenge*.[2] The planned route was around the north of Scotland, past the west coast of Ireland to the Cape of Good Hope, then to make for Batavia (Djakarta), calling in at Ceylon. This northern route, known by the Dutch as the 'Achter-Om', was considered the safest passage. During the winter months it was less perilous than beating the contrary winds of the English Channel and avoid the English and French pirates.

On the morning of 8 November a fierce gale blew up, as the ships neared the Shetland Islands, and *De Liefde* was caught sailing too far south.

The precise circumstances of her loss are not known; she went on to the rocks of Mio Ness near the southern tip of the Outer Skerries. Out of 200 crew and 100 soldiers only one seaman survived; he was found wandering and dazed by the islanders on the morning following the shipwreck.

News of the loss of *De Liefde* reached Amsterdam and was duly recorded in the Resolution Book of the Amsterdam Chamber: '. . . From letters we received from Laarwijk [Lerwick] in Hitland [Shetland] on the 17 and 19 December last, we learned that the company's ships which sailed from Texel on the 3 November ran into a bad storm off Hitland, as a result of which one of them, De Liefde, was wrecked by sailing onto a reef named Mioni [Mio Ness] off Uutscheren (Outer Skerries). There was only one survivor, the shipwreck was not far from the shore, and the bow of the ship under water.'[3]

The Dutch East India Company sent two small salvage ships under the command of Luijtje Bontchoe. The *Arent* and the *Otter* arrived at the wreck site in April 1712 but only a few ship's timbers and some of the rigging were found.

Between 1729 and 1735 Captain Jacob Rowe of London had some success by recovering 2160 gold coins. William Irvine, the Lerwick customs officer who attempted the *Lastdrager* salvage in 1736, was also reported to have recovered a few gold coins.

Two hundred years later, in 1964, the minesweeper HMS *Shoulten* anchored off Mio Ness at 'Dregging Geo' (the local name for the wreck site where the islanders would drag the seabed for coins; 'geo' means a narrow rock gully). Navy divers discovered two silver coins and an iron cannon.

Scientific Survey & Location

SSL was a small company which primarily worked in the field of underwater research technology. An agreement was arranged in 1967 between the Dutch Government which owned the wreck, and SSL to excavate the site.

Alan Bax and Owen Gander surveyed a small area that was to become known as 'silver gully'. They cleared tons of boulders and shingle, finding a chest which contained 3300 silver ducatoons, plus a wide variety of everyday artifacts.

Operations ceased and were not resumed until 1978. The main wreck site was shown to be at the Long Gully at 'Dregging Geo' near the entrance to Renelip Sound. This is an area of large rocks covered by kelp, making excavation extremely difficult. Over an area of 40 by 90 feet the divers found 300 silver coins concealed in crevices and fissures. In total, 4000 silver and twenty gold coins were found. It is impossible to estimate just how much of De Liefde's treasure still lies on the seabed around 'Dregging Geo'.

SLOT TER HOOGE

The Slot Ter Hooge *(Castle of Hope) was a 850-ton, thirty-four gun square-rigged merchantship belonging to the Zeeland Chamber of the Dutch East India Company. The ship was commanded by Captain Steven Boghoute with a crew of 254 men.*

AREA: Wrecked during a storm in a small bay called Porto do Guilhermo on the north coast of the island of Porto Santo, near the Madeira Islands, Atlantic Ocean.

The *Slot Ter Hooge* departed on her maiden voyage on 19 November 1724 bound for Batavia (Djakarta): 'There was aboard cooking oil, wine, brandy, foodstuffs and miscellaneous . . . there was also aboard 19 chests, 15 of which containing 100 bars of silver of 4 pounds each, 3 chests of mexicaenen pieces (pieces of eight from Mexico) and one chest containing thirty bags of 100 guilden each.'[1]

Sailing south of the coast of Portugal the *Slot Ter Hooge* encountered a fierce Atlantic gale which drove the ship off course, west towards the Madeira Islands, where she was wrecked on the rocks of the small bay at Porto do Guilhermo with the loss of 221 of her crew.

John Lethbridge

John Lethbridge, the Devon inventor, constructed a diving-engine and completed his first test of it in 1715.

An extract from *Read's Journal* of April 1720 states: 'Last Tuesday, Wednesday & Thursday, Mr Lethbridge of Devonshire, the famous Diver, was let down into the Thames near Whitehall-Stairs, in an Engine & kept under Water half an hour. He took with him Meat & Drink, and had his Dinner under Water; He had also Fire in the Engine, & baked a Cake, bored several Holes in a Piece of Wood, besides other Performances, in a small Quantity of Air, without the use of Air Pipes.'[2]

Lethbridge describes his engine:

> My engine ... constructed by a Cooper in Stanhope Street, London ... of wainscot perfectly round, about six feet in length, about two foot and a half diameter at the head, and about eighteen inches diameter at the foot, and contains about thirty gallons; It is hoop'd with iron hoops without and within to guard against pressure. There are two holes for the arms and a glass about four inches diameter, and an inch and a quarter thick, to look thro', which is fixed in the bottom part, so as to be in a direct line with the eye, two air-holes upon the upper part, into one of which air is conveyed by a pair of bellows, both which are stopt with plugs immediately before going down to the bottom. At the foot part there is a hole to let out water. Sometimes there is a large rope fixed to the back or upper part, by which the people above are directed what to do, and under is a fixed piece of timber as a guard for the glass. I go in with my feet foremost and when my arms are got thro' the holes, then the head is put, which is fastened with screws. It requires 500 weight to sink it and take but 15 pound weight from it and it will buoy upon the surface of the water. I lie straight upon my breast all the time I am in the engine, which hath many times been more than six hours, being frequently refreshed upon the surface by a pair of bellows. I can move it about 12 foot square at the bottom, where I have stayed many times 34 minutes.[3]

Ten years later Lethbridge was a well-known and successful salvage diver.

In a report by the Dutch Consul at Lisbon, who sent the news of the loss of the *Slot Ter Hooge* to the Dutch East India Company, he added: 'I know not how well acquainted the Dutch are with the machines but the English are most certainly capable of fishing all (the treasure) up ... the depth being 10 to 12 fathoms [60 to 72 feet].'[4]

Lethbridge was contracted by the Dutch East India Company in 1725 to salvage the wreck. According to the records, in his first expedition to Porto do Guilhermo Lethbridge recovered 349 silver bars, most of the silver pieces-of-eight and over 9000 Dutch guilders.[5]

On subsequent expeditions to the wreck site, in 1726, 1732, 1733 and on his final expedition in 1734, Lethbridge wrote: 'Came back with less than one could have hoped for, but still with a reasonable success.'[6]

Robert Stenuit

Robert Stenuit, the well-known Belgian diver who salvaged the treasure from the Spanish galleon *Girona* (see p. 177), organized a salvage expedition to recover the remaining silver of the *Slot Ter Hooge*. Stenuit estimated that there still remained between 100 to 250 silver bars with a large number of silver coins still unaccounted for. In 1975, after months of research and with financial backing from the National Geographic Society and support from the French undersea engineering company, COMEX of Marseilles, Stenuit and his team set out for Porto Santo.

During Stenuit's research Rex Cowan, another well-known diver, showed Stenuit a document which illustrated an engraving on a lost silver tankard. On one side of the tankard was an illustration of Lethbridge's boat and his diving-engine suspended below. On the other side was an engraved map of an island with the inscription 'Port Santo Island Lat 33 N Lon 5' the exact location of the wreck. Using inflatable boats Stenuit's divers anchored in 60 feet of clear water in the small bay of Porto do Guilhermo. When surveying the seabed the divers located a large anchor and two iron cannons; the following day, the first silver coin was recovered and identified as a Dutch Dubbelstuiver with the coat of arms of the Zeeland Chamber on the obverse side and, on the reverse side, the word ZEE-LEE-DIA and the date 1724.

In the next five months, using an airlift, the divers found more coins and their first silver bar clearly stamped with the symbol of the Dutch East India Company.

At a depth of 10 feet below the sand the divers found a chest with neatly packed 6 x 2 inch silver bars. Commenting on the silver coins recovered, Stenuit said, 'We found an incredible variety . . . Spanish pieces of eight, Ducatoons, tiny Dubbelstuivers.'[7]

At the end of Stenuit's expedition he estimated that perhaps 100 silver bars were still to be recovered from the wreck.

HOLLANDIA

The Hollandia, of 750 tons, was built in Amsterdam in 1742 for the Amsterdam Chamber of the Dutch East India Company. She carried 195 Company soldiers and passengers, with a crew of 80 commanded by Captain Jan Kelder.

AREA: *The Hollandia was wrecked during a storm when she struck the Gunner Rock in Broad Sound, off St Agnes Island, Isles of Scilly, Atlantic Ocean.*

On 3 July 1743 the *Hollandia* departed Texel on her maiden voyage to Batavia (Djakarta), accompanied by two other ships, her sister ship, the *Overnes*, and the *Den Heuvel*. The *Hollandia* carried '300 Mexican Marks as payment of salary and expenses; value, 796 guilders. Specie for India: twelve chests containing 4,000 Marks Mexican and 8,000 silver ducatoons to hand over to the Governor of Batavia, value 121,712 Guilders, 18 stuivers. Finally, monthly payments on hand for 2/3 of wages, value 4,284 Guilders (for the sailors) and 2,922 guilders for the militiamen.'[1]

On board were a number of important passengers, among them Baron van Imhoff, Governor of the Dutch East Indies, his brother Hendrik Francois and his wife, Mechteld Bentinck, and her sister.

Sailing instructions were given by the Company directors that '... Ships' masters of the summer fleet travelling from the Netherlands to Batavia ... shall firstly sail down the Channel and arrive at Lands End or the Lizard shall set a south-westerly course to latitude 43° in order to bypass Cape Finisterre by 60 miles, except when otherwise ordered in written instructions.'[2]

The three ships sailed into the English Channel. The captain of a homeward-bound Dutch ship on entering the English Channel reported that between 9 July and 13 July he was struck by a severe south-westerly gale. On 13 July at 6.30am he sighted two ships near the Scillies 'In thick weather and heavy seas, the wind westerly'.[3]

Exact details of the loss of the *Hollandia* are unknown but she found herself blown off course, north of the Scillies. The captain, probably thinking he was clear of the Scillies, turned south and struck Gunner Rock. With part of her hull shattered and leaking badly, she then sailed east where she sank about a mile east of Gunner Rock in Broad Sound; all her passengers and crew perished.

Captain Robert Heath, an Engineer Officer stationed in the Garrison at St Mary's, wrote: '. . . About the year 1743 a Dutch East Indiaman outward bound, was lost off St Agnes in about 20 or 22 fathoms of water, with all the people. Their firing of guns as a signal of distress . . . was heard in the night but none could give assistance.'[4]

A brief notice appeared in the *London Gazette*: 'The Dutch East-India Company had just lost a new ship bound from Amsterdam to Batavia, with M. Imhoff, brother to the Governor of that name, and his whole family, on board, and with a very rich lading, which ship was cast away upon the rocks of Scilly and not a man saved.'[5]

John Lethbridge

The Dutch East India Company approached John Lethbridge in 1745 to salvage the *Hollandia*. Heath recorded Lethbridge's lack of success: 'A diver there upon was sent by the Dutch Merchants to discover and Weigh the Plate, of considerable Value, but the Tide Running strong at Bottom and the Sea appearing thick the Diver could not see distinctly through the Glass of his Engine so he returned without success.'[6]

Rex Cowan

In 1967 Rex Cowan began research on the *Hollandia* but it was not until 1971 that Cowan and his team of divers began a detailed search around Gunner Rock. When searching an area 2000 feet east of Gunner Rock Cowan picked up anomalies on the magnetometer. On investigating the anomalies the divers located cannons, lead ingots and an anchor; next day they found a bronze cannon stamped with the monogram of the Dutch East India Company. Proof that the wreck was the *Hollandia* was confirmed when a silver spoon was found with the crest of the arms of the Imhoff-Bentinck family.

Towards the end of the diving season, the divers discovered a 10–12-foot mound of calcified silver coins covered in sea growth. The mound was made up of newly minted 1743 silver ducatoons known as 'silver riders'. The coins depicted a mounted knight on horseback, and were minted exclusively for the Company's Asian trade. Cowan and his divers recovered over 35,000 silver coins, sold in auction by Christie's in Amsterdam.

LUTINE

La Lutine was originally a French twenty-six-gun frigate launched at Toulon in 1785. Although, by 1792, France had declared herself a republic, much of the country was still in revolt. In a forward-looking move the Royalists handed sixteen French men-of-war over to the British for safekeeping — should the rebellion fail. In 1793 Lord Hood took delivery of the ships, including the Lutine *(the 'tease' or 'tormentress'). In 1795 she was refitted to carry thirty-two guns and was incorporated into the British Navy.*

AREA: *Ran aground and sank on the Noorwest Gat between the islands of Vlieland and Terschelling, off the coast of Holland, North Sea.*

In 1795 Britain was at war both with Napoleonic France and with Holland. From 1799 British and Russian troops occupied the Dutch coastal island of Texel with a view to establishing a base for a mainland invasion. The occupying armies were much in need of funds; the troops had not been paid and an urgent request for money to meet the payroll was sent to the Secretary of the Treasury. He stated to the Lords of the Admiralty 'that a sum of money in silver will be ready for transmission to Texel, for the use of the army in Holland' and also mentioned 'a quantity of bullion for Hamburgh'.[1]

The Bank of England approached the Admiralty for a ship capable of transporting bullion, both for troops in Holland and to support the Hamburg Stock Exchange which was heading towards a financial crisis. In a letter to Admiral Duncan, Commander of the North Sea Fleet, the request was detailed: 'We take the liberty most earnestly to request your Lordship as a particular favour, should you not think it improper, if there is no packet in harbour when the mail of 8 October reaches Yarmouth to have the goodness to appoint any of His Majesty's ships of war to take the specie and the mail of the above date — we submit the necessity of speedy assistance.'[2]

Admiral Lord Duncan reported back to the Admiralty on 9 October: 'The merchants interested in making remittances to the Continent for the support of their credit, having made application to me for a King's ship to carry over a considerable sum of money on account of their being no packet for that purpose, I complied with their request, and ordered the Lutine to Cuxhaven.'[3]

The exact value of the two consignments of bullion and specie varies between £1,000,000 and £1,400,000. Documents relating to the precise amounts were destroyed in the London Stock Exchange fire of 1838. John

Admiral Andrew Mitchell, Commander of the British fleet at Texel, who reported to
the Admiralty the loss of the *Lutine* on a sandbank north of Texel, while carrying
over £1 million in specie and bullion

Mayor Still, chief Lloyd's agent (Amsterdam) in 1858, submitted a note that
still survives: '. . . the total value of the cargo was put at £1,200,000 including
£900,000 in Lloyd's gold and silver bars, £160,000 for Hamburg's account
and £140,000 for soldiers' pay.'[4]

The *Lutine* sailed from Great Yarmouth, Norfolk on 9 October 1799 under
the command of Captain Lancelott Skyner with 240 passengers and crew
under his charge as well as an 'estimated 1900 gold bars, 500 silver bars'[5] and
a large number of gold and silver coins.

As the ship approached the Dutch coast a north-northwesterly gale blew
up; the *Lutine* was caught on the lee shore and relentlessly pushed towards
shallow waters. In the early hours of 10 October she ran hard aground and

sank on a sandbank north of Texel between the islands of Vlieland and Terschelling. Two British ships, the twenty-eight-gun *Arrow* and the corvette *Wolverine*, were in the area; Captain Portlock of the latter reported sighting distress signals in the Vlieland Waterway. The ships searched the area and before dawn found three bodies, wreckage and one survivor.

Later that same day Admiral Andrew Mitchell, Commander of the British fleet at Texel, wrote to the Admiralty:

> It is with extreme pain that I have to state the melancholy fate of HMS *Lutine*, which ship ran onto the outer bank of the Fly Island Passage on the night of the 9 inst. in a heavy gale of wind from the NNW, and I am much afraid that her crew with the one exception of one man, who was saved on a part of the wreck, have perished. This man, when taken up, was almost exhausted. He is at present tolerably recovered, and relates that the *Lutine* left Yarmouth Roads on the morning of the 9 inst. bound for Texel, and that she had on board a considerable quantity of money.[6]

The Admiralty instructed Portlock to continue to make every effort to salvage anything of value. The sole survivor was to be returned to England 'by the first opportunity, that such information may be given to the persons concerned in the property as may be necessary for the benefit of the insurers'.[7]

No enquiry was held as to the loss of the *Lutine* and Lloyds paid in full the entire loss.

In early 1800 Mr F.P. Robbé, Receiver of Wrecks at Terschelling Island, commissioned three salvors to begin salvage operations. Robbé promised that one third of the value of everything recovered would be paid to the salvors, provided items were promptly declared. Anyone caught disregarding this rule would forfeit all rights to his share and would also be dealt with under strict salvage laws. The salvors used grabs, hooks and pincers to bring the treasure to the surface: 'Between June 1800 to November 1801: 58 Bars of Gold; 35 Bars of Silver; 41,697 Spanish Silver Pistoles [an old Spanish coin] and 212 Spanish Silver Half-Pistoles; 179 Spanish Gold Pistoles, 20 Gold Half-Pistoles, 24 Gold Quarter Pistoles; 18 Gold One-Eighth Pistoles, 28 Gold One-Sixteenth Pistoles; 81 Double Louis 'D' or 138 Single Louis D'Or, 4 English Guineas and 2 Half Guineas.'[8]

The wreck was lying in approximately 25 feet of water and the men dug and groped their way around the site. By the end of 1801 the treasure had become scattered about the seabed and further salvage was very difficult. Sporadic operations that continued into the following year produced little yield. Frequent storms and strong currents had gradually broken up the *Lutine*; one whole side had split away from the hull and other timbers were buried in the sand. Eventually, all salvage attempts were abandoned.

Pierre Eschauzier

Robbé's successor, Pierre Eschauzier, was appointed Receiver of Wrecks in 1810. In June 1814 the President of the Council of Crown Lands gave his permission to Eschauzier for the recovery of gold and silver from the *Lutine*. After twelve attempts he had recovered '8 Louis D'Or and 7 Spanish Piastres'.[9]

Further salvage attempts were abandoned until 1821 when Eschauzier convinced the Dutch Government to grant him credits (loans), thus enabling him to finance further treasure-seeking operations. He worked for another seven years, but only managed to recover seventeen more gold coins.

J.P. Brand-Eschauzier and L.J.M. Taurel

Two Dutchmen, Jean-Pierre Brand Eschauzier (a retired military captain with some knowledge of salvage) and Louis Taurel, a retired mechanical engineer, formed a partnership to salvage the *Lutine*.

In August 1857 when Brand-Eschauzier and Taurel went to investigate the wreck site, they discovered that a channel had been created across the site by the constantly changing currents. The two men decided that the bulk of the wreck must be lying on the Goudplaat Sandbank. Diving began towards the end of August; by October they had recovered a quantity of gold and silver coins. Over the winter months operations were suspended and then resumed in June 1858. On the second dive the first silver bar was recovered and, over the next two years, a total of forty-one gold bars, sixty-six silver bars, 15,350 gold and silver coins were recovered along with the now famous bronze bell of the *Lutine*.

Lutine Syndicate

The Lutine Syndicate was founded by Mr. W.R. Kinipple of Brighton, who signed a two-year contract with Lloyds in 1893. Salvage work began in 1895 and extended to 1900. No gold or silver was found but a large quantity of copper coins was recovered – of no value.

New Lutine Company

At the end of 1900 Kinipple launched a new company and obtained an extended licence until 1904 with further extensions to 1911. In 1910 the New Lutine Company employed the British National Salvage Association which sent its salvage vessel, *Lyons*, fitted with sand-sucking equipment. *Lyons* arrived at Texel on 31 January 1911: 'On the night of 31 January 1911, the Lyons commenced sucking sand from the Lutine site. She worked for eight hours, after which she had to stop owing to a N.W. wind coming up very suddenly. The first attempt was rather promising, two small shot about 1¾ inches in diameter, a few small pieces of wood and two small iron bolts being recovered . . . copper nails, human bones . . . and many silver and gold coins, two anchors, weighing 3900 kilos were recovered.'[10]

The value of objects and coins recovered from 1911 to 1913 was approximately £135; operations ceased in 1915.

Between 1924 and 1938 a number of salvage companies were granted licenses by Lloyds: Van Der Wallen & Colenbrander (1924–5), the Texel Steamship Co. Ltd with G. Doeksen and Sons (1928–9), Frans Becker (1933) and the Van Wienen Salvage Company (1937–8). No gold or silver was recovered.

Karimata

The *Karimata* of the Doeksen Shipping Company in Terschelling was a tin-dredger weighing 4200 tons. Built by the Billiton Collective Mining Company, she was the largest dredger in the world, carried 160 buckets, had a depth capability of 98 feet, and could dredge 523 cubic feet per hour. *Karimata* had been due to work in the Dutch East Indies but, as the voyage was postponed, the company signed a salvage agreement with Lloyds on 4 June 1938. The company engineer wrote in the Dutch magazine *De Ingenier*: 'Thus to the beginning of the year 1938 one was faced with the following situation: There were well-founded reasons for assuming that assets worth between eight to eighteen million guilders lay hidden at the Lutine site. There was no certainty on this score, so one had to take into account the fact that one might recover less, or even nothing at all.'[11]

On 9 June, the *Karimata* was anchored above the wreck. The remains of the *Lutine* were thought to be 20–30 feet below the seabed. The dredger began working her buckets and the first gold bar was recovered on 29 July. Lloyd's

List reported this on 30 July: 'Amsterdam 29 July: the first bar of gold from the wreck of the Lutine was brought up by the dredger Karimata at 2:30 this morning. The bar was nearly 9 inches long and 22 inches broad. It weighed about 120 ounces valued at approximately £840 at the present value of bar gold.'[12]

(The value today would be in the region of £39,000 or $58,000.) The following day a single gold coin was found. By 12 September the total amount recovered was 'one gold bar; 8 gold coins; 123 silver coins and 10 copper coins.'[12]

After excavating an area 180 to 230 yards long by 70 to 140 yards wide, with a depth of up to 60 feet, the company decided to suspend operations; costs ran to 442,554 guilders (approximately £40,000). The company's annual report for 1938 stated: 'We need hardly add that we shall not be repeating the attempt.'[14]

An article published in the *Sunday Times* on 20 June 1993 stated:

> There is now growing optimism from Lloyd's that the entire gold bullion hoard, worth an estimated £28 million could be raised from the seabed. . . . The latest recovery operations, carried out in dangerous conditions by Dutch divers, is being undertaken amid much secrecy. Ane Jan Duif, head of the 10 strong amateur archaeological diving team working with Lloyd's and the Dutch Ministry of Culture, will eventually publish his finds . . . 'We have had success, we have found many, many artefacts' . . . The archaeologists have identified the 300 yard 'track' that the sinking craft followed before it finally reached its resting place less than 40 feet from the surface.[15]

COLOSSUS

The warship, HMS Colossus, *was launched at Gravesend on 4 April 1787. Commanded by Captain George Murray and attached to Admiral Nelson's Mediterranean fleet, the* Colossus *subsequently took part in the Battle of Cape St Vincent in which she sustained severe damage from enemy fire. After the battle she was refitted as an armed storeship.*

AREA: *Sank on the Southward Well Reef off Sampson Isle, Isles of Scilly, Atlantic Ocean.*

As a storeship the *Colossus* assisted in the Battle of the Nile in 1795 and was subsequently ordered to Lisbon to rendezvous with other ships returning to England. En route, she accompanied Nelson's flagship *Vanguard*, to Naples.

Sir William Hamilton, Envoy Extraordinary to the court of Naples and a connoisseur and collector of Greek and Roman statues, bronzes, glass and other valuable objects, became increasingly concerned for the safety of his collection.

Napoleon was penetrating deep into North Italy. As the political and military situation deteriorated Sir William approached Admiral Nelson and obtained permission for his precious vases to be shipped safely to England on board the *Colossus*.

In addition to Hamilton's treasures there was 'scarcely an officer in Lord Nelson's fleet but had put on board some presents for their friends, which had been taken on board off the French fleet'.[1]

Captain Murray set sail for Lisbon and joined the fleet of British merchantships. In addition to fresh water and provisions, he also took on the embalmed body of Lord Shuldham who had died in Lisbon. Many of the accompanying ships were not yet ready, however, to make the voyage back to England. Due to the apparent unseaworthiness of *Colossus*, Captain Murray was anxious to return home for repairs. He had previously written a letter to Lord Spenser the first Lord of the Admiralty expressing grave concern at the ship's many defects: '. . . several timbers on the starboard side broke . . . timbers for the security of the anchor on the larboard side broke . . . main deck decay . . . boats and copper on the bottom wants repairs . . . lower mast complains much . . . ship complains much and when on larboard tack blowing a fresh gale makes from 2 to three feet water a hour.'[2]

The *Colossus* finally set sail on 25 November accompanied by eight loaded ships. The small convoy sailed down the Tagus, made for the open Atlantic and headed for the English Channel across the Bay of Biscay.

As the wind was blowing strongly from the east, the fleet was forced to change tack and to head for the Scilly Isles. At dawn on 7 December *Colossus* reached St Mary's Island where she made for St Mary's Pool, dropped anchor, furled and lashed her sails and prepared to ride out the storm at anchor on an even keel. On 12 December the Captain reported to the Admiralty:

> In my letter of the 8th I informed you of my having put into St. Mary's with the convoy, the wind being from the eastward. On the 9th it blew strong from the ESE and SE but as the wind was from the shores and the water in consequence smooth, I had not the smallest apprehension that the ship would drive. On the 10th the wind considerably increased
> . . .

About four in the afternoon, the cable parted, the small bower was immediately let go and after veering to a cable she brought up having then the sheet anchor only left, and every appearance of it continuing to blow hard – I wished to go to sea but the pilot told me it was impossible as we should not have daylight to go through the rocks ... about half past five the small bower anchor came home and we were obliged to veer and let her ride between both ... about six she struck the ground but not so hard as to be of consequence ... it then blew a high very hard gale of wind ... she again struck with great violence ... about midnight the rudder went, it still continued to blow very hard and the night very dark. Signals of distress were repeatedly made.... But situated as we were, we could expect no relief until daylight.... Before daylight in the morning ... the water then being up to the cills of the ports of the upper deck and with her rolling, frequently struck the quarter deck with great force – About 8 we saw boats coming to our assistance. ... I am happy to say that before three o'clock in the afternoon I saw the last man out of the ship ...

A postscript was added by the Captain: 'I have further to observe that since my writing the above, the Colossus main mast is gone, part of her larboard side appears beat in, and guns of course fell over ... I am therefore apprehensive there will not be many of the stores saved.'[3] The gale continued to blow for two more days before the *Colossus* finally sank.

Upon hearing of the disaster Sir William Hamilton wrote to Charles Grenville: 'As to my eight cases, all the best vases in my collection that were on board the Colossus, I fear none will be recovered, and it is a pity, for never in this world will such a collection be made again.'[4]

In another letter to Grenville, Hamilton wrote with much bitterness: 'My Phylosophy has been put on Trial by the loss of the Colossus. You give me but little hopes, but I have learnt that the body of insolvent Admiral Shuldham has been saved from the wreck. ... Damn his body, it can be of no use but to the worms, but my collection would have given information to the most learned ...'[5]

Roland Morris

Roland Morris was born in Cornwall and, by the age of twenty, he had had lessons in helmet diving. By late 1940 he had become a partner in a salvage company that specialized in the recovery of scrap metals.

Morris was familiar with old wrecks and HMS *Colossus* became of particular interest to him. He began a concentrated search for her in 1968, but it was not until 1974 that Morris and his divers discovered three anchors of the period, on the gravel seabottom in the area off Sampson Island at Southward Well Rock. They also found a variety of ship's artifacts: pulley wheels, a sounding lead, coppers pins, nails, and a number of copper sheathing tacks indicating that a wooden vessel had, sometime before, lain on the seabed. Morris complied with the correct legal procedure and reported his discovery to Her Majesty's Receiver of Wrecks. In due course permission was granted by the Secretary of State for Defence, under the Protection of Wrecks Act of 1973, to carry out salvage operations on the wreck site. Roland Morris continued diving operations on the Southward Well Rock. The team, diving to fixed parallel compass lines along the rock reefs, discovered five cast-iron cannons and two carronades, bronze rudder pintles and the first piece of Greek pottery.

Although nothing remained of the ship's timbers, the wreck site did give clues as to the position of the ship as she laid on the seabed. The carronades were an important find as they were usually bolted to the forecastle deck and mounted on swivels for easy firing. Thus the bow section was identified. Marble fireslabs marked the ship's galley; the pintles which turned the rudder pointed to the stern section.

It was in the stern that the eight cases containing the priceless Hamilton cargo of 1000 vases had been stowed. As the divers excavated and cleared the surface of the seabed they began to find vast numbers of vase fragments. Two British Museum experts from the Department of Greek & Roman Antiquities were able to identify some of the decorated pottery pieces: Hamilton had prudently commissioned Wilhelm Tischbein in 1787 to illustrate many of the scenes painted on the vases; these illustrations were to play an important part in piecing the find together.

The divers methodically laid down a 30-foot grid which enabled precise numbering and recording of the sherds before they were actually brought to the surface. Between 1975 and 1976 Morris and his team excavated 35,000 pieces of Greek vases. These fragments were carefully washed and then reassembled according to Tischbein's drawings. The most famous of these vases is one called the 'Colossus Vase' which can now be viewed in the British Museum.

EARL OF ABERGAVENNY

The Earl of Abergavenny was a three-masted schooner of 1400 tons, armed with thirty guns. She was built at the Pitcher yard in Northfleet, Kent, in 1796, for the East India Company to trade between England and China.

AREA: *Struck the Shambles Bank. When freed, her hull was discovered to be badly damaged and she sank a mile off Weymouth in the English Channel.*

The Captain of the *Earl of Abergavenny* was John Wordsworth, brother of the poet William Wordsworth. The Wordsworth family had long associations with the East India Company and had invested £20,000 in private trade goods aboard the ship on her voyages to Bengal and China.[1]

The *Abergavenny* sailed out of Portsmouth Harbour in February 1805 in the company of four other East Indian merchantships: *Wexford, Henry Addington, Bombay Castle* and the *Royal George.* The armed frigate *Weymouth* sailed as escort.

The *Abergavenny* carried fifty-nine soldiers of the East India Company, 100 of the King's troops, thirty-two Chinese and fifty-one passengers, and a crew of 160, a total of 402 persons.[2] 'Her cargo consisted of £67,000 value in dollars.[3] Packed in 62 chests, copper, tin, lead and iron, 200 tons each — a vast quantity of cloth, haberdashery, millinery, glass, Wedgwood ware, harnesses, saddles, military stores, wines, liqueurs etc.'[4]

The convoy made its way around the Isle of Wight and into the English Channel. Upon reaching St Alban's Head the winds from the south and west increased and the *Weymouth* separated from the other ships. As the remaining ships approached Portland Bill, Captain Clarke of the *Wexford*, as senior Commander, signalled that they head for Portland Roads and await the *Weymouth*.

At 3pm the *Abergavenny* took aboard her pilot and sailed towards Portland Roads for safe anchorage. The strong wind on her port suddenly dropped, the tide setting in fast, and she struck the Shambles Bank, a large area of shallows, comprised of sand and rocks lying off Portland Bill. After an hour, the crew managed to free the hull and clear the rocks. Upon investigation, the ship's carpenter found that the water level in the hold had risen from 6 inches to 6 feet:

The East Indiaman *Earl of Abergavenny*, captained by John Wordsworth, brother of the poet William Wordsworth. En route to China carrying a cargo of coins, metals and a vast quantity of other trade goods, she struck the Shambles Bank and sank a mile off Weymouth in the English Channel

The Carpenter announced that a considerable leak was discovered near the bottom of the chain pumps, which was not in his power to stop. The pumps were set a-going, and part of the crew endeavored to bail her at the fore-hatch, but all attempts were in vain. At six pm, the inevitable loss of the ship became apparent, other leaks were discovered. The wind had increased to a gale, and the severe beating of the vessel upon the rocks threatened immediate destruction. As the night advanced, the situation of all onboard became more terrible.[5]

Captain Wordsworth, realizing the seriousness of the situation, fired distress signals and sent the ship's boat, manned by the purser, the third mate and six seamen for help; they were never seen again. The pilot's sloop arrived, and managed to take off two women and three men passengers but, s the seas were so rough, the sloop was unable to make further rescue attempts. The few ship's boats that had managed to be launched were either capsized or dashed to pieces against the sinking *Abergavenny*. 'At seven, the company was nearly exhausted . . . about nine o'clock, the dreadful cries approached. The passengers were informed of their situation and every man was aware of his fate.'[6]

As the ship began to settle in the water, Mr Baggot, the chief officer, went on the quarter-deck and told the Captain: 'We have done all we can, sir, she will sink in a moment.' The Captain replied, 'It cannot be helped, God's will be done.'

At 11pm, the sea gave the *Abergavenny* a sudden shock and she sank in 12 fathoms of water; eighty to ninety persons were clinging to the top of the masts and were afterwards taken off. When the ship sank, she did not go down the usual way by falling upon her beam ends, but went down by the head. This deviation is supposed to have arisen from her being laden with treasure and porcelain ware.[7]

Two hundred and seventy-one passengers, soldiers and crew drowned. Of the 131 who survived, only five were passengers.

John Braithwaite

Shortly after the *Abergavenny* sank, the East India Company received a number of offers to salvage the ship.

John Braithwaite and his brother William had successfully salvaged the rich cargo of the *Haleswell*, lost after a mutiny in the Cape Verde Islands in 1785.

At the time of the sinking of the *Abergavenny* John Braithwaite came out of retirement and was awarded the contract on the basis of 12½ per cent of the value of the silver recovered, and the sale of much of the other cargo.

Captain Braithwaite in his ship *Endeavour* began diving on the wreck on 15 February 1805 and continued at intervals, depending on the weather conditions. Captain Braithwaite brought to the surface pigs of lead, pieces of cloth, boxes of shot and general cargo – all of which were sold at auction in Weymouth.

The *Gentlemen's Magazine* of October 1805 published a report on the progress of salvage operations: 'Mr Braithwaite continues to be very successful in fishing up the property from the Abergavenny, East Indiaman. The sales of sundry articles recovered from it usually take place every fortnight by public auction, and furnish curious contrasts of bargains to the purchasers . . . '[8]

It was not until 30 April that the first chests of dollars were recovered, quickly followed by other chests. In his journal, dated 17 May Captain Braithwaite recorded: 'I chest of dollars and the last, making in all 62 chests, I believe about £1200 in each chest.'[9]

Salvage work continued intermittently until March the following year. On 28 March 1806 Braithwaite wrote in his journal 'Fixed the windlass and other machinery, then we went to work and had a prosperous summer, worked as long till the cargo got so thin, not worth getting up. After succeeding in breaking of the ship "The Earl of Abergavenny", by the assistance of gunpowder and weighing the cargo as above, and setting all things at Weymouth, we return in the *"Endevour"* to London.'[10]

ROYAL CHARTER

The Royal Charter *was built in 1855 at the Sandycroft Ironworks located on the River Dee near Liverpool. The Eagle Line commissioned the clipper ship for the Liverpool-Australian Steam Navigation Co.* Royal Charter *was built for both sail and steam and was registered at 2719 tons, carrying a crew of 112 with accommodation for 500 passengers. Captained by Thomas Taylor, she was advertised as the 'Magnificent steam clipper,* Royal Charter *– Australia in under 60 days. The* Royal Charter's *extraordinary passage of 59 days to Melbourne is the fastest ever made.'*

AREA: *Sank off the rocky shore between Lligny Bay and the Moelfre Headland, Anglesey, North Wales, Irish Sea.*

At the end of August 1859 the *Royal Charter* lay at the Melbourne roadstead off Port Phillip ready for departure. She had on board a large consignment of '68,397 ozs of gold sovereigns' (£322,440 at the then existing prices).[1] The sovereigns were packed in wooden boxes and stored in the strongroom which lay in her stern section.

There was a passenger list of 376 and a full crew of 112; many of the passengers were successful gold miners returning to England with the results of their diggings from the Ballarat Mines north of Melbourne.

On 26 August the *Royal Charter* departed Melbourne for Liverpool. She headed for open sea and sailed east around Cape Horn, following the prevailing trade winds and the westerlies. On Monday, 24 October, she passed the Old Head of Kinsale off the south coast of Ireland, then hove to off Queenstown where fourteen Irish passengers disembarked. The ship continued up the St Georges Channel; she was expected in Liverpool within twenty-four hours. At about 1.30pm she was within sight of Holyhead, the small island off the Anglesey coast.

The wind was moderately strong, coming from the southeast. At 6.30 the *Royal Charter* rounded the Skerries; she was then about sixty miles from Liverpool.

Suddenly, the barometric pressure dropped.

The Reverend Scoresby wrote:

The wind gradually freshened during the afternoon, though not very much, till over the mountain came a thin black haze, which rose into the air with ominous rapidity and overspread the sky. The sea and wind kept rising as the glass fell, and before eight it blew a heavy gale from the eastward, with fierce squalls and storms of rain. As night wore on, the wind increased and came in fearful gusts, tearing away among the spars and rigging with a hoarse sustained roar that was awful to listen to, especially when one bore in mind that the glass was still falling, and that what we saw was only the commencement of the gale![2]

The wind changed direction and, at the same time, increased to force 10; the *Royal Charter* was caught off the lee shore. Realizing that he desperately needed room to manoeuvre, the Captain signalled for a pilot with the aim to be led further out to the open sea.

By 10.30 the winds were blowing force 12, the tide began to ebb and the ship was set both by the rushing tide and the terrible winds. She could no longer make any headway and the coastline loomed closer and closer. Captain Taylor ordered the port anchor to be set, but the ship's drift was not stopped and her engines simply did not have the necessary pulling power. Taylor set the starboard anchor and it held. At 1.30 the port anchor-chain parted at the hawser hole and an hour later, the starboard anchor parted. The *Royal Charter* heeled over and quickly drifted towards the rocky coastline. Three masts were cut to reduce windage and every conceivable effort was made to save the ship but, at 3.30am, fifty yards from shore, the *Royal Charter* struck a rock ledge.

Able Seaman Edward Wilson was later to describe the tragic scenario: '. . . Nothing but confusion on deck, fore and aft passengers, saloon, cabin and steerage all mixed together, fathers and mothers clasping their children in their arms, wives clinging to their husbands, shrieking and crying, 'Save me, save me', 'Don't leave me' and so on.'[3]

Sea was breaking over the ship and no lifeboats could be launched. Mountainous waves, 60-foot high, hit the ship broadside, the force smashing the metal hull in two. Hundreds of passengers and crew were swept overboard to be dashed on to the rocks, then flung back on to the wreck. By 8am little remained of the ship. The *Illustrated London News* described the aftermath: 'The ironwork of the vessel was in mere shreds; the woodwork was in chips. The coast and the fields above the cliffs were strewn with fragments of the cargo and of the bedding and clothing. Worse still, the rocks were covered with corpses of men and women frightfully mutilated, and strewn with the sovereigns which the poor creatures had gone so far to seek, and were now torn from them in such a painful way.'[4]

Many of the bodies washed up had tied round their waists money-belts that were crammed full of gold. Many pockets were filled with gold coins.

On the cliff overlooking the wreck site lies a stone monument to those 400 passengers and crew who perished on board the *Royal Charter*.

In November 1859 salvage operations were begun using a lighter (equipped with heavy lifting cranes) anchored near the wreck. Divers searched amongst the tangled mass of ironwork, trying to locate the bullion room. The gold had been packed in small mahogany boxes, some had already been found washed up on the rocks. By 7 December the divers had located the bullion room and had recovered twelve boxes of gold and twelve bags of gold dust, all valued at £100,000. By the end of 1859 the total amount salvaged was between £275,000 and £370,000.[5]

Underwriters sold the wreck to Messrs Gibbs Bright for £1000. Salvage work was continued, the divers finding an additional £30,000 in gold and sovereigns. They also stripped the wreck and were able to claim value for brass, iron and other ship's fittings. The total savage value over the initial £322,440 was rumoured to have reached nearly £500,000. Gibbs Bright then went on to sell the wreck to a small consortium of Anglesey islanders. This group continued to work on the wreck until 1873; when they removed the sternpost 500 gold sovereigns were found.

Wignall Reynolds

In 1958 the marine archaeologist, Sydney Wignall, and fellow diver, Eric Reynolds, explored the *Royal Charter*:

> Within a few yards of our entry into the water, we were swimming amongst broken iron ribs and frames, and buckled iron plates, embedded in the sand. With curiosity we examined and discarded the odd porthole, stanchion and deck fitting, and it was then that I chanced on a large yellow ingot

protruding from the sand, jammed between an iron frame and a huge piece of jagged iron plate. It seemed to be a copper bar, and I struggled to free my wreck souvenir. Reynolds joined me and we struggled away at the metal ingot until we eventually ran out of air. Reynolds was first to surface, leaving me struggling alone. In the end, in desperation, I drew my knife and, using its saw edge, sawed into the ingot. The metal was soft and yellow. At that moment I realized that I had found a gold bullion bar.[6]

Royal Charter Salvage Expedition

Jack Smart and Peter Day founded the Royal Charter Salvage Expedition in 1972. When the group investigated the site it was discovered that the wreck had now broken into three parts. As they methodically excavated the site using airlifts and carefully probing around the rusting structures, they were able to recover a gold watch, a tiepin, a gold ring and a variety of ship's artifacts.

Diggings were made to a depth of 12 feet but only a few copper coins and gold sovereigns were found; the location of the strongroom was never discovered as much of the wreck was now embedded in the encroaching sand.

Bestspeed

In the summer of 1985 Joseph McCormack and Bernie McDonald formed Bestspeed to salvage the remaining Royal Charter cargo. Establishing a base on the clifftop overlooking the rocky shore of the wreck site, they proceeded to blast their way through 30 feet of silt and rock. They then used a 6-inch airlift and exposed a section of lower hull and rusted plating. Over the following months six gold sovereigns, a few gold nuggets and a gold ring were recovered.

By mid-November it was decided to suspend operations; in accordance with the salvage laws, the finds were handed over to the Receiver of Wrecks.

Royal Charter Salvage Expedition

In 1986 Jack Smart and Peter Day once again resumed their search for what remained of the Royal Charter's treasure. They spent many months excavating and clearing tons of sand and shingle; their efforts were totally destroyed by

Hurricane Charlie which struck the Anglesey coast on 25 August 1986. Further excavations were abandoned. From his research, Peter Day believes more gold was aboard the *Royal Charter* than was publicly admitted; he is sure that lying in, or near, the elusive strongroom is a fortune in gold.

LUSITANIA

The Lusitania *was built in 1907 by the John Brown shipyard in Clydebank, Scotland, for the Cunard Steamship Company. One of Cunard's first luxury liners, she was 787 feet long with an 88-foot beam, and could accommodate 563 first-class passengers, 464 second-class and 1138 third-class with a crew of 750. With a cruising speed of twenty-four knots, she was the fastest, largest most elegant ship in the world.*

AREA: *Torpedoed by the German submarine U-20 as she was off Old Head of Kinsale, forty miles from the south coast of Eire, Atlantic Ocean.*

The *Lusitania* made her maiden voyage on 7 September 1907 when she sailed from Liverpool to New York. On her third voyage she won the Blue Riband for England by crossing the Atlantic with an average speed of 23.61 knots. Her sistership, *Mauritania*, took the record from her in 1909 and held it for the next twenty-two years.

In May 1913 the possibility of war with Germany prompted Cunard to authorize a secret re-fit for the *Lusitania*. The number one boiler-room was converted into a magazine for explosives and ammunition and the mailroom on the shelterdeck was modified to carry four 6-inch guns mounted on each side of the ship.[1]

On 4 August 1914 Britain declared war on Germany. The German Government immediately stated that all ships carrying war material would be considered legitimate naval targets; during the early part of 1915 a number of British and Allied ships were subsequently attacked and torpedoed by German U-boats. The first sinking of an American vessel was that of the *US Gulflight*, a tanker, torpedoed on the day the *Lusitania* left New York on what was to be her final voyage.

On 1 May 1915 the Cunard Shipping Company ran the following advertisement in the *New York Times*: 'Lusitania, Europe via Liverpool, the fastest and largest steamer now in the Atlantic service.'

Next to the advertisement, in heavy black type, was a 'Notice' from the Imperial German Embassy in Washington, DC, which stated:

The *Lusitania* was the first of Cunard's luxury liners, one of the most elegant ships in the world. She was torpedoed by a German U-boat off the coast of Ireland on 7 May 1915; 1198 of the 1959 people on board perished. Her sinking helped to bring the United States into World War I

Travellers intending to embark on the Atlantic voyage are reminded that a state of war exists between Germany and her allies and Great Britain and her allies; that the zone of war includes the waters adjacent to the British Isles; that, in accordance with formal notice given by the Imperial German Government, vessels flying the flag of Great Britain, or any of her allies, are liable to destruction in those waters and that travellers sailing in the war zone on ships of Great Britain or her allies do so at their own risk.[2]

Two weeks before the *Lusitania*'s departure the British Admiralty sent two confidential warnings to her Captain, William Turner:

Confidential Daily Voyage Notice April 15, 1915, issued under Government War Risks Scheme: German submarines appear to be operating chiefly off prominent headlands and landfalls. Ships should give prominent headlands a wide berth.

The second notice was issued a day later:

Confidential memo issued April 16, 1915: War experience has shown that fast steamers can considerably reduce the chance of successful surprise attacks by zigzagging – that is to say, altering the course at short and irregular intervals, say in ten minutes to half an hour. This course is almost invariably adopted by warships when cruising in an area known to be infested by submarines. The underwater speed of a submarine is very slow and it is exceedingly difficult for her to get into position to deliver an attack unless she can observe and predict the course of the ship attacked.[3]

On 1 May US Customs signed a brief one-page manifest and clearance was given for the *Lusitania* to depart New York City on 2 May. On 5 May, three days after her departure, Mr N.L. Mead, Cunard's customs agent submitted a twenty-four-page supplementary manifest for goods taken on board at the last minute.

The *Lusitania*'s manifests have been the focal point of much speculation and controversy. C. Simpson, in his book *Lusitania*, mentions that three manifests (all copies), each one showing different information have been found.[4] General cargo listed was a mixture of sheet metal, copper, beef, butter, lard, cheese and bacon but a supplementary manifest listed a consignment of military weapons and supplies. These were stored in the main orlop deck. Two versions with regard to this particular cargo are in dispute: one states that 51 tons of 3-inch shrapnel shells, packed into 1248 cases, were actually live ammunition; the second manifest states that the shells were empty casings accompanied by a consignment of 4927 boxes of small-calibre rifle ammunition weighing 173 tons. All figures continue to be unsubstantiated.

$6,000,000 in gold bullion was rumoured to be stored in the ship's strongroom along with a collection of Reubens's paintings; the latter items were rolled into waterproof zinc containers and were destined in the Lane Bequest for the Dublin Museum. Diamonds, worth over one million dollars, were also said to be stored in the strongroom.[5]

At 9am on 2 May 1915 the *Lusitania* left pier 54 at the foot of New York's 14th Street. Crowds of relatives, friends and wellwishers bid her farewell at the quayside. On board were 290 first-class passengers, 600 second-class and 367 third-class with a crew of 702.

By the second day out she was making a steady twenty knots and had logged 501 nautical miles. She was then south of Nova Scotia, the weather was fine, the seas calm – an uneventful voyage. On the morning of 6 May, as the *Lusitania* neared the war-zone, the crew uncovered the lifeboats and swung them out from their davits, ready for launch in the case of any hostilities. The ship had forty-eight lifeboats, as well as rafts and lifejackets for 3205 individuals. The Captain was assured that the ship could manage any emergency.

At 7.50pm, approximately 375 miles from the English coast, Captain Turner received a radio communiqué from the British Admiralty: 'Submarines active off south coast of Ireland.'

At 8.30pm a further radio report was received: 'To all British ships 0005: Take Liverpool pilot at bar and avoid headlands. Pass harbours at full speed, steer mid-channel course; submarines off Fastnet.'[7]

On Thursday morning, 7 May, the *Lusitania* had to reduce her speed to eighteen knots due to heavy fog patches. The fog lifted as the ship passed Fastnet Rock off Cape Clear. Captain Turner was about to have lunch when he received a further Admiralty message, relayed through Spain: 'Submarine five miles south of Cape Clear, proceeding west when sighted at 10 am.'[8]

As the Old Head of Kinsale came into view, on the Irish coast, Turner ordered the helmsman on a straight 87-degree easterly course.

Ten miles off the Irish coast Kaptleutnant Schwieger, Commander of the German U-boat, U-20, sighted the *Lusitania* approaching from south-south-west, making towards Galley Head. The Captain entered in his log: 'Proceeded at high speed to obtain position ahead.'[9]

At 2.10pm, ten miles from the Irish coast, the Commander of U-20 gave orders to fire one torpedo at a distance of 700 yards at a depth of 9 feet.

The torpedo hit the *Lusitania* and exploded amidships to starboard. Within seconds a second explosion followed as the ship's boilers blew up. Schwieger entered in his log:

> ... shot hits starboard side right behind bridge. An unusually heavy deto-nation follows with a very strong explosion cloud (high in the air over the first smokestack). Added to the explosion of the torpedo there must have been a second explosion (boiler, coal, or powder). The superstructure over point struck and the high bridge are rent asunder and fire breaks out and envelops the high bridge. The ship stops immediately and quickly heels to starboard. At the same time diving deeper at the bow ... .[10]

Minutes after the explosion the *Lusitania*'s radio operator tapped out a distress message: 'Come at once, big list, ten miles south Old Head Kinsale.'[11]

Although listing badly the ship continued to plough through the water; under such momentum, due to speed and weight, it was not possible to launch the lifeboats. As the list increased to 25 degrees, the port-side lifeboats could not be lowered at all. Many of the lifeboats on the starboard side capsized as they were lowered, hurling their terrified occupants into the sea.

The radio operator continued to send messages; at 2.15pm Admiralty House in London received a message for Sir Charles Coke: 'Lusitania in distress off Kinsale. Believed sinking.'[12]

At 2.28pm, eighteen minutes after she was torpedoed, the *Lusitania*'s bow dipped downwards, lifting her stern high above the water. Hundreds of passengers, unable to jump, clung to her stern, only to be sucked into the vortex created as the ship slipped below the surface.

Captain Schwieger wrote: 'Go to 11 metres and take look around. In the distance astern are drifting a number of lifeboats. Of the Lusitania nothing is to be seen. The wreck must lie off Old Head of Kinsale Lighthouse, 14 sea miles distant, in 90 metres of water, 358 degrees (bearing to the lighthouse), 27 miles from Queenstown ... 51°22.6', 8°32 'W. The shore and lighthouse are clearly seen.'[13]

Of the 1959 passengers and crew 1198 drowned. On 9 May, two days after the sinking, the *Chicago Tribune*, in a special report, stated:

> In the strong box of the *Lusitania* at the bottom of the sea off the Irish coast is approximately $5 million of money, foreign exchange and other valuables belonging to the Chicago people. Of this treasure $3,000,000 consists of foreign exchange belonging to the First National Bank. ... Had the P.O. Department not prescribed shortly before the *Lusitania*'s departure that mails intended for her be specifically directed to the ship, the amount of Chicago treasure aboard her would have been much greater.

Royal Navy

In the years following the sinking, lighthousemen at the Old Head of Kinsale reported numerous vessels over the wreck. In 1936 the well-known Italian salvage company, Sorima, was in the area of the wreck, but was warned away by coastguard ships.

The British Government indirectly owns the salvage rights of the *Lusitania* through the Receiver of Wrecks and the Department of Trade. The Royal Navy salvage vessel, *Reclaim*, was reported to be working over the wreck in 1946, conducting blasting operations a number of years later: 'A number of years later two Royal Navy divers admitted they had been to the wreck but felt obligated not to elaborate. The Admiralty still deny any involvement with Lusitania operations.'[14]

According to Colin Simpson, in his book *Lusitania*, he 'traced two members of the crew of the *Reclaim* and have spoken at length to them. Both freely admitted that they had been to the *Lusitania* but could not say anything else without permission of the Admiralty.'[15]

Risdon Beazley Ltd

In 1954 the *Recovery*, a salvage ship owned by Risdon Beazley Ltd of Southampton, acknowledged that they were under charter by the Admiralty and had conducted a series of blasting and diving operations.

John Light

John Light, an American ex-naval diver, made frequent dives between 1960 and 1962. He and his associates made over 100 dives on the *Lusitania* and were able to draw some interesting conclusions about the overall state of the wreck. He decided that an internal explosion had caused far greater damage in the forward hull than the obvious external explosion and destruction caused by the torpedo. Light went on to find evidence that cutting operations had taken place after the sinking. Steel cables were found near a rectangular hole some 8 by 15 feet which had been cut into her bulkhead.

In 1967 Light purchased the *Lusitania* from the British War Risks Association for £1000. He then formed a salvage company with the hope of salvaging part of the wreck but the project came to nothing. Light sold his interest to two other American businessmen who, in turn, sold on the salvage rights.

Oceaneering Ltd

In April 1982 Oceaneering Ltd, the largest salvage company in the world, began investigating and surveying the wreck. An agreement was made with the *Sunday Times* to monitor the operation; television coverage was also to be arranged. The salvage ship, *Myrevag*, used a remote-control submarine named *Scorpio* to transmit pictures. Oceaneering's operational headquarters confirmed Light's earlier observations that a massive explosion had taken place deep in the *Lusitania's* hold. The rectangular hole was relocated and, as the remaining hold plating was examined, it became evident that grab marks, caused by salvage grapples, had scored the steel surfaces. The divers moved to the purser's office and the bullion room, but found nothing. Whatever live ammunition, explosives, paintings, diamonds and bullion that the *Lusitania* is reputed to have been transporting, all proof of their recovery – or even existence – has been shrouded in secrecy.

It is interesting to note that the Ministry of Defence has closed some of the *Lusitania*'s files held at the Public Records Office until the year 2016.

HAMPSHIRE

HMS Hampshire *was a cruiser of the Devonshire Class, weighing 10,850 tons and commissioned in August 1905. Although heavily armed, she was one of the fastest of the Royal Navy cruisers with a capability of 23 knots. She carried a crew of 665 and was captained by Herbert Savill.*

AREA: *Struck a mine and sank a few miles west of Marwich Head off the Orkney Islands, Scotland, North Atlantic Ocean.*

When the First World War broke out in 1914 the military leaders and politicians of Great Britain, France and Russia all expected hostilities to last only a matter of months. But by 1916 Russia was not only desperately short of armaments, her political situation was rapidly deteriorating, much to the concern of Britain and France. The Prime Minister, Herbert Asquith, appointed Field Marshal Lord Kitchener as Secretary of War. Kitchener stressed the importance of bolstering Russia and her ailing battle fronts, and emphasized the dangers of Russia being forced to seek a separate armistice with Germany.

As a direct result of Kitchener's diplomatic approaches a communique was sent to the British Government via the British Ambassador in Amsterdam: 'Lord Kitchener's urgent representations and inspiriting messages have induced the Czar to consider the whole matter of munitions supplies from a new angle. The Czar now believes that a visit from Lord Kitchener can boost morale in Russia among the faint hearts at Court. The Czar wants advice and thinks it might help if the control of certain things, possibly supplies, were taken into British hands.'[1]

The Prime Minister agreed that Kitchener should depart for Petrograd: 'The secret of Lord Kitchener's Mission was strictly guarded at the Admiralty where only five or six persons who were actually concerned with the arrangements, knew what was in contemplation. The number that knew of the programme in any detail was still smaller.'[2]

In mid May 1916 a German decoding officer picked up a British naval communication that had been repeated three times within one hour. The message was from a minesweeper and advised the Admiralty that orders had been followed and completed: a path west of the Orkneys, south to north, had been swept and was now declared clear of mines.

German Naval Command became suspicious and decided that a shipment of munitions must be due to pass through Scapa Flow. Acting on this information, a German submarine, U-75, was sent to mine the area that ran northeast from Noup Head between Marwick Head and the Brough of Birsay. A series of mines was laid in a scattered pattern about 21 feet below high water.[3]

The Admiralty gave its orders:

Secret sailing orders to Archangel had been given by the Commander-in-Chief to the Captain of the Hampshire on the previous day (4 June). These orders directed her to proceed by a route to the east of the Orkneys, and to maintain a speed of 18 knots until reaching the latitude of 62°N, after which a speed of at least 16 knots was to be maintained, and stated that, weather permitting two destroyers were to screen her as far as that latitude, where they were to be detached to return to Scapa.[4]

On 5 June at 4.45pm Lord Kitchener set sail from Scapa Flow on the cruiser *HMS Hampshire* and escorted by two destroyers, *HMS Unity* and *HMS Victor*. The weather was severe – gale force winds. *Hampshire* was making 18 knots but, in the face of raging winds and seas, reduced her speed to 15 knots. The escort vessels found that they could not keep up with the cruiser. *Hampshire*'s captain signalled the *Unity* and *Victor* to return to base. The *Hampshire* kept to her course, sailing N30°E, keeping one and a half miles off shore between the Brough of Birsay and Marwick Head.

It was just after 7.40pm that the *Hampshire* struck a mine:

The explosion seems to have occurred under the forward half of the ship and probably near the keel. There is evidence that some of the stokers on duty on the port side sustained bad burns; and that the fumes of high explosive penetrated on to the stokers' mess deck. The ship at once began to settle down. The survivor who was on the bridge stated that the explosion seemed to tear the centre part of her right out, and that she could be seen going right away from the start. She was unable to steer; the electric power failed; all lights went out; and no wireless communication was possible. Between ten and twenty minutes after the explosion, approximately therefore at 8 o'clock, she sank, bows first, her propellers still revolving.[5]

No lifeboats could be launched; a few survivors made it to the floats, some clung on to wreckage but the rough seas, coupled with bitterly cold water, gave very long odds for any survival. An extract from one such survivor reads:

> It was so rough that the sea beat down on us and many men (i.e., in the float) were killed by the buffeting they received. Many others died from the fearful cold. I was quite benumbed. An almost overpowering desire to sleep came upon us, and to get over this we thumped each other on the back, for no man who went to sleep ever woke again. When men died it was just as though they were falling asleep . . .
>
> I got them singing, but they still keep dropping off the raft. They were clustered round you, dying as you looked at them. They were people of fine physique, I was quite surprised at. It was very cold. . . . It was impossible to swim in that sea.[6]

Of the survivors that were washed ashore on the floats only twelve men survived; 650 men drowned, Kitchener's body was never recovered.

Shortly after the mining of the *Hampshire* rumours began to circulate that spies had been involved in the sinking of the ship. A spy scandal, one of international dimension, was then suspected. It was further suggested that *Hampshire* had been torpedoed and that large quantities of gold were also stowed on board. Ten years later the Admiralty issued *The Official Narrative: The loss of the HMS* Hampshire.

Sir Basil Zaharoff

Sir Basil Zaharoff, born in Constantinople in 1850, was a wealthy businessman of Greek origins who had a variety of interests, including oil, engineering and arms sales. During the early 1930s Zaharoff 'officially' chartered a salvage vessel and employed a number of divers to attempt to recover £2 million in gold[7] reputed to be lodged aboard the *Hampshire*.

By 1932 the Zaharoff team had located the *Hampshire's* position. She lay, covered in mud and silt, 240 feet deep near Marwick Head. Armed with this

Lord Kitchener became Secretary of State for War on the outbreak of World War I in 1914. He was drowned while on a mission to Russia when the HMS *Hampshire* struck a mine and sank off Scotland on June 5 1916

information, Zaharoff arranged for a second vessel to sail out of Kiel, Germany. Captain Brandt had on board a crew of highly professional divers: an Australian, Costello; Whitefield, an American; two Germans, Kruger and Lt Max Weissfelt (the latter had served on a mine layer, A-10, in the Marwick Head Bank area); and an Englishman, C. Courtney.

When the salvage vessels reached Marwick Head Costello and Whitefield made the initial dive and confirmed that the *Hampshire* was indeed lying beneath the salvage ships. Costello was quoted: 'She is three fathoms deeper than she was last summer, there is a mountain of sand to be got away.'[8]

The cross-currents were contentious, but diving proceeded. Over the first week sand and silt were removed, using airlifts, and a way was cleared through the first bulkhead in order to reach the strongroom situated behind the captain's cabin. In 1983, in a *Times* article, Noel Wentworth, a London lecturer who has made a special study of *HMS Hampshire*, stated: 'The vessel went into the Harland & Wolff shipyard in Belfast in 1916 for what was described at the time as a refit, but research has disclosed that a strongroom was built.'[9]

The divers took three days to cut their way into the strongroom: '... Forcing the bulkhead door further back, we crawled into the bullion room where we found chest after chest of gold coins, twenty-rouble pieces. The chests were too heavy to drag out, so Costello and I broke them open, filling

our bags with as many as we could manage and passing them back to
Whitefield and Weissfelt.'[10]

Gold coins worth £60,000[11] were brought to the surface, as were paper
money and ship's documents.

The weather suddenly deteriorated and Captain Brandt was forced to seek
shelter in Stromness. The expedition was able to return to the wreck after
three days of waiting; by then, the hull was covered in mud and sand. The
divers set to work with pressure hoses and cleared a passage back to the strongroom.

By 23 April the weather was still not ideal, but Courtney, Costello and
Whitefield decided to go ahead and dive. When they reached the wreck they
found that visibility was poor and the notorious cross-currents seemed to have
increased. As they reached the strongroom a sudden surge of water caused a
huge mudslide. The divers were slammed against the metal hull. All three divers
were terribly injured, but they managed to get to the surface. Further inspec-
tions of the wreck revealed just how hazardous future diving conditions would
be; it was decided to abandon the operation.

On 26 January 1951 a Mr Lloyd Knight of Lethbridge (Alberta, Canada)
wrote to the Admiralty requesting permission to salvage the *Hampshire*. The
Admiralty replied in a letter dated 13 March: 'With reference to your letter
dated 26 January 1951 concerning salvage of H.M.S. Hampshire, I am
commanded by my Lords Commissioners of the Admiralty to inform you that
the wreck of this vessel is Admiralty property and they are not prepared to
entertain proposals for salvage operations on this wreck.'[12]

Wharton Williams Taylor

Nothing further was heard of salvage operations until 1983. It had been
reported in the British press, however, that Wharton Williams Taylor, a salvage
company from Aberdeen, along with a German film company (AGUF from
Frankfurt) were given permission by the Ministry of Defence to dive and to
film 'external features of the wreck' from 1977 to 1979.

In 1983 Wharton Williams Taylor again went diving on the *Hampshire*, but
this time without prior permission. Diving from a Swedish vessel, *Sterna Workhorse*,
they recovered a phosphor-bronze propeller, valued at £30,000 ($45,000),
along with other unspecified items. The Ministry of Defence stopped further
operations, stating: 'All we gave permission for originally was for filming outside
the wreck but not for bringing up artefacts.'[13]

And in another article, in *The Times*: 'The situation is that now we have asked the consortium to cease diving at the wreck and have asked them to return the artefacts as reverently as possible.'[14]

In a *Times* report Wharton Williams Taylor denied 'that they had any knowledge of gold on board the vessel'. On the following day an additional article was published: 'The co-producer for the film makers admitted that they were looking for gold as well as searching for evidence on how the ship had gone down.'[15]

Numerous books and articles have been written on the subject of HMS *Hampshire* and her gold. In order that the legend and rumours be laid to rest it is necessary that a serious salvage operation take place and that the documentation of the cargo be publicized so that proper conclusions may be reached regarding the £2 million.

LAURENTIC

Ordered by the Dominion Line for transatlantic service between New York and Liverpool, built by Harland and Wolfe in 1908, the Laurentic *weighed 15,000 tons and was constructed to accommodate 260 first-class, 420 second-class and 1000 third-class passengers. She was subsequently allocated to the White Star Line.*

At the beginning of the First World War the Laurentic *was commissioned by the British Admiralty and converted to an armed merchant cruiser.*

AREA: *Struck a German mine off Lough Swilly, two miles east of Fanad Head Lighthouse, north coast of Ireland, Atlantic Ocean.*

The *Laurentic* sailed out of Liverpool on 23 January 1917 with a complement of 470 officers and men, along with a large consignment of 3211 bars of gold weighing 35 tons (1,285,000 oz) and valued at £4,996,317.[1] The gold was packed in wooden boxes bound for the Bank of Canada in Nova Scotia.

The *Laurentic* was directed to sail to Lough Swilly in Northern Ireland. She arrived at 7.45am on 25 January and anchored two miles inside the boom. At 5pm the *Laurentic* sailed from Lough Swilly, passing Danree Head at a speed of 17½ knots.

About 5.55 p.m., when in a position outside Lough Swilly two miles east from Fanad Head Lighthouse, a loud explosion was heard and felt on the port side just abreast of the foremast. This was very short followed by a second explosion on the port side abreast of the engine room. All the electric lights were at once extinguished and, the ship not being fitted with secondary lighting, she was at once plunged into darkness... the Captain then ordered the boats to be turned out and endeavoured to send out the 'SOS' call for assistance. The engine room was immediately flooded and this made it impossible to work any of the pumps which were situated there. Apparently no-one on duty survived. Subsequently the boats were lowered and all persons alive on board, as far as could be ascertained, left the ship in them, the last boat leaving at about 6:45 pm.

The ship was then in a sinking condition and undoubtedly sank shortly afterwards in a position 62° east (mag.) about two miles from Fanad Head Lighthouse ... the majority of the loss of life occurred from exposure in the boats after the ship was abandoned.[2]

The *Laurentic* sank in 132 feet of water. Of the 470 officers and men, 354 perished.

Commander F. Damant: Royal Navy

The loss of the gold was a severe blow to the British war effort and salvage operations were implemented almost immediately.

Commander Damant, a salvage expert in the Royal Navy, was placed in charge of operations. Working from the *Volunteer*, a mooring lighter converted into a salvage vessel, Damant and his team of divers located the wreck. On the first survey the divers found that the *Laurentic* had broken her back and was lying on her port bilge at an angle of 60 degrees, her top deck 60 feet below the surface.

The wreck site was situated in an exposed position. Lough Swilly gave the wind and sea a twenty-mile-long 'funnel', causing divers to be swept to and fro by the heavy surges of the waves; combined with strong currents and high tides, conditions were extremely dangerous.

The gold bullion was stored in the second-class baggage room. The easiest point of access had to be through the watertight entry door where the gold had been originally loaded, halfway down the starboard side.

The divers blasted open the entry door with a charge of gun cotton. Upon gaining entry they found their way blocked by fallen debris: 'Operations were continued on the 16, 17, 18, 19, 20, 21 and 22 May 1917, large pieces of deck and bulk heads being dislodged, slung and hoisted; by the afternoon of the 22 part of the specie could be reached by divers crawling in through a rent in the deck. The boxes were found broken up, but their ingots appeared quite undamaged though buried in masses of debris . . .'[3]

The divers brought to the surface the first gold bars and a box of silver florins. Operations were always at the mercy of the weather; sudden storms would appear and divers would have to be brought up. On one occasion, in July, the wind strengthened to a full gale and diving operations were suspended for a week with the *Volunteer* forced to return to port. When the team finally returned to the *Laurentic* they discovered 'that the starboard side instead of being 64 feet above the sea bottom, is now only 26 feet above it, in other words, her beam has shrunk from 64 feet to 26 feet. The consequence is that the bulkheads have crumpled up accordion fashion.'[4]

The entry door was now at a depth of 103 feet. Under hazardous conditions the divers set explosive charges against the twisted steel bulkhead and the metal debris. On reaching the baggage room the divers found that the floor had collapsed and the room due to the slope, had emptied itself of the gold It took a further two months to locate the gold which had slipped downwards to a depth of 120 feet and a passage had to be blasted through the ship's superstructure. The gold had separated into two parts; the majority lay under the ship's smoking and dining salon, the remainder was scattered over the seabed. By September £836,000 in gold ingots had been recovered.

The Admiralty decided to discontinue operations until after the war. In April 1919 Damant resumed his work with a new salvage vessel, the *Racer*, he managed to recover gold to the value of £484,209. After the winter gales of 1920 Damant was to report: 'The wreck has greatly changed its aspect since I last surveyed it in 1919, much destruction having being caused by last winter's gales. The shell of the ship has crumbled down flat in most parts and boilers have broken out and scattered at some distance on the sea floor.'[5]

In a letter to Mr Blackett of the Bank of England the Admiralty quoted comments by Damant: 'It is impossible to be sure how much there is to be recovered from this particular place, as experience in previous years has shown that the gold is scattered all along the remains of the vessel like a trail, so that there may be a great deal that can never be recovered.'[6] Salvage continued until 1924 when the Admiralty halted operations.

The Bank of England reported that the value of gold recovered from seven years of salvage was as follows:[7]

	£	s	d
1917	836,000	0	0
1918	No operations		
1919	484,209	2	10
1920	11,707	10	2
1921	66,018	2	6
1922	1,390,603	8	11
1923	1,970,638	0	0
1924	199,469	9	4
	£4,958,708	15	9

Total amount of gold lost	£4,996,318.00
Recovered	4,958,708.00
Unrecovered gold	37,610.00

The value of gold in 1917 was around £3.10 per oz. As the *Laurentic* was carrying £1,285,226 standard oz valued at £4,996,318, at today's prices (£260 per oz) the gold would be worth £334,158,760 ($501,240,000) and the twenty-five unrecovered gold bars would now be valued at £2,516,000 ($3,774,000).

EGYPT

The Egypt *was a passenger liner of 7941 tons gross, 499 feet in length and 55 feet in beam, with a maximum speed of eighteen knots, built in Scotland in 1899 for the Peninsular and Oriental Steam Navigation Company of London (P&O Line). During the First World War the* Egypt *was converted into a hospital ship; after the war she was refitted back to a liner, capable of carrying 301 first-class passengers, 208 second-class, with a crew of 298. She was captained by Andrew Collyer.*

AREA: *In collision with a French cargo steamer, the* Seine, Egypt *sank off the coast of France twenty-five miles south of Ushant and thirty miles west of Pointe du Raz, Atlantic Ocean.*

The *Egypt* departed from Tilbury Docks, London, on 19 May 1922 bound for Bombay, and carrying forty-four passengers and a crew of 294. She was due to stop at Marseilles to pick up most of her passengers.

Besides her general cargo was a large consignment of gold and silver, 119 boxes containing 1089 bars of gold, thirty-seven boxes holding 164,979 gold sovereigns and 1229 loose bars of silver[1] – all stacked in the strongroom.

The consignment was valued at £1,058,879 and was insured by Lloyd's of London. On 20 May the *Egypt* passed the Channel Islands and continued down the English Channel, taking a navigational fix from the French coast and altering course towards the island of Ushant; as she passed Ushant fog patches began to appear. By late afternoon, in a calm sea, the *Egypt* entered a thick fog bank where visibility was reduced to 20 or 30 yards.

The captain ordered that the ship's horn be sounded at three-minute intervals; he reduced speed to dead slow. At 7pm the *Egypt* was about twenty-five miles south of Ushant when a ship's horn sounded very closely on the port beam; suddenly, the bows of a large cargo steamer rammed her below the waterline, aft of midships. The ship heeled to starboard and then listed to port as water rushed into her lower decks through the jagged hole below her waterline.

The *Egypt* had been struck by the French cargo steamer, *Seine*, from La Pallice bound for Le Havre. *Seine* had specially constructed bows that were strengthened to push through ice. Although badly damaged, she was still capable of steaming on but, as soon as her captain realized what had happened, she was turned back to assist the rescue and help with survivors.

Captain Collyer ordered the radio operator to transmit an SOS signal giving *Egypt's* position. The mayday was picked up by three ships: the *Andes*, the *Cahiraon*, and the *Akabo*. None could reach the *Egypt* in time to attempt any rescue. Orders were given to abandon ship. As the *Egypt* was listing so heavily, it was only possible to lower five of the sixteen lifeboats; one of these capsized, drowning many of the occupants. Most of the crew and passengers jumped into the sea and clung to liferafts and other wreckage.

Captain Le Barzac of the *Seine* later described the disaster:

I was proceeding from La Pallice to Havre. The fog was dense. I was on the bridge and looking out. I had already passed several ships, and, as a measure of protection, had reduced my speed to five knots. About 7 o'clock, without any previous warning, I saw bearing down upon me a large steamer. It was the *Egypt* right ahead of my ship. We struck her in the side. She was going at great speed, and continued her course. I realised the danger which she ran, and although my ship was considerably damaged I went after her. Twenty minutes later I succeeded in catching her up. The scene was terrible. On all sides we heard fearful cries and calls for help. A man and a woman were struggling in the sea, which fortunately was very calm. I quickly launched several lifeboats. My men displayed great courage in rescuing the passengers. We remained on the spot for three hours. I saw from my bridge a man crying for help with two children in his arms. I proceeded to Brest, where I arrived at noon today.[2]

The purser of the *Egypt* stated 'that the vessel was stationary at the moment of collision, and was sounding her siren. The *Seine* was steaming at five knots and was also sounding her siren.'[3] Of the 338 passengers and crew ninety-six drowned.

The recovery of 10 tons of silver and gold[4] at a depth of 396 feet was well beyond the diving capabilities of the time. Lloyd's underwriters paid out in full, believing the gold and silver impossible to recover.

Giovanni Quaglia and Sorima

Giovanni Quaglia, a successful Genoese lawyer, became interested in shipping, subsequently gave up his law practice and bought a number of merchantships. After the First World War he became the first Italian owner of a fleet of tankers.

In 1924 Quaglia formed Sorima (Societa Ricuperi Marittimi), a salvage organization working in Italian waters.

In 1925 Peter Sandberg and James Swinburne successfully applied to Lloyd's for the salvage concession for the *Egypt*'s gold and silver. They contracted the Gothenburg Towing and Salvage Company, along with the Salvage Association, then began operations to locate the *Egypt*. They spent the first months searching an area south of Ushant with no results. They continued searching for a further two years before approaching Sorima.

The Italian salvage organization had recently developed up-to-date diving techniques that had been proven whilst salvaging the *Elisabethville*. Sorima took on the contract to locate and recover *Egypt*'s lost bullion.

The Sorima organization searched the French maritime archives at Brest, and found the radio transmissions sent by various radio stations giving coordinates on the *Egypt*'s location on the evening of 20 May 1922:

a) From Pointe du Raz Station to Prefet Maritime, Brest: 'Have located steamship in distress bearing 277° at 19.01.'
b) Ushant Station to Wireless Service, Brest: 'SOS from MMG Egypt bearing 217° at 19.08.'
c) Ushant Station to Prefet Maritime, Brest: 'Received from Egypt MMG SOS position 48° 10' N.,5°30'W.'[5]

Also, a British destroyer picked up mail bags from the *Egypt* in Lat 48°
14'N. Long 5° 30'30" West. These bearings marked off a rectangular search
area of approximately ten by six miles.

The salvage operations began in June 1929 with two ships: the *Artiglio* and
a support ship, *Rostro*. A sweep was made with a cable 6500 feet long attached
to two 4-ton weights, one at each end. The cable was designed to sweep over
the seabed 25 feet from the bottom. Every time contact was made with an
object, the divers would go down and investigate. By August 1930 they had
located the *Egypt*: Lat 48° 6'N. Long 5° 30'W.

The *Egypt* was resting on a seabed of hard sand and scattered rocks. Her
bullion-room, 25 feet by 5 feet, had been situated on the Orlop deck, below
the main deck between the forward deck and the bridge.

After long discussions, it was finally decided that the most suitable solu-
tion to the problem of reaching the bullion was to use explosives to blast
through the four decks above the strongroom, and specially designed auto-
matic grabs and hooks would be used to bring up the gold and silver. The
whole operation would be guided by a diver operating inside an observational
bell fitted with six windows; the whole structure would be suspended from a
400-foot hawser. The diver relayed instructions by telephone up to the mother
ship, directing the laying of explosives and the use of the hooks and grabs.

As mid-September approached, rough seas and impending winter weather
forced the postponement of salvage operations until the following year. Over the
winter the *Artiglio* was transferred to another project in safer waters, that of salvaging munitions from a wreck. During operations she blew up, killing a number of her crew and divers.

A Newfoundland Banks fish carrier was purchased, refitted and renamed
Artiglio II. Salvage operations began on 23 May 1931 when *Artiglio II* dropped
anchor at the marker buoys above the wreck. Six concrete blocks, each weighing
7 tons, were winched to the seabed. Heavy chains were run up from the blocks
to 1-ton anchors; these blocks ensured the *Artiglio* would not be pulled from
her moorings over the *Egypt*. With the ship firmly in position the observation
bell was lowered with the diver inside: 'After the removal of all superstructure,
three decks, with all the complications presented by stairways, bulkheads and
stanchions were gradually broken down and cleared away for a space of about
98 feet of the vessel's length, for 54 feet of her beam, and to a depth of 33
feet. To achieve this result a total of more than 11,000 lbs of 'T.N.T.' in steel
tubes of various lengths and diameters, were gradually placed on the wreck
and electronically detonated.'[6]

By the end of November the grabs had removed over 500 tons of metal plate and debris. The deck above the strongroom was cleared and one third of the length of this covering deck was ripped open. A diver was lowered through a hole into the darkness but was unable to reach the strongroom. With changing weather operations were again suspended until the following spring.

Salvage work was resumed at the beginning of May 1932. The roof of the strongroom was removed and, finally, a few weeks later, the divers in their 'observation shells' directed the first grab into the now exposed room. On 22 June the first two gold ingots and sovereigns were brought to the surface. David Scott, a journalist on board the *Artiglio* described the first finds:

> The grab rises out of the sea, a stream of silvery water pouring from it. It swings high overhead, drenching heedless men to the skin. As the outer casing opens and the grab comes down, we see the usual jumble of wreckage in its jaws. They open with a rattle. Among the mud and wood and paper two bright yellow bricks fall with a double thump on the deck. They lie there shining, while a great shout bursts from the men of the *Artiglio*.
>
> '*Lingotti! Lingotti! Oro! Oro, ragazzi!*'
>
> Now the flood-gates are open. The months of waiting and striving are at an end. Pent-up hope and patience burst forth in a rush of emotions that sweeps us off our feet. They throw themselves on the golden bars, laughing and crying together, scrambling to touch them, embracing one another at the sight of them. They pass them from hand to hand, stroking their cold smoothness with calloused palms, laying them against unshaven cheeks, swinging them aloft to feel their weight. They shout and dance and shout again. Four years of effort, patience, tragedy and reward at last![7]

The value of *Egypt*'s treasure when she sank was £1,054,000 and by 1932 the value had increased to over £1,200,000; today, the value would be many millions of pounds. Each time a grab came to the surface, gold sovereigns and gold ingots of varying sizes all fell on to the *Artiglio*'s waiting decks.

It was not until 1935 that Giovanni Quaglia and his crew ceased their methodical salvage of the *Egypt*. In all, they recovered £1,001,300 of the sunken treasure. Sir Percy Mackinnon, the Chairman of Lloyd's sent a telegram to Mussolini: 'The Chairman of Lloyd's on behalf of the Corporation of Lloyd's sends congratulations to all Italians upon the magnificent success which has been achieved by their fellow countrymen in salving the gold from the *Egypt*. Their success is a practical illustration of the advantages of international

The *Egypt* collided with the French cargo vessel, *Seine*, in a dense fog off the coast of France on 20 May 1922, while carrying a consignment of gold and silver valued at over £1 million

co-operation, and if all nations would join together in the same spirit to salve the world from the deep waters in which it is now submerged, success would be speedily attained.'[8]

The remaining £52,000 in gold ingots and gold sovereigns, valued today at around £2–300,000 ($300,000–$450,000) lies scattered in and around the remains of the strongroom.

EDINBURGH

HMS Edinburgh *was launched at Wallsend-on-Tyne in 1938. A cruiser of 10,000 tons, with a speed of 32.5 knots, she was heavily armed with 12/6-inch, 12/4-inch guns and 6/12-inch torpedoes. She carried four Walrus aircraft and a crew of 800, commanded by Hugh Faulkner.*

AREA: *Torpedoed 170 miles north of Murmansk, Russia, in the Barents Sea, Arctic Ocean.*

The Barents Sea takes its name from William Barendz, a Dutch navigator, who explored this part of the Arctic Ocean in the sixteenth century. Weather conditions in the area are usually severe.

When Germany invaded Russia on 22 June 1941, Stalin appealed both to
Roosevelt and to Churchill for military aid. It was agreed that the United
States and Great Britain would send armaments to the value of $1 billion.
Payment would be in dollars and gold: Churchill would arrange the shipments
from England to Russia. The Barents Sea thus became an important supply
route for the Arctic convoys destined for the Russian ports of Murmansk and
Archangel. The shortest route to these ports was across the Arctic Ocean from
Iceland. The Allied forces established bases in Iceland in 1941 and Reykjavik
became a major centre for convoy operations. The first convoy, PQ 1, left
Reykjavik bound for Murmansk on 28 September 1941. Convoys were
numbered and prefixed: PQ outward-bound and QP homeward-bound. By the
end of 1941 350,000 tons of war supplies had been shipped to the northern
Arctic ports with the loss of only two ships. By March 1942 the situation
had changed.

With the German invasion and subsequent occupation of Norway (in 1940)
the German Naval Command established naval and air bases at Kirkenes,
Petsamo, Banak and Bardufoss, all in northern Norway. German U-boats and
aircraft began to concentrate their efforts on attacking the convoys, with some
success. Convoys PQ13 and PQ17 were badly depleted; out of fifty-two ships
only twenty-nine arrived at Murmansk.

Convoy PQ14 comprised twenty-three merchantmen and ten other
escort destroyers and minesweepers; her main escort was the cruiser
HMS *Edinburgh*. The ships assembled off the northeast coast of Iceland on
12 April 1942. They came under heavy attack by German U-boats and aircraft, several ships were lost and damaged, but the convoy arrived at Kola Inlet,
the entrance to Murmansk, on 19 April. On 28 April the *Edinburgh* was due
to escort Convoy QP11, consisting of thirteen merchantmen returning to
England.

Two days prior to departure, two canvas-covered barges came alongside and,
under armed Russian guard, ninety-three heavy wooden crates were loaded
aboard the *Edinburgh*. Captain Hugh Faulkner signed an official receipt for
5 tons of gold; five bars, each weighing 28 lbs, were packed in each crate. This
made up the manifest of 465 gold bars, each numbered and stamped with the
official Russian assay mark and the hammer and sickle.

This was not the first occasion that British ships had carried gold from
Russia. The first shipment was in 1941 when 10 tons of bullion were shipped
from Archangel aboard HMS *Suffolk* and, again, in the early part of 1942,
HMS *Kenya* carried another shipment, also 10 tons.

On 28 April, HMS *Edinburgh*, loaded with the bullion, sailed out of Murmansk. She sailed north along the Kola Inlet to rendezvous with her merchantships that made up Convoy QP 11, before heading for the open seas. The assembling convoy had been spotted two days before by German reconnaissance planes. Admiral Schmundt of German Navy Group North, based at Kirkenes, ordered seven of his U-boats, supported by three destroyers, to prepare to attack the convoy.

On the morning of 29 April a Junkers reconnaissance plane located the homeward-bound ships. The German command at Kirkenes received the report of the convoy's speed and position and, the following day, as the *Edinburgh* zigzagged ahead of the merchantships, the convoy was attacked by destroyers and U-boats. The *Edinburgh* was spotted at periscope depth by the German U-boat, 456, under Lieutenant Teichert. Closing in to 1000 yards he ordered the firing of his last two torpedoes. Captain Faulkner, in his report to the British Admiralty, noted:

39   At 0652 torpedoes were seen breaking surface about 5000 yards on the starboard beam and it seemed certain that they would pass well astern.
40   The ship's head, however was swinging very slowly to port and the tracks were lost sight of. The ship started to swing rapidly to port and tracks were again sighted on the port side and it was thought they would pass astern, which, in fact two of them did.
41   One torpedo struck the ship between frames Nos.87 and 108 and she listed rapidly to port to an angle of 12' and continued slowly to increase the list. The Engineer Officer reported that the steam was failing.
44   The list had by this time increased to 17' and orders were given to transfer all sick and wounded to minesweepers and men not required to man the armament also to embark.[1]

With only her forward guns in action she managed to hit and sink the German destroyer *Hermann Schoemann*. Captain Faulkner's report continued:

47   When I had been informed by the Master-at-Arms and Executive Officer that all men were up from below, that all upper deck hatches that could be reached had been opened, I then left the ship myself and boarded Harrier. In accordance with your orders Harrier lay off to wait for the ship to sink.
48   The wind having gone down and there being no sea, the list only increased very slowly and as the action with the destroyers was still in

progress, attempts were made to hasten the end by firing a few 4" shells from Harrier and dropping depth charges close alongside. This proved unsuccessful and Foresight who had one torpedo remaining and was now again under way was ordered to sink her.

49 On being hit by Foresight's torpedo the ship immediately started to turn over and within three minutes was completely submerged.

50 I have no doubt from seeing the effect of the final torpedo, that the ship had previously been in a very bad state; had another torpedo hit her before the ship's company was taken off, only a very small proportion would have been saved; the temperature of the water being so low that no men could have lived if not picked up within a few minutes, and even those who could have been saved would probably have been maimed by frostbite as they would not have been given proper attention in the limited space available in the minesweepers.[2]

The Captain made notes on board HMS *Harrier* stating:

The Edinburgh though slowly sinking was sunk by the remaining torpedo of the Foresight. A hateful signal to make to the Foresight but though sinking slowly I considered it necessary to hasten her sinking in case the enemy destroyer returned. At the time none were in sight. Edinburgh had had all she could take. She rolled over to port, her back broke and the last seen of her was her bows rising vertically in the air and then disappearing. The after part just rolled over.[3]

HMS *Edinburgh* sank in 800 feet of icy water, carrying with her £45 million in gold bars.

Risdon-Beazley Salvage Co.

In 1954 a British firm, the Risdon-Beazley Salvage Company, was the first to research the possibility of recovering the gold bullion from HMS *Edinburgh*.

The company had been British Admiralty salvors since the early thirties but, after long negotiations, they withdrew their application, having decided that 800 feet was really beyond the then current (1950s) diving or salvage capabilities. In 1957 the British War Graves Commission designated HMS *Edinburgh* as an official wartime cemetery; however, as the wreck was in international waters, any unauthorized diver or nation could claim her salvage rights.

By the late 1970s diving techniques and equipment had become more advanced. The Risdon-Beazley Company revived its interest in the search for, and the salvage of, the *Edinburgh*. A Norwegian company, Stolt-Nielsen, had made a preliminary sea-search covering an area of over 1000 square nautical miles, but found nothing. In 1978 the Russians searched the targeted area but were forced to abandon their attempt.

Jessop Marine Recoveries Ltd

In 1980 Keith Jessop formed Jessop Marine Recoveries Ltd with a registered capital of £100. Jessop, a Yorkshireman, was an experienced diver both in salvage and on the North Sea oil rigs and had spent years researching the possibilities of salvaging the gold bullion from the *Edinburgh*.

As an established and experienced deep-sea diver he was able to put together a consortium of highly qualified contractors and specialists in deep-sea salvage. It was agreed that Offshore Supply Association (OSA), London agents for the German shipping company, Vereinigte Tanklager und Transportmittel (VTG), would assign operation and support vessels. Racal Decca would supply navigational and sonar equipment and Wharton Williams Taylor would provide advanced diving technology along with £2 million for expenses. Jessop Marine was the third company in 1980 to submit an application to the British and Russian governments for the proposed salvage of the *Edinburgh*.

After many months of delicate negotiations and in the face of fierce competition, Jessop was awarded the contract for the recovery attempt. The agreement was formally approved by both governments on the basis that they would be collectively awarded 55 per cent, '37.22% to the Russian government and 17.78% to the British government. 45% was to go to the salvors.'[4]

It was, in its time, the most elaborate, expensive and politically complex operation ever organized at such unprecedented depths.

Preparations were made at Peterhead, Scotland, the base headquarters. The OSA survey ship, *Dammator*, equipped with Klein 50KHz sidescan sonar as well as the then most current wreck detection and position-location equipment, was standing by ready to depart for the Barents Sea.

The area of search was based on naval records, logs from *Edinburgh*'s escort destroyer, *Foresight*, and the two minesweepers, *Harrier* and *Gossamer*; and the position of the German U-boat (456) as she attacked the *Edinburgh* was also taken into account. All the evidence indicated a position within a five nautical-mile radius.

On 30 April 1981 the *Dammator* left Peterhead. On board were two Russian observers from the Ministry of Merchant Marines. Two weeks later, on 14 May, a contact made by the sonar beam indicated that a large wreck was present far below on the ocean floor. Hopes were high but were tempered by the knowledge that the wreck could be that of the German destroyer, *Hermann Schoemann*, which the *Edinburgh* had engaged and sunk just before she, herself, was finally torpedoed.

Two days later *Scorpio*, a remote-controlled robot, was lowered and a video film confirmed that the wreck was that of the *Edinburgh*. The *Dammator* returned to Scotland on 22 May.

Stephaniturm was the OSA's 1400-ton salvage vessel with deep-dive capacity to reach 1316 feet. She carried a three-man diving bell, two large decompression chambers and was the most up-to-date vessel of her type.

She sailed out of Peterhead on 30 August bound for the Barents Sea. Three days later she was located in position 72'04 North by 35'01 West, directly above the wreck of the *Edinburgh*. Twelve divers, working in pairs, began to survey the wreck which lay on her port side. The divers had to cut through the armour-plated hull using thermal lances to get into the bomb-room where the gold was stored. Conditions were extremely dangerous; two divers cut a hole through the ship's fuel tank, adjacent to the bomb-room cutting, and removed jagged metal and debris as they worked.

As the divers cut through the bulkhead and entered the bomb-room, unexploded shells and bombs were scattered all around them. Visibility was poor but, through the gloom and stacked to one side, were the wooden boxes containing five tons of gold bars.

By 7 October 431 gold bars had been brought to the surface. The weather did not hold and freezing conditions and exhaustion served to prevent the recovery of the remaining thirty-four gold bars. *Stephaniturm* headed for the port of Murmansk. There, the agreed 37.22 per cent (£16 million) in gold bars was handed over to officials of the Moscow State Bank.

Upon return to Britain, the 17.78 per cent was delivered to the vaults of the Bank of England and the remaining 45 per cent was divided '22.68% to OPA; 16.6% to Wharton Williams, 1.12% to Racal Decca and to Keith Jessop went the first bar of gold brought to the surface, marked KP 0620 and 4.5%.'[5]

The remaining thirty-four bars, valued at approximately £4 million ($6 million), still lie in the deep and dark bomb-room of HMS *Edinburgh*.

NOTES

AFRICA

Witte Leeuw

1. Napier, W., *Land of Spice and Treasure* (Aldus Books, London 1971), p.111.
2. Williams, M. 'Deep Sea Treasure', *National Geographic Magazine*, vol. 154, no. 14 (1978), p.562.
3. ibid., p.566.
4. ibid., p.576.

Bredenhof

1. Christie's sales catalogue, 'Bredenhof Bullion' (Amsterdam, 4 December 1986), p.8.
2. ibid., p.12.

Doddington

1. Allen, G. & D., *Clive's Lost Treasure* (R. Garton, London 1978), p.12.
2. ibid., Apendix II.
3. ibid., Appendix V, Order No.2.
4. ibid., Appendix V, Order No.18., Order No.24.
5. ibid., p.16, p.17.
6. *Public Advertiser*, London, 8 June 1757.
7. Allen, op.cit., p.21.
8. *Public Advertiser*, op.cit.
9. Allen, op.cit., p.48.
10. Webb, W.A., 'Journal of the Proceedings of the Doddington East Indiaman' in Plasted, A., *Remarkable Voyages and Shipwrecks* (T. Kinnersly, London 1758), p.357.
11. 'Loss of the Doddington on Bird Island – 1755', *Cape Monthly*, vol. I, p.276.
12. *Public Advertiser*, op.cit.
13. Webb, op.cit., p.273.
14. ibid., p.287.
15. *Gentleman's Magazine*, Sept. 1749.
16. Allen, op.cit., pp.61–2.
17. Turner, M., *Shipwrecks and Salvage in South Africa* (Struik Publishers, Cape Town 1988), p.91.
18. 'For the Guidance of Commanders of Steamers and Sailing Vessels' in *India Directory* (Smith Elder & Co., London 1891), p.84, section III.
19. Allen, op.cit., p.78.

Grosvenor

1. A Star Pagoda was a small gold coin first minted by the East India Company in 1641. Its approximate worth in 1782 was 8s.
2. Kirby, P.R., *True Story of the* Grosvenor (Oxford University Press, 1960), p.181.
3. Rochlin, S.A., 'The Wreck of the *Grosvenor*', *Africana Notes & News*, Cape Town, vol. III–IV (1944–6), p.53.
4. Dalrymple, A., *An Account of the Loss of the* Grosvenor *Indiaman*, (Official report to the East India Company, London 1783), p.10.
5. Kirby, op. cit., pp.61–7, Journal of William Hubberly.
6. ibid., pp.183–4.
7. ibid., p.184.
8. Holt, B., 'The Grosvenor Treasure': Turner's Discoveries, *Africana Notes & News*, Cape Town, vol. XII (1956–7), p.131.
9. Kirby, op. cit., p.185.
10. ibid., p.189.
11. ibid., p.191.
12. ibid., p.195.
13. Kirby, P.R., *Source Book on the Wreck of the* Grosvenor (Jan Riebeeck Society, Cape Town 1953), p.199.

Winterton

1. *The Times*, 23 August 1793.
2. Burman, J., *Great Shipwrecks off the Coast of South Africa* (Struik Publishing, Cape Town 1967), p.89.
3. Barrington, G.W., *Remarkable Voyages & Shipwrecks* (Simpkin, Marshall, Hamilton, Kent & Co., London), p.243.
4. Fox-Smith, C., *Adventures & Perils* (Michael Joseph, London 1936), p.215.
5. *Narrative of the Loss of the* Winterton, *East Indiaman* (Waugh & Innes, Edinburgh 1820), pp.13–14.
6. ibid., p.32.
7. ibid., p.17.
8. ibid., p.52.

Birkenhead

1. Hocking, C.A., *A Dictionary of Disasters at Sea in the Age of Steam 1824–1962* (London Stamp Exchange, London 1969), vol.I, p.85.
2. Bevan, D., *Drums of* Birkenhead (Prunell, Cape Town 1972), p.83.
3. Addison, A.C., *The Story of the* Birkenhead (Simpkin, Marshall Hamilton Kent & Co., London 1902), pp. 17–18.
4. Bevan, op. cit., p.82.
5. Burman, J., *Great Shipwrecks* (Struik Publishing, Cape Town 1967), p.110.
6. Addison, op.cit., pp.2–3.
7. Kayle, A., *Salvage of the* Birkenhead (Southern Book Publishers, Johannesburg 1990), p.39.
8. ibid., p.32.
9. Bevan, op. cit., p.198.
10. Kayle, op. cit., pp.41–2.
11. Bevan, op. cit., p.193.
12. Kayle, op. cit., pp.34–5.
13. Bevan, op. cit., p.204.
14 *Weekend Argus*, 8 March 1986.

THE AMERICAS

Nuestra Senora de Atocha

1. Mathewson, R.D., *Treasure of the* Atocha (Sidgwick & Jackson, London 1986), p.33.
2. Lyon, E., 'The Trouble with Treasure', *National Geographic Magazine*, vol. 149, no.6 (1976), p.797.
3. ibid., p.797.
4. Potter, J., *Treasure Diver's Guide* (Robert Hale, London 1973), p.216.
5. Horner, D., *Treasure Galleons* (Robert Hale, London 1973), p.135.
6. *New York Times*, 15 June 1988, section C, p.27.
7. Lyon, op. cit., p.809.
8. *Chicago Tribune*, 31 July 1986, 'Tempo' section, p.1.
9. *New York Times*, 23 September 1986.
10. ibid.
11. *New York Times*, 15 June 1988, section C, p.27.
12. *Chicago Tribune*, 20 July 1990, 'Tempo' section, p.11.

Santa Margarita

1. Mathewson, R.D., *Treasure of the* Atocha (Sidgwick & Jackson, London 1986), p.92.
2. Horner, D., *Treasure Galleons* (Robert Hale, London 1973), p.134.
3. ibid., p.135.
4. ibid., p.134.

Nuestra Senora de la Pura y Limpia Concepcion

1. Earle, P., *The Wreck of the Altmiranta* (Macmillan, London 1979), pp.47-8.
2. ibid., p.47.
3. Haring, C.H., *Trade and Navigation between Spain and the Indies* (Harvard University Press, 1918), p.120.
4. Earle, op. cit., p.60.
5. ibid., p.119.
6. ibid., p.123.
7. ibid., p.132.
8. ibid., p.140.
9. PRO COI/57 XC 1274.
10. Earle, op. cit., p.138.
11. PRO COI/57 XC 1274.
12. PRO CO 138/5.
13. PRO T 52/12 XC 1382.
14. Earle, op. cit., p.173, quoted from J. Taylor, 'Multum in Parvo' MS, Institute of Jamaica, vol iii, 705 and 808.
15. ibid., p.173.
16. Latil, P. de and Rivoire, J., *Sunken Treasure* (Hart-Davis, London 1962), p.48.
17. Earle, op. cit., p.173.
18. ibid., p.178.
19. ibid., pp. 192–3.
20. *Christian Science Monitor*. 9 June 1981.
21. *New York Times*, 23 August 1979.
22. *Herald Tribune*, 4 January 1979.
23. *New York Times*, 23 August 1979.

Nuestra Senora De Las Maravillas

1. Christie's Press Release: The Hunt for the Treasure of the Nuestra Senora de Las Maravillas, 28th and 29th May 1992, p.4.
2. *Telegraph* Magazine, 6 February 1993, p.26.
3. Marx, R.F. and Marx, J., *The Search for Sunken Treasure* (Swan Hill Press, Shrewsbury 1993), p.83.
4. *Los Angeles Times*, 2 December 1972.
5. ibid.
6. ibid.
7. ibid.
8. *Financial Times*, 6 June 1992.

San Jose

1. Phillips, C.R., 'The Galleon *San José*, Treasure Ship of the Spanish Indies' *Mariner's Mirror*, vol. 77, no. 4 (1991), p.357.
2. ibid., p.357.
3. PRO, ADM/51/4233.
4. ibid.
5. Horner, D., *Treasure Galleons* (Hale and Co., London 1973), p.170–71.

6. ibid., p.172.
7. PRO, ADM/SEC/1/5267.
8. ibid.
9. ibid.
10. Phillips, op. cit., p.358.
11. Phillips, op. cit., p.357.
12. Horner, op. cit., p.175.
13. 'Washington Post', 8 September 1983.
14. ibid.

Whydah
1. It is possible that Louis Lebous was Oliver le Vasseur, alias *La Buse*, 'the Buzzard', who joined the pirate Edward England plundering ships in the West Indies. With Spain's inclusion in the quadruple Alliance they sailed to the unprotected routes of the Indian Ocean. *La Buse* was captured and hanged on 17 July 1730.
2. Jameson, J.F., *Privateering and Piracy in the Colonial Period* (Macmillan, London 1923), p.294.
3. Course, A.G., *Pirates of the Western Seas* (Muller, London 1969), p.167.
4. Jesuit's bark is another name for Chinchona from which quinine is made.
5. One of the small islands in the Bahamas.
6. Jameson, op. cit., p.295.
7. Snow: a small vessel like a brig, with a trysail.
8. Jameson, op. cit., p.295.
9. Pink or pinkie: a small sailing ship with a narrow stern.
10. Jameson, op. cit., p.296–7.
11. Dethlefson, E., *Cape Cod's Mystery Treasure Ship* (Seafarer's Heritage Library, Woodstock 1984), pp. 138–9.
12. Course, op.cit., p.172.
13. ibid., p.172.
14. Jameson, op. cit., p.292.
15. *New York Times*, 8 January 1985.
16. ibid., 4 December 1988.

Le Chameau
1. Potter, J.S., *Treasure Diver's Guide* (Robert Hale, London 1973), p.472.
2. Edmonds, A., 'Treasure! How the *Chameau* gave up its fortune', *Macleans Magazine*. Canada, vol. 79, part I (18 July 1966), p.38.
3. ibid., p.38.
4. ibid., p.39.

La Genovesa
1. Weller, R., *Galleon Hunt* (Florida Treasure Brokers, West Palm Beach 1992), p.144.
2. ibid., p.142.
3. PRO, ADM 51/1008.

Nuestra Senora de la Luz
1. Sotheby's Catalogue, 'The Uruguayan Treasure of the River Plate', New York, 24 March 1993, p.20.
2. *Independent*, 14 November 1992.
3. Sotheby's Press Release, 24 March 1993.

Nuevo Constante
1. Pearson, C.E., *El Nuevo Constante, Investigation of an 18th century Spanish shipwreck off the Louisiana Coast* (Dept. of Culture, Recreation and Tourism, Louisiana 1981), p.3.
2. ibid., p.5
3. ibid., p.12.
4. *Times-Picayune Newspaper*, 1 March 1981.

De Braak
1. Gentle, G., *Shipwrecks of Delaware* (Gentle Publishing, Philadelphia 1990), p.55.
2. Potter, J.S., *Treasure Diver's Guide* (Robert Hale, London 1973), p.483.
3. Wilkins, H.T., *Treasure Hunting* (Nicholson & Watson, London 1932), p.182–183.
4. PRO, ADM/5121/3.
5. ibid., Document 638.
6. Gentle, op. cit., p.57.
7. *Los Angeles Times*, 4 November 1984.
8. ibid.
9. Gentle, op. cit., p.71.
10. ibid., p.72.

Thetis
1. Gough, B.M., 'Specie Conveyance from the West Coast of Mexico in British Warships c.1820–1870, *Mariners Mirror*, vol. 69 (1983), p.421.
2. Thomas Dickinson, *A Narrative of Operations for the Recovery of Public Stores and Treasures sunk in HMS* Thetis (Longman, Rees, Orne, Brown, Green and Longman, London 1834), p.2.
3. PRO, ADM1/5476. XC 16077.
4. ibid.
5. ibid.
6. Gilly, J., *Shipwrecks of the Royal Navy between 1793–1849* (J.W. Parker, London 1850), p.282.
7. Dickinson, op. cit., p.59.
8. ibid., p.62.
9. ibid., Appendix IV, p.184.
10. ibid., p.153.

Lexington
1. Wagner, R., 'The Lexington's Gold', *Skin Diver Magazine*, vol. 10 (1961), p.35.

2. Snow, E. R., *Storms and Shipwrecks of New England* (Yankee Publishing, Boston 1943), p.110–12.
3. ibid., p.121.
4. Wagner, op. cit., p.35.

Yankee Blade
1. US Congress, House, Executive Documents, 30th Congress, 2nd session, 1848, 1:4.
2. Knight, G.D. and Wheeler, E.D., *Agony and Death on a Gold Rush Steamer* (Pathfinder Publishing, California 1990), p.58.
3. ibid., pp.67–8.
4. *New York Daily Tribune*, 11 November 1854.
5. Knight and Wheeler, op. cit, pp.108–9.

Central America
1. *The Numismatist*, July 1990, p.1066.
2. Conrad, Judy (edit.), *Story of an American Tragedy* (Columbus-America Discovery Group, Ohio 1988), p.13.
3. *New York Daily Tribune*, 9 September 1857, p.5.
4. Conrad, op. cit., pp. 75–6.
5. *New York Journal of Commerce*, 21 September 1857, p.2.
6. *Los Angeles Times*, 10 August 1987.
7. ibid.
8. *Los Angeles Times*, 3 April 1990.
9. ibid.

Brother Jonathan
1. Hollister, F., *San Francisco Magazine*, vol. 27, May 1985, p.37.
2. ibid., p.40.
3. ibid., p.41.
4. ibid., p.112.

Republic
1. Atlantic Constitution July 17 1987 and Lonsdale A.L. and Kaplin, H.R., *A Guide to Sunken Ships in American Waters* (Compass Pub. Inc., Virginia 1964), p.26.
2. Eaton, J.P. and Hass, C.A., *Falling Star* (Patrick Stephens Ltd, London 1989), p.105.
3. ibid., p.109.
4. ibid., p.105.
5. The distress signal 'CQD' was implemented on 1 February 1904. In 1908 the International Conference ratified 'SOS' as the new distress signal, but this was not in general use in 1909.
6. Eaton and Haas, op. cit., p.110.
7. ibid.
8. ibid., p.113.
9. *New York Times*, 19 July 1987.

10. Atlantic Constitution 17 July 1987.
11. *New York Times*, 15 September 1987.

Andrea Doria
1. *Newsweek*, 3 September 1973, p.57.
2. Mosco, A., *Collision Course* (Longmans, London 1959), p.76.
3. ibid., p.104.
4. ibid., p.100.
5. *New York Times*, 18 August 1973.
6. *Popular Mechanics*, January 1975, p.72.
7. *New York Times*, 18 August 1973.
8. ibid.
9. *Newsweek*, 3 September 1973, p.57.
10. *The Times*, 27 August 1981.
11. ibid., 1 September 1981.
12. ibid., 18 August 1984.

AUSTRALASIA AND THE FAR EAST

Flor de la Mar
1. News International Database, 18 December 1991. Time 154846.
2. The *Sunday Times*, 26 September 1989.
3. ibid.
4. News International Database, op. cit.

Batavia
1. Drake-Brockman, H., *Voyage to Disaster : The Life and Times of Francisco Pelsaert* (Angus & Robertson, Sydney 1963), p. 86. ('The Great Cameo of Gaspar Boudaen' is in the Royal Coin cabinet in the Hague, Holland.)
2. The 'Rubens Vase' is now in the Walters Art Gallery, Baltimore, MA., U.S.A.
3. Drake-Brockman, op. cit., pp.248-50.
4. ibid., p.248.
5. ibid., p.41.
6. ibid., pp.62-3.
7. ibid., pp.122-3.
8. ibid., pp.124-5.
9. ibid., p.130.
10. ibid., p.131.
11. ibid., p.133.
12. ibid., p.46.
13. Edwards, H., *Island of Angry Ghosts* (Hodder & Stoughton, London, 1966), pp.64–5.
14. Drake-Brockman, op. cit., pp. 141–2.
15. ibid., pp.176-7.
16. ibid., p.82.

Nuestra Senora de la Concepcion
1. Boxer, C.R., 'The Manila Galleons: 1565–1815', *History Today* (August 1958).

2. Mathers, W.M., 'Track of the Manila Galleons', *National Geographic Magazine* (Sept 1990), p.45.
3. ibid., p.40.
4. ibid., p.50.
5. ibid., p.44.

Vergulde Draeck
1. Byron, K.W., *Lost Treasures in Australia and New Zealand* (Angus & Robertson, London 1964), p.48.
2. Henderson, J.A., *Marooned* (St George's Books, Perth 1982), p.52.
3. A small boat with a mainsail and jib, generally towed astern, and used to carry stores and passengers from ship to shore.
4. Henderson, op.cit., p.52.
5. ibid., p.53
6. Green, J., 'The Loss of the Verenigda', *British Archaeological Report*, Supplementary series no.36 (London 1977), p.50.
7. Henderson, op. cit., p.54.
8. Green, op. cit., p.52.
9. Henderson, op. cit., p.96.
10. Green, op. cit., pp.59–60.
11. Potter, J.S., *Treasure Diver's Guide* (Robert Hale, London 1973), p.425.
12. Green, J., 'The Wreck of the Dutch East Indiaman, the Vergulde Draeck, 1656' *Nautical Journal of Archaeology and Underwater Exploration* 2.2 (1973), p.279.

Chinese Trading Junk
1. Jongsma, Hetti, *Christie's Press Release*, 7-8 April 1992.
2. 'The Vung Tau Cargo: A Shipwreck of Chinese Export Porcelain, *Christie's Auction Catalogue*, 7–8 April 1992.

Zuytdorp
1. Playford P.E., 'The Wreck of the Zuytdorp', *The Western Australian Historical Society*, vol. V, part V (1959), p.24.
2. ibid.
3. Bateson, C., *Australian Shipwrecks 1622–1850* (A.H. & A.W. Reed, London 1972), p.21.

Zeewijk
1. Edwards, H., *The Wreck on the Half Moon Reef* (Robert Hale, London 1971) p.123.
2. Boxer, C.R., *The Dutch Seaborne Empire 1600–1800* (Hutchinson, London 1975), p.243.
3. Thunberg, C.P., *Travels in Europe, Africa, & Asia 1770–1779* (London 1795), Vol. I, p.228.

4. The 'Land of Eendracht' was named after Captain Dirk Hartog's Dutch ship, *Eendracht*, on sighting the coast of what is now known as Australia.
5. Edwards, op.cit., p.56.
6. Charnley, W., 'The Story of the Zeewyjk', *Walkabout Magazine*, Melbourne (April 1956), p.29.
7. Edwards, op. cit., p.82.
8. Charnley, op. cit., p.29.
9. ibid., p.32.
10. Edwards, op. cit., p.110.
11. ibid., p.127.
12. ibid., p.130.
13. ibid., p.131.
14. Charnley, op. cit., p.32.
15. Edwards, op. cit., p.159.
16. ibid., p.163.

Geldermalsen
1. Jorg, C.J.A., *The Geldermalsen: History of Porcelain* (Kimber, London 1986), p.57.
2. Sheaf, C., and Kilburn, R., *The Hatcher Porcelain Cargoes* (Phaidon, Christie's, Oxford 1988), p.97.

Favorite
1. *Melbourne Morning Herald*, 17 June 1852.
2. *Melbourne Argus*, 26 June 1852.
3. ibid., 25 May 1853.

General Grant
1. Eunson, K., *The Wreck of the General Grant* (A.H. & A.W. Reed, Sydney 1974), p.29.
2. ibid., p.42.
3. ibid., p.52.
4. ibid., p.80.
5. ibid., p.125.
6. ibid., pp.125–6.
7. ibid., pp.135–6.
8. ibid., p.147.
9. Potter, J.S., *Treasure Diver's Guide* (Robert Hale, London 1973), p.429.

Admiral Nakhimov
1. Potter, J.S., *Treasure Diver's Guide* (Robert Hale, London 1973), p.452.
2. ibid., p.452.
3. ibid., p.454.
4. *New York Times*, 10 October 1980.
5. *Japan Quarterly*, January–March 1981.
6. *The Times*, 23 October 1980.
7. *The Times*, 1 November 1980.
8. *The Times*, 26 September 1981.

Niagara

1. Taylor, J., *Gold from the Sea* (Harrap, London 1943), p.10.
2. Public Records Office, T/1101/FI7109 xc 16077.
3. Taylor, op. cit., p.17.
4. Taylor, J., *Spoils from the Sea* (Harrap, London 1943), p.115.
5. ibid., p.116.
6. Gores, V.N., *Marine Salvage* (David & Charles, Newton Abbot 1973), p.59.
7. De Latil, P. & Rivoire, J., *Sunken Treasure* (Hart-Davis, London 1962), p.194.
8. ibid., pp.197–8.
9. ibid., p.197.
10. PRO, op. cit.
11. ibid.
12. ibid.
13. ibid.
14. *The Australian Encyclopedia*, vol. 7, p.546.

EUROPE

San Juan de Sicilia

1. Wilkins, H.T., *Treasure Hunting* (Ivor Nicholson & Watson, London 1932), p.22.
2. Stenuit, R., *Treasures of the Armada* (David & Charles, Newton Abbot 1972), p.36.
3. Marx, R., *Deep Sea Treasure* (Heinemann, London 1981), p.27.
4. Wilkins, op.cit., pp. 20-21.
5. ibid., p.21.
6. Mcleay, A., *The Tobermory Treasure* (Conway Maritime Press, London 1986), p.32.
7. ibid., p.33.
8. Masters, D., *When Ships go Down* (Eyre Spottiswoode, London 1932), p.183.
9. Mcleay, op.cit., p.39.
10. ibid., p.40.
11. Armstrong, W., *Last Voyage* (Frederick Muller, London 1956), pp.40-50.
12. Mcleay, op.cit., p.46.
13. ibid., p.57.
14. ibid., pp.57-62.

Girona

1. Galleass was a name applied to a large war galley powered both by oars and sail.
2. Fallon, N., *The Armada in Ireland* (Standford Maritime, London 1978), p.89.
3. Stenuit, R., *Treasures of the Armada* (David & Charles, Newton Abbot 1972), p.36.
4. Thomas, D.A., *The Illustrated Armada Handbook* (Harrap, London 1988), p.180.

5. Stenuit, op.cit., p.35.
6. Fallon, op.cit., p.94.
7. Thomas, op.cit., p.154.
8. Fernandez-Armesto, F., *The Spanish Armada* (OUP, Oxford 1988), p.209.
9. Thomas, op.cit., p.163.
10. Fernandez-Armesto, op. cit., p.210.
11. ibid., p.215.
12. Stenuit, op.cit., p.123.
13. Fernandez-Armesto, op.cit., p.252.
14. Fallon, op.cit., p.87.
15. ibid., p.98.

Cinque Chagas

1. Another Portuguese carrack, of the same name, was built in Goa in 1560.
2. Oppenheim, M., *Royal Naval Records*, vol. I, p.311.
3. The *Sampson* was in company with the *Mayflower* and the *Royal Exchange*.
4. Hakluyt, R., *Principal Navigations* (AMS, New York 1965), vol. II, p.374.
5. Oppenheim, op.cit., p.311.
6. ibid., p.311.
7. Greek fire is a combustible composition of naphtha, nitre and sulphur, first used by the Byzantine Greeks for setting fire to enemy ships.
8. Horner, D., *Treasure Galleons* (Robert Hale, London, 1973), pp.105–6.

Lastdrager

1. Larn, R., *Shipwrecks of Great Britain and Ireland* (David & Charles, Newton Abbot 1981), p.49.
2. 'Early Relics of the VOC trade from Shetland. The Wreck of the Flute Lastdrager lost off Yell, 1653', *International Journal of Nautical Archaeology & Underwater Exploration*, vol. 2 (1974), p.215.
3. ibid.
4. ibid., p.218.
5. Stenuit, R., *The Loss of the Lastdrager*, Appendix I, British Archaeological Report, Part I, 1977, p.409.
6. ibid., p.441.
7. IJNA, op.cit., p.218.

Kronan

1. Franzen, A., 'Kronan, Remnants of a Warship Past', vol. 175, no.4 (April 1989), p.464.

De Liefde

1. Bax, A., and Martin, J.M.C., 'The Dutch East Indiaman', *International Journal of Nautical*

Archaeology & Underwater Exploration, vol. 3.1 (1974), p.89.

2. The *Kockenge* arrived at Batavia on 4 July 1712; she sailed from the Cape in April 1712 in company with *Zuytdorp* which was lost on the coast of Western Australia (see p.133).
3. Bax and Martin, op.cit., pp.82–83.

Slot Ter Hooge

1. Christie's Sale Catalogue, 16 March 1983, p.29.
2. Cowan, Z., 'John Lethbridge, Diver', *History Today*, December 1978, p.827.
3. Cowan, Z., *Early Divers*, Treasure World, Norfolk, p.32.
4. Stenuit, R., 'The Treasure of Porto Santo', *National Geographic Magazine*, vol. 148, no.2 (August 1975), p.262.
5. Burgess, R.F., *They Found Treasure*, (Dodd Mead & Co, New York 1977) p.164.
6. Stenuit, op.cit., p.267.
7. ibid., p.271.

Hollandia

1. Cowan, Z., 'The Dutch East Indiaman Hollandia, wrecked on the Isles of Scilly 1743', *International Journal of Nautical Archaeology and Underwater Exploration*, vol. 4.2 (1975), p.275.
2. Williams, M., *Deep Sea Treasure* (Heinemann, London, 1981), p.101.
3. ibid., p.102.
4. ibid., p.102.
5. Boxer, C.R., *History Today*, November 1973, p.774.
6. Cowan, Z., op. cit., p.276.

Lutine

1. van der Molen, S.J., *The Lutine Treasure* (Adlard Coles, London 1970), p.25.
2. Williams, L.N., 'Sav'd from the Wreck of the "Lutine Frigate"', *Stamp Collecting*, London (28 December 1978), p.675.
3. ibid.
4. van der Molen, op.cit., p.24.
5. ibid., p.29.
6. ibid., p.37.
7. Williams, op.cit., p.681.
8. Latil P. de and Rivoire J., *Sunken Treasure* (Hart-Davis, London 1962), p.99.
9. van der Molen, op.cit., p.63.
10. Binnendijk, N.S., Lloyd's Log (August, September, October 1938), p..8.
11. van der Molen, op. cit., p.140.

12. Lloyd's List, 3 July 1938.
13. van der Molen, op.cit., p.144.
14. ibid., p.145.
15. The *Sunday Times*, 30 June 1993.

Colossus

1. *Morning Herald*, 9 December 1798.
2. PRO, BT 99/2073.
3. ibid.
4. Morris, R., *HMS Colossus* (Hutchinson, London 1979), p.78.
5. *Mariners Mirror*, vol. XLVI (1960), p.105.

Earl of Abergavenny

1. Cumming, E.H. and Carter, D.J., 'The *Earl of Abergavenny*', *International Journal of Nautical Archaeology and Underwater Exploration*, vol. 19.1 (1990), p.31.
2. Thomas, R., *Narratives of Remarkable Shipwrecks* (Books for Libraries Press, Freeport, New York 1835), p.133.
3. Dollar: large quantity of Spanish pieces-of-eight were held by the Bank of England; two million of these were restruck. They bore the head of George III on the obverse side, with the figure of Britannia, the legend 'Bank of England' and 'five shillings dollar' on the reverse side.
4. *Journal of the* Endevour by J. Braithwaite.
5. *Gentlemen's Magazine*, Vol. 75 February 1805, p.174.
6. ibid. p.174.
7. ibid. p.174.
8. *Gentlemen's Magazine*, Vol. 22, p.307.
9. *Journal of the* Endevour, op. cit.
10. ibid.

Royal Charter

1. McKee, A., *The Golden Wreck* (New English Library, London 1961), p.182.
2. ibid., p.44.
3. ibid., p.71.
4, *Illustrated London News*, 5 November 1859.
5. McKee, op.cit., p.180.
6. Wilson, I., *Undiscovered* (Michael O'Mara Books, London 1987), p.178.

Lusitania

1. Simpson, C., *Lusitania* (Longman, London 1972), p.31.
2. Cunard Advertisement in the *New York Times*, 1 May 1915.
3. Hoehling, A.A. & Hoehling, H., *The Last Voyage of the Lusitania* (Longman Green & Co, London

1956), p.74.
4. Simpson, op. cit., p.11.
5. Knowlton, D., *The Titanic Communicator*, vol. 14 no. 1 (1990), p.19.
6. Hickey, D. and Smith, G., *Seven Days to Disaster* (Collins, London 1981), p.153.
7. Hoehling and Hoehling, op. cit., p.65.
8. Hickey and Smith, op. cit., p.168.
9. ibid., p.172.
10. Hoehling and Hoehling, op. cit., p.79.
11. Hickey and Smith, op. cit., p.192.
12. ibid., p.213.
13. Hoehling & Hoehling, op. cit., p.137.
14. Knowlton, op. cit., p.15.
15. Simpson, op. cit., p.10.

Hampshire
1. McCormick, D., *The Mystery of Lord Kitchener's Death* (Putnams, London 1959), p.94.
2. British Admiralty, *The Loss of HMS* Hampshire: *The Official Narrative* (HMSO, London 1926), p.4.
3. Courtney, C., *Unlocking Adventure* (Robert Hale, London 1951), p.166.
4. *The Loss of HMS Hampshire*, op. cit., p.5.
5. ibid., p.9.
6. ibid., p.18.
7. Courtney, op. cit., p.165.
8. ibid., p.161.
9. *The Times*, 10 August 1983.
10. Courtney, op. cit., p.174.
11. ibid., p.171.
12. PRO, ADM/22774 WS61/1951.

13. *The Times*, 11 August 1983.
14. ibid., 10 August 1983.
15. ibid.

Laurentic
1. PRO, Adm 116/1740.
2. ibid., Adm 116/1553.
3. ibid., Adm 116/1740.
4. ibid.
5. ibid., Adm 116/1741.
6. ibid.
7. ibid.

Egypt
1. *Smith's Dock Journal*, North Shields (January 1933), p.3.
2. *The Times*, 22 May 1922.
3. ibid.
4. Scott, D., *The Egypt's Gold* (Faber & Faber, London 1932), p.296.
5. *Smith's Dock Journal*, op. cit., p.5.
6. ibid., p.15.
7. Latil, P. de and Rivoire, J. *Sunken Treasure* (Hart-Davis, London 1962), p.130.
8. Scott, op. cit., p.266.

Edinburgh
1. PRO, ADM/1/12275
2. ibid.
3. ibid. Notes made on board *Harrier* on the way back to Kola.
4. Penrose, Barry, *Stalin's Gold* (Granada Publishing, London 1982), p.218.
5. ibid.

BIBLIOGRAPHY

ADDISON, A.C. *The Story of the Birkenhead*, Simpkin, Marshall, Hamilton, Kent & Co, London 1902

ALLEN, G. *Clive's Lost Treasure*, Garton, London 1978

ANDREWS, K.R. *Drake's Voyages*, Weidenfeld & Nicolson, London 1956

ARMSTRONG, W. *Lost Voyages*, F. Muller, London 1956

BATESON, C. *Australian Shipwrecks 1622–1850* A.H. & A.W. Reed, London 1972

BARRINGTON, G.W. *Remarkable Voyages and Shipwrecks*, Simpkin, Marshall, Hamilton, Kent & Co., London

BEVAN, D. *Drums of Birkenhead*, Prunell Publishers, Cape Town 1972

BOXER, C.R. *The Dutch Seaborne Empire 1600–1800*, Hutchinson, London 1975

BOXER, C.R. *The Manila Galleons 1565–1815*, History Today, London, August 1958

BOXER, C.R. *The Verguide Draeck*, History Today, London, March 1968

BURMAN, J. *Great Shipwrecks Off The Coast of South Africa*, Struik Publishing, Cape Town 1967

BURGESS, R.F. *They Found Treasure*, Dodd, Mead & Co, New York 1977

BYRON, K.W. *Lost Treasures in Australia and New Zealand*, Angus & Robertson, London 1964

CONRAD, J. *The Story of an American Tragedy*, Columbus–American Discovery Group, Ohio 1988

COURSE, A.G. *Pirates of the Western Seas*, F. Muller, London 1969

CHARNLEY, W. *The Story of the Zeewyjk*, Walkabout Magazine, Melbourne, April 1956

DALRYMPLE, A. *An Account of the Loss of the Grosvenor, Indiaman* (Official Report to the East India Company), London 1783

DETHLEFSON, E. *Cape Cod's Mystery Treasure Ship*, Seafarer's Heritage Library, Woodstock 1984

DICKINSON, T. *A Narrative of Operations for the Recovery of Public Stores and Treasures Sunk in HMS Thetis*, Longman, Rees Orne, Brown, Green, Longman, London 1834

DRAKE-BROCKMAN, H. *Voyage to Disaster*, Angus & Robertson, London 1964

EARLE, P. *The Wreck of the Altmiranta*, Macmillan, London 1979

EATON, J.P. & HASS, C.A. *Falling Star*, P. Stevens Ltd, London 1989

EDWARDS, H. *The Wreck on Half Moon Reef*, R. Hale, London 1971

EDWARDS, H. *The Isle of Angry Ghosts*, Hodder & Stoughton, London 1966

EUNSON, K. *The Wreck of The General Grant*, A.H. & A.W. Reed, Sydney 1974

FALLON, N. *The Armada in Ireland*, Standford Maritime, London 1978

FERNANDEZ-ARMESTO, F. *The Spanish Armada*, Oxford University Press 1988

FOX-SMITH, C. *Adventures and Perils*, Michael Joseph, London 1936

GENTLE, G. *Shipwrecks of Delaware*, Gentle Publications, Philadelphia 1990

GILLY, J. *Shipwrecks in the Royal Navy between 1793–1849*, J.W. Parker, London 1850

GORES, V.N. *Marine Salvage*, David & Charles, Newton Abbot 1973

GOUGH, B.M. *Specie Conveyance from the West Coast of Mexico in British Warships c 1820–1870*, Mariner's Mirror, Vol. 69 1983

HARING, C.H. *Trade and Navigation between Spain and the Indies*, Harvard University Press, 1918

HAKLUYT, R. *Principal Navigations* Vol. 2, Arms Publishing, New York 1965

HENDERSON, J.A. *Marooned*, St George's Books, Perth, Australia 1982

HICKLEY, D. & SMITH, G. *Seven Days to Disaster*, Collins, London 1981

HOCKING, C.A. *A Dictionary of Disasters at Sea in the Age of Steam 1824–1962*, London Stamp Exchange, London 1969 (two Volumes)

HORNER, D. *Treasure Galleons*, R. Hale, London 1973

HOEHLING, A.A. & HOEHLING, H. *The Last Voyage of the Lusitania*, Longman Green & Co, London 1956

JAMESON, J.F. *Privateering and Piracy in the Colonial Period*, Macmillan, London 1923

JORG, C.J.A. *The Geldermalsen – History of Porcelain*, Kimber, London 1986

KAYLE, A. *Salvage of the Birkenhead*, Southern Book Publishers, Johannesburg 1990

KNIGHT, G.D. & WHEELER, E.D. *Agony and Death on a Gold Rush Steamer*, Pathfinders Publishing, California 1990

KIRBY, P.R. *The True Story of the Grosvenor*, Oxford University Press 1960

KNOWLTON, D. *75 Years on the Seabed – Diving on the Lusitania*, Titanic Communicator Vol. 14 No I, 1990

DE LATIL, P. & RIVOIRE, J. *Sunken Treasure*, Hart-Davis, London 1962

LARN, R. *Shipwrecks of Great Britain and Ireland*, David & Charles, Newton Abbot 1981

MARX, R.F. *Deep Sea Treasure*, Heinemann, London 1981

MARX, R.F. & MARX J. *The Search for Sunken Treasure*, Swan Hill Press, Shrewsbury 1993

MASTERS, D. *When Ships Go Down*, Eyre and Spottiswoode, London 1932

MATHEWSON, R.D. *Treasure of the Atocha*, Sidgwick & Jackson 1986

MCCORMICK, D. *The Mystery of Lord Kitchener's Death*, Putmans, London 1959

MCKEE, A. *The Golden Wreck*, New English Library, London 1961

MCLEAY, A. *The Tobermory Treasure*, Conway Maritime Press, London 1986

NAPIER, W. *Land of Spice and Treasure*, Aldus Books, London 1971

OPPENHEIM, M. *Naval Tracts of Sir William Monson*, Admiralty List of Lost Ships, Naval Records Society 1902–1914, Vol. I

PEARSON, C.E. *El Nuevo Constante, Investigation of an 18th century Shipwreck off the Louisiana Coast*, Dept. of Culture, Recreation & Tourism, Louisiana 1981

PENROSE, B. *Stalin's Gold*, Granada Publishing, London 1982

PHILLIPS, C.R. *The Galleon San Jose, Treasure Ship of the Spanish Indies*, Mariner's Mirror, Vol. 77 No. 4, 1991

POTTER, J.S. *Treasure Diver's Guide*, R. Hale, London 1973

SCOTT, D. *The Egypt's Gold*, Faber & Faber, London 1932

SIMPSON, C. *Lusitania*, Longman, London 1972

SNOW, E.R. *Storms and Shipwrecks of New England*, Yankee Publishing, Boston 1943

STENUIT, R. *Treasures of the Armada*, David & Charles, Newton Abbot 1972

STENUIT, R. *The Loss of the Lastdrager*, British Archaeological Report, Part One, Appendix One

SHEAF, C. & KILBURN, R. *The Hatcher Porcelain Cargo*, Phaidon/Christie's, Oxford 1988

THUNBERG, C.P. *Travels in Europe, Africa and Asia 1770–1779*, London 1795

TAYLOR, J. *Gold from the Sea*, Harrap, London 1943

TAYLOR, J. *Spoils from the Sea*, Harrap, London 1943

THOMAS, D.A. *The Illustrated Armada Handbook*, Harrap, London 1988

VAN DER MOLEN, S.J. *The Lutine Treasure*, Dodd Mead & Co, New York 1977

WILSON, I. *Undiscovered*, Michael O'Mara Books, London 1987

WILKINS, H.T. *Treasure Hunting*, Nicholson & Watson, London 1932

WEBB, W.A. `Journal of the Proceedings of the Doddington East Indiaman' in Plasted, A., *Remarkable Voyages and Shipwrecks*, T. Kinnersly, London 1758

INDEX